# HOW TO PUBLISH YOUR NONFICTION BOOK

# HOW TO PUBLISH YOUR NONFICTION BOOK

RUDY SHUR

Cover Designer: Phaedra Mastrocola
In-House Editors: Joanne Abrams and Marie Caratozzolo
Typesetter: Gary A. Rosenberg

**Square One Publishers**
Garden City Park, NY 11040
(516) 535–2010
www.squareonepublishers.com

**Publisher's Cataloging-in-Publication Data**
Shur, Rudy, 1946 –
How to publish your nonfiction book : a complete guide to making the right publisher say yes / by Rudy Shur.
p. cm. — (A Square One writer's guide)
Includes bibliographical references (p. ) and index.
ISBN 0-7570-0000-2 (alk. paper)
1. Authorship—Marketing. I. Title. II. Series.
PN161 .S56 2001
070.5'2—dc21 00-010138



Printed in the United States of America

10 9 8 7 6 5 4 3 2 1

# Contents

*To all writers*
*who are looking for a voice.*

# ACKNOWLEDGMENTS

There are four groups of people to whom I would like to express my gratitude. First, there are those individuals who have provided me with the opportunity to learn as much as I could in the world of publishing. Second, there are those people who have given freely of themselves in providing me with valuable information, suggestions, and ideas in the preparation of this work. Third, there are those in-house folks who have worked with me throughout this project. And last, but certainly not least, are those people who have provided me with support and encouragement throughout my life and my career.

## My Publishing World

To Ian O'Leary, who gave me my first opportunity to work for a publisher. Thank you for being so different and for seeing past my ill-fitting suit. To Larry Brown, who unintentionally gave me both the chance and motivation to start my own company. To my former publishing partners, Lee Solomon and Ken Rajman, for helping me achieve my first dream, and giving me the incentive to put this book together. To John Banks and Seymour Goldberg of Reflex Offset, for providing my first company with its first real office. To Steve Porpora, my old printing partner at Paragon Press, for his patience, skills, and humor.

To Nathan Keats, for inspiring me to be the best publisher I could be. To Norman Goldfind, for filling in so many of the fine points of publishing. To Eugene Schwartz, the direct mail wizard, who I knew only over the phone. Thank you for showing me how powerful the written word can be. To Neil Brody, my attorney. Thank you for your wise counsel and caring heart over the years. To Art Rogen, my highly sought-after sales consultant, who never lets me forget the basics. To David and Nikki Goldbeck of Ceres Press, Bob and Cindy Holzapfel of the Book Publishing Company, and Marty and Judy Shepard of Permanent Press, for proving that you *can* publish books on your own terms. To all my authors, for trusting me with their words, and teaching me more than they realized.

And to Bennett Cerf, the cofounder of Random House, whom I knew only through his appearances on *What's My Line?* Thanks for planting the seed.

## My Publishing Experts

To Ken Kaiman, salesman par excellence, as well as Square One's sales director, for his insights and expertise about book sales and the selling operatus. To Rena Wolner, former president of Avon Books, for taking the time out of her very busy schedule to provide me with a more exacting look at the inner workings of large publishing houses. To Steve Berman, Director of Marketing, Sales, and Membership for the Jewish Publication Society; Henri Hardison, Product Specialist for R.H. Boyd; and Allen McVicker of Victory Marketing Group, for explaining the ins and outs of religious publishing. To Helene Ciaravino, talented editor and author, for her invaluable information on writers' groups, conferences, and workshops. And to Jayne Alexander of the Parkville Branch of the Great Neck Library, for her "inside" information on both research techniques and the world of library acquisitions.

## People in the Square

To Joanne Abrams and Marie Caratozzolo, my very talented and demanding in-house editors, without whom this book would never be what it is. To Gary Rosenberg, my typesetter, whose skills allowed this book's complicated layout to become a visual asset. To Phaedra Mastrocola, my art director, whose artistic vision consistently turns ideas and suggestions into beautiful realities. To Karen Hay, my skillful managing editor, who provided the correct answers to so many of my annoying questions. To Bob Love, my business manager, whose passion for publishing and business savvy provide us with a firm anchor. Thanks to all of you.

## Personal People

To Izzy and Sonia, my parents, who provided me with a different point of view of the world at a very early age. It was my father who instilled in me a love of books, and my mom who showed me just how important it is to maintain a sense of humor. To my children, Shoshana and Justin, for turning out the way I hoped they would—passionate, caring, and smart. And finally, to my wife, Erica, who, fortunately, my kids have taken after. Thank you for your love, support, and steadfastness. You have always been and will always be the light of my life.

# Preface

Over the past twenty years, I have lectured to hundreds of writers at colleges and universities throughout New York State. The topic of my lectures? How you can get your nonfiction book published. And I must say that I have always enjoyed the experience. Not only have I learned a great deal from the people who attended, but I have also gotten some great book leads.

It's not always easy to get your nonfiction book into publication. However, if you understand some of the basics of publishing and then use a solid system to apply what you've learned, you can definitely increase your odds of getting your work into print. Well, at least that's the main thrust of my speech. In the question-and-answer session I hold after each lecture, at least one member of the audience has always asked, "So, how come you haven't written a book yourself?" And my response has always been pat: "I am the publisher. You are the writers. Your job is to write, mine is to publish." It was always that simple to get out of it.

However, more recently, when two of my editors posed the same question, I had a bit more trouble escaping—possibly because they had me cornered in my office. "If you know so much about publishing," they said, "why not put it down in a book? That's what you always tell other people who know a lot about a subject. Hey, we'll even edit it for you." Ten months later, with the help of these two skilled editors, Joanne Abrams and Marie Caratozzolo, the manuscript was completed.

Of course, those ten months were not easy ones. From the beginning, I certainly felt that I knew my subject; after all, I'd been in the business long enough. And I'd not only published hundreds of books, but also guided many writers in getting their books published with other companies. Still, I was aware of the challenges involved in writing a book that really accomplishes what it sets out to do. The very first thing I did was to look at the books that were already out there on publishing. (As you'll find out, it's always wise to check out the competition.) What did I find? Well, there certainly are plenty of books out there on the subject, but oddly, very few of them focus on works of nonfiction. Instead, most of them talk about all kinds of publications, from works of fiction to magazine articles to short stories. The information that directly pertains to the nonfiction book is scattered and skimpy, at best.

And then there are the few books that specifically address the nonfiction writer. Surprisingly, even these books typically have a host of drawbacks. For instance, most provide little information to help the author understand the category into which his or her book falls—a step that is critical if the writer is to target those publishers that might even *consider* looking at the project. Some of the categories mentioned in these books don't even exist as a classification within publishing houses! Moreover, few books provide the author with an accurate picture of how the business of book publishing actually works. And none of the books presents clear, step-by-step instructions for writing an effective submission package; picking the best publishers to receive the package; sending the package out in the most efficient way possible; and tracking—and understanding—the results.

My work was cut out for me. So, laptop computer in hand, I set out to create a truly useful book—a book that would provide you with the information you need about the book publishing business, and carefully guide you in applying that information to your particular work of nonfiction, whether it's a trade book, a textbook, a scholarly work, or a reference work. I do this through eight chapters, each of which adds more pieces to the puzzle that is publishing, and guides you further along the steps involved in getting your book into publication.

Rightly called "An Introduction," Chapter 1 introduces you to the world of publishing and to the Square One System for getting your nonfiction work into print. Chapter 1 also presents the first of many rules that you must learn and follow to get your book published. These rules will pop up now and then throughout the book, helping to steer you toward your goal.

Chapter 2 explains what book categories are, and why it's so important to understand the category into which your book falls before you determine the publishers who will receive your proposal. It then presents the Square One Book Classification System—a system I devised to help writers easily and accurately identify the category in which their books belong. This important chapter also acquaints you with the marketplace, and explains the importance of identifying your audience, all with the goal of improving your ability to pinpoint the best companies for your book.

Chapter 3 looks at the business of publishing. You'll learn what happens when you send a book proposal to each of the many types of publishers that are out there—small, medium-sized, and large commercial publishers; university presses; and foundation presses. And you'll learn which types of publishers are most likely to seriously consider your project.

Chapter 4 further helps you determine the type of publisher you need—this time by helping you assess your personal goals. Are you most interested in gaining enhanced status by getting your book into publication? Are you more concerned with additional income? Depending on the goals you've pinpointed and on the nature of your project, the chapter then guides you in compiling a list of thirty to forty appropriate publishers—publishers who can help you realize your dream. It even explains how you can take the sometimes-confusing resource books you'll find at your local library, and easily navigate the reams of listings to locate the specific data that you need on the companies you want to contact.

You now know who will be receiving your submission package. But what exactly should you be sending out? Enter Chapter 5, "Preparing the Package." Working with you on a paragraph-by-paragraph basis, this chapter will guide you through the writing of an effective submission package—a package designed to get results. Then Chapter 6 presents a step-by-step system for sending out that package in a way that will maximize your chance of success; minimize your effort, time, and costs; and even allow you to fine-tune your submission package along the way.

If all goes well, you may soon be receiving a publishing agreement in the mail. That's right—a contract. Using clear English, Chapter 7 helps you cut through the intimidating legalese so that you can truly understand your agreement. Throughout, I have tried to give you the benefit of my many years as a publisher by telling you not only what your contract *states*, but also what it *implies*. You'll then know exactly what your responsibilities and rights are according to your agreement, and will be able to make informed decisions throughout the negotiations process.

Let's say you've followed the Square One System to the letter, but haven't had any bites. Is there anything you can do? Chapter 8 helps you pinpoint the possible cause of the problem, and presents a variety of ways in which it can be solved. And if there are still no bites, this chapter fills you in on some fascinating alternatives, from electronic publishing to self-publishing. You may be surprised to learn that you, like many writers before you, can get your book out to your audience *without* the help of a publishing company. In fact, a number of authors have enjoyed success by going it alone.

In the writing of this book, I have done all that I can to make sure that my information is as up-to-date and accurate as possible. I have done the research, and have used my friendships with publishing people unabashedly to make certain my facts were straight and my points on the mark. If, however, any errors remain, they are solely my responsibility, and I promise to correct them in the next printing.

In closing, let me say that I believe that books have tremendous power. They have the ability to inform, enlighten, and entertain. They can make us laugh and cry. They can open doors to new and exciting ideas. They can transport us to distant places in an instant. They can make an important and crucial difference in our lives. From one new writer to another, I hope this book allows you the opportunity to have your book unleash its own power in its own way.

Rudy Shur
*Publisher*
*Garden City Park, New York*

# A Note on Gender

To avoid long and awkward phrasing within sentences, the publisher has chosen to alternate the use of male and female pronouns according to chapter. Therefore, when referring to the third-person writer or editor, odd-numbered chapters use male pronouns, while even-numbered chapters employ female pronouns, to give acknowledgment to writers and editors of both genders.

# CHAPTER 1

# AN INTRODUCTION

*The wall clock reads 6:30 PM. My phone has finally stopped ringing, and no one has come into my office for the past half hour. Finally, some quiet time. I look at the stack of manuscript proposals that have been left on my desk. There, on top, is a beautifully prepared submission package. I rip it open and start reading the cover letter, which begins, "Dear Mathematics Editor." I stop reading. I write "kill" on the top of the page and toss it onto the rejection pile. I think to myself, "The writer didn't even bother to check if we did math books. What is this guy thinking?"*

I am an acquisitions editor. I'm the person who is on the receiving end of all those manuscript proposals sent out by potential authors. And it has always amazed me how little most writers know about getting their books accepted by a publishing house. Without realizing it, so many writers send out material that actually decreases their odds of getting a positive response from an editor.

However, every once in a while, I receive a manuscript proposal that does everything right. I finish reading the proposal, and I can't send out a request for additional material quickly enough. God bless e-mail! Consciously or unconsciously, the writer has done everything he can to increase the odds of getting me to react positively. And it has worked.

Is it magic? Prayer? Blind luck? No. It is a matter of knowing what an editor is really looking for—of knowing what to say to turn him on, and what not to say. Unfortunately, the process of having a book published is a real mystery to most people outside the world of book publishing. To these people, the submissions process seems a hit-or-miss system based on a random selection of presses. In fact, while an element of chance is always involved, the rules for increasing your success are very clear. All you have to do is know the rules and understand how to use them.

While an element of chance is involved in getting a book into print, you can greatly improve your odds of success by following a few simple rules.

That's why I wrote this book—to let you in on the rules of getting a nonfiction book successfully published. The system I devised is based on years of experience publishing over one thousand titles, upon many candid conversations with authors and other editors, and upon much success in guiding authors to the right publishing houses. Finally, after the umpteenth person asked, "Why don't you put it into a book?," I decided I would. I had certainly asked the same thing of hundreds of professionals who offered great advice in person and on the air, but never thought of putting their valuable information down on paper. And besides, I knew I had an open slot in my fall list. (If you don't know what a fall list is, don't worry, you will. It's covered later in the book.)

The book you are about to read will provide you with a proven system of submissions that will (1) avoid the common mistakes that turn editors off, (2) allow you to find those houses best suited for your title, (3) save you valuable time and money, and (4) increase your odds of having your manuscript proposal accepted. Let's look at each of these points in turn.

## AVOIDING MISTAKES THAT TURN EDITORS OFF

Many authors unwittingly sprinkle their proposals with words and phrases that are almost guaranteed to trigger negative reactions on the part of an editor. Always remember that editors are busy people. If they see something in a proposal that tries their patience or raises questions about the abilities of the writer or the marketability of a book, they will instantly reject the proposal. I will show you how to clear your submission package of all unintentional land mines.

## SAVING TIME AND MONEY

It costs a lot of money to mail those heavy manuscript proposals to editors, not to mention the high costs of duplication. You can also spend a great deal of time putting those elaborate submission packages together. I will show you how to create submission packages that don't take hours to put together, and don't cost an arm and a leg to mail.

## FINDING THE HOUSES BEST SUITED TO YOUR TITLE

Most writers in search of a publisher pay little attention to the fine points of choosing a house that would best serve their needs. Instead, they concentrate their energies on finding any "legitimate" house interested in their work. This could be a big mistake. I will explain what you should be looking for, and what the right publisher should offer based upon your needs.

## INCREASING YOUR ODDS OF ACCEPTANCE

Just as there are many ways to kill an editor's interest in your proposal, there are numerous ways to turn an editor on to your project. Some are quite simple; others require more work. But the result should be a positive response from the editor. In this book, you will find out how it's done.

## WHAT'S IN THIS BOOK?

I have designed *How to Publish Your Nonfiction Book* to provide you with all the information you need to put my system into practice. I have attempted to write this book in nontechnical language. However, whenever I do use a technical term that's commonly utilized *in-house*—in other words, within the publishing company—it is explained the first time it appears. And if you miss it the first time, you can check the handy glossary at the back of the book.

Following this introductory chapter, the book is divided into seven chapters, each of which contains a crucial piece of the publishing puzzle. Since a good deal of the publishing business is camouflaged by smoke and mirrors—that is, advertising and publicity—the general public rarely has an opportunity to learn how a publishing company actually functions. What you usually hear about is the sizeable advance just paid to a first-time author living in a remote part of the Australian outback; or how a best-selling horror writer's book has just presold over a million copies; or how the endorsement of a famous television celebrity has rocketed a book to the top of the bestsellers list. But while these success stories sound wonderful, they have nothing to do with the everyday workload of an editor, nor do they increase your chances of getting published. The material in this book will. You will no longer have to guess what you need to do. You will *know* what to do and why you are doing it.

The book begins at the beginning by helping you avoid one of the most common land mines of all. Among the most frequent problems I have found is the new writer's lack of knowledge about his book's category designation, audience, and marketplace. Believe it or not, every day, hundreds—perhaps thousands—of writers tell editors that they have written a book for a category that does not exist or for a marketplace that is very hard to reach. Of course, each of these writers believes that the experienced editor will be able see the merit of the work and position the book appropriately to overcome any marketing problems that may arise. Unfortunately, the editor does not see the book's merit, and automatically rejects the proposal. You, not the editor, should be able to explain how and to whom your book will sell.

Chapter 2, "Where Does Your Book Fit In?," explains what book categories are, and what they mean to an editor and the marketplace. It then helps you determine the book category into which your project falls. You will also learn how to sort out who your book's readers will be. Within nonfiction, there are many markets that focus on different audiences, including trade, educational, professional, and scholarly audiences. Some of these marketplaces cross over. Many do not. Chapter 2 explains the importance of identifying your audience and keeping it in mind as you write your book.

Large, moderate-sized, and small publishers each have their own way of publishing books. Some aspects of the publishing process are the same regardless of the company's size; others are very different. Chapter 3, "The Business of Publishing," looks at the types of publishers that are out there—including commercial presses, university presses, and foundation presses—and explains the publishing process as it is determined by the size and structure of a company. And it helps steer you to the type of house that is most likely to accept your book proposal.

Before I sign an author up, I always ask, "Why do you want your book published?" I ask this question because I do not want to establish a publishing relationship with an author who expects something that my company could never provide. Whether your goal is additional income, enhanced status, or some other personal need, matching up the realities of publishing with your own expectations will help you determine the type of company for which you should be looking. Chapter 4, "Choosing the Right Publisher," first addresses the most common reasons authors write books, and helps sort out the motivations behind your own writing efforts. Once you understand your personal goals, the chapter helps you develop criteria for selecting publishers that can help you meet these goals. Finally, based upon your criteria, the chapter guides you in compiling a list of thirty to forty appropriate publishers.

It is important to understand what you hope to gain by getting your book into print. Do you want additional income? Enhanced status? Greater public awareness of a growing problem? Knowledge of your personal goals will help you choose the best publisher for your project.

As the opening paragraphs of this chapter indicated, the vast majority of submission packages I receive may have been composed with the best of intentions, but were not put together with any understanding of what an editor needs and wants in a submission package. Many times, the proposal simply doesn't provide me with even the most *basic* information I need to make an initial decision. In other cases, the author presents me with such a towering stack of material that my response is simply to get it off my desk—and into the kill pile—before it can do some damage. And nine times out of ten, the cover letter shows all too clearly that the writer doesn't understand his book's category, audience, or marketplace.

Chapter 5, "Preparing the Package," provides step-by-step guidelines for composing a short but effective submission package—a package that will be opened and read. You'll learn exactly what to include, and, perhaps just as important, you'll learn how to avoid the pitfalls that keep so many writers from realizing their

**Helpful Hint**

To maximize your chance of success, you'll want to craft a submission package that provides the editor with all the basic information he needs to make an initial decision, but doesn't overwhelm him with unnecessary material.

dream of publication. Following this, Chapter 6, "Using the Square One System," will show you how to send your letter-perfect package out in a way that will maximize your chance of success, while minimizing your effort, time, and costs.

Most authors dream of finding that longed-for publishing contract in their mailbox. But when the contract finally arrives, too often, the author's elation is replaced by confusion. I won't deny that to the uninitiated, a publishing contract is a real bear—full of legal mumbo-jumbo that makes most people want to run the other way. But, in fact, it is possible for even the most contract-challenged person to understand a standard publishing agreement, and—in many cases—to negotiate more favorable terms. Chapter 7, "The Deal," explains the terms of a standard agreement in plain English, and provides some guidelines for negotiation. It also helps you decide whether you want to handle the negotiation process alone, or enlist the aid of a lawyer or literary agent.

You know what they say about the best-laid schemes of mice and men? Well, even if you try to do everything right, you may find that none of the publishers you contact is interested in your proposal. This could happen for any number of reasons. Chapter 8, "When It Doesn't Happen," first helps you pinpoint the cause of the problem. It then presents a variety of ways in which the problem can be fixed. And if there are still no "takers," the chapter fills you in on some great options such as self-publishing—options that may allow you to get your manuscript out of the desk drawer and into a bookstore.

Do you need to read this whole book to get your book into print? Not necessarily. You can always jump to the chapters that you think best meet your specific needs. However, since the system is based on a steppingstone approach, by reading all the chapters, you will be sure to equip yourself with the tools you need to become the type of author that editors seek. Will it take some work? Absolutely. Once you know what you must do, you will have to invest the time and do the work necessary to make it happen. Will you really get your work published? I make it a practice never to lie to my authors, and I will not lie to any of my readers by providing a guarantee. But I will say this: By reading this book, you can greatly increase the odds of getting your book into publication. You can become a more knowledgeable author, and can begin to make choices that are based on fact, not wishful thinking.

## RULE #1

## *There are exceptions to every rule*

A little earlier, I said there were rules to learn and follow in order to get your book published. At this point, I'd like to introduce you to one of my favorite rules—there are exceptions to every rule. It is this rule of exceptions that turns paupers into kings, dark horses into champion thoroughbreds, and struggling writers into best-selling authors. That's what makes publishing so exciting—the books that become surprise hits. The problem is that when viewed from outside the industry, these best-selling exceptions may be considered the norm. But for every exception that takes off in a marketplace, there are literally thousands of exceptions that fail. Experienced editors know this. This does not mean that editors will not take on an exception in which they strongly believe. Many do take chances. However, by positioning your book as the next best-selling exception to the rule, you will greatly reduce your odds of getting your work into print.

This book was written for the vast majority of writers who simply want to get their work published by a good house, and is designed to help you work *within* the system of rules that most editors follow. What if you feel that your book is one of the exceptions mentioned above? Well, you may be right. Nevertheless, I encourage you to learn about the rules I've laid out in this book. Like my mother always said, "It couldn't hurt."

With that out of the way, let's get the show on the road.

## CHAPTER 2

# Where Does Your Book Fit In?

*The phone rings, and picking it up, I hear the voice of my secretary. She says, "There's a gentleman on the line who says he's a friend of a friend who told him you might be able to help him with his book." I look at the pile of work on my desk, take a deep breath, and accept the call. Who knows? It could be the next Carl Sagan.*

*The writer tells me that he doesn't have a clue about how he can get his book into publication. I ask him what type of book he has written, and he responds, "I've written a novel. Yes, I know you don't publish novels, but this is different—it's based on a true story. It's not really a novel because it tries to teach some very important lessons about life. It's a type of how-to book in that sense. It's perfect for college students who are confused about their future, not to mention those people who are looking for some kind of change in their lives. I really believe most everyone can gain something from it."*

*I think to myself, "Definitely not another Carl Sagan. Not even close."*

If you were to call me at my office, as the writer did in the above story, would you be able to tell me what type of book you're writing? Could you tell me the audience at which your book is aimed? How about the marketplace for which it's geared?

At this point, you might be saying to yourself, "Well, I think I can answer those questions. I *definitely* know what kind of book I'm writing. And I'm pretty sure who my readers are going to be and where my book will sell." If you are like most writers, though, you have only a general notion of where your book fits in—and you probably think that this is adequate. After all, you're a writer, not an editor, and you shouldn't have to know every little detail about the book business. But the fact is that in the world of publishing, general impressions just aren't enough. If you send a proposal to an editor and rely on that editor to fill in the details of where your book fits in, you will most certainly decrease your chance of getting your work reviewed. As an author, it is absolutely vital that you understand your book in terms of its category, audience, and marketplace. And it is equally important to communicate this information to the publisher if you hope to get your work into print.

This chapter will help you pinpoint the category into which your book fits, the audience to which it should be directed, and the outlets through which it may be sold. By identifying these three elements, you will be better able not only to find a publisher who produces books in the appropriate area, but also to convince that publishing house that your book does, indeed, have an existing audience that can readily be reached.

## RULE #2

## *Know your book's category*

There are three important reasons to learn where your title belongs in the often confusing world of publishing. First, you must know your book's category if you are to create a list of those publishing houses that are best positioned to accept and market your work. Second, in many cases, you have to know your book's category to address your manuscript proposal to the right editor at these companies, instead of trusting that fate will deliver your package into the right hands. And third, pinpointing your book's category will enable you to identify and analyze any competing books now in the marketplace. How—and why—are books categorized? The discussion below will answer that question. Following this, we'll look at the Square One Book Classification System—a system designed to help you easily and accurately identify where your book belongs.

## WHAT ARE BOOK CATEGORIES?

Book categories were created to help people organize and locate books. The average writer finds it no easy task to understand book categories—and for good reason. You see, today, there are several *different* book classification systems in use. First, there are the systems used by libraries. Based on either the Library of Congress or Dewey decimal system, these methods of classification allow libraries to keep track of thousands of volumes. Then, there are the categories used by bookstores. These are designed as a promotional tool that enables consumers to find the books they want. Finally, there are the categories created by publishers to identify the types of titles in which they specialize, and—in some cases—to indicate the outlets through which their books will be sold.

Knowing the category into which your book falls will help you to:

- ❑ Create a list of publishing houses that are best suited to accept and market your work.
- ❑ Send your manuscript proposal to the appropriate editor within the company.
- ❑ Identify and analyze competing books in the marketplace.

Clearly, many of the book categories created by these systems overlap. They have many of the same names, and, to a degree, use the same criteria to arrange titles. However—and this is an important point—many have created book categories that are unique to their own needs. For example, bookstores have classifications such as "New Adult Fiction" and "New York Times Best Sellers." Publishers, on the other hand, have categories such as "Book Club," "Mail Order," "Mass Market Paperback," "Subscription Reference," and "University Press." So what's the problem? Well, if you're simply browsing the shelves of a bookstore, there is none. But if you're an author who's trying to determine your own book's category, you may find it difficult to use the existing systems to describe your book to a publisher. Do you know of any writers who set out to write a mass market paperback, or a bestseller mail order title? I certainly hope not! First of all, most mass market paperback publishers buy the rights to books that were first published as hardbound books. And many mail order book companies either have their own in-house people write books, or they, too, buy the mail order reprint rights for previously produced works. Just as important, if a writer did describe her book using one of these labels, the label would fail to tell the publisher anything she needs to know about the book.

Where does that leave you? It leaves you in search of a classification system that meets your specific needs. It therefore gives me great pleasure to introduce you to the Square One Book Classification System.

## THE SQUARE ONE BOOK CLASSIFICATION SYSTEM

The Square One Book Classification System was specifically designed for authors who must explain their projects to publishers. It presents book categories that editors both understand and are looking for. Just as important, the system avoids those categories that only confuse and bewilder editors—and make you look as if you don't have a clue about your own book.

The Square One system is composed of twelve main categories, each of which is further divided into three levels. The twelve categories include:

1. Trade books
2. Elementary and secondary school textbooks
3. College textbooks
4. Professional books
5. Scholarly books
6. Reference books
7. Religious trade books
8. Religious elementary and secondary school textbooks
9. Religious college textbooks
10. Religious professional books
11. Religious scholarly books
12. Religious reference books

Below, you will find a detailed description of each of the Square One system's basic categories. As an author, you must select no more than one of these twelve categories for your project. As you learn about these categories, keep in mind that they reflect the basic classifications into which most book publishers fall. That is, a publisher can be a trade book house, a college textbook company, a professional book publisher, and so on. That's why pinpointing your book's category is such an important step in the selection of an appropriate publisher. Of course, some large publishers are composed of several divisions, and thus may publish more than one category of books. But—and this is an important but—these divisions usually operate as separate entities. In most cases, each has its own editors, catalogue, and marketing operation.

The different levels of each main category break down that class of books into subcategories. These subcategories will help you further narrow your search for an appropriate publishing house. They will also help you pinpoint the type of information an editor needs to make an initial decision about a title's suitability for her publishing company.

So what type of book are you writing? Let's find out.

## I. Trade Books

Trade books are designed to sell to the general public. They include paperbacks and hardbacks, large-sized editions such as coffee table titles, medium-sized books such as standard novels, and small books such as mass market paperbacks. They can be prose, poetry, or a combination of both. They can be illustrated, or they can be straight text.

Trade books are priced to appeal to the average reader. Because of this, these titles are sold through retailers such as bookstores, drugstores, and dot.com companies, to mention just a few outlets. In fact, these books can be sold in almost any high-traffic area where there are shoppers. Trade books are the types found on almost every bestsellers list. *Of the twelve categories, is this the most appropriate for your title?*

**SAMPLE**
*How to Publish Your Nonfiction Book*
by Rudy Shur

**Category #1**

Trade Book

**Level One**

Adult nonfiction

**Level Two**

Reference/Writing

**Level Three**

A how-to book on getting your nonfiction book into publication. It is geared for the first-time writer who needs a step-by-step system for pinpointing appropriate publishers, writing a winning submission package, and sending the package out in the most effective way possible.

## Level One

At level one, trade books are divided into six classifications: children's fiction, which is also called juvenile fiction; young adult fiction; adult fiction; children's (juvenile) nonfiction; young adult nonfiction; and adult nonfiction. Since our book is not focused on fiction, we will concern ourselves only with nonfiction from this point on. *Select one classification only from this level.*

## Level Two

At level two of nonfiction trade books, we group books specifically within subject categories. These level-two categories reflect the breakdown you would most likely find in bookstores and libraries. They include antiques, architecture, art, biography, business, collectibles, computers, cooking, crafts and hobbies, current affairs, education, etiquette, fitness, foreign languages, gardening, health, history, home schooling, law, mathematics, medicine, metaphysics, military, music, nature, occult, parapsychology, parenting, performing arts, pets, philosophy, photography, political science, psychology, reference, religion, science, self-help, sports and recreation, study aids, technology, travel, true crime, and writing. Please note that some books on the subjects just listed—education, medicine, reference, and religion—may appear to fit into other main categories listed on page 12. However, if these titles are written specifically for the general public, they would be considered trade books. *You can select up to two classifications from this level.*

## Level Three

While level two of this category provides the general subject area, level three focuses on the specific topic of your work. For example, if you have written a history book, your level-three category should clarify what your book is the history of, including the time period covered. Although you may be tempted to use the title of your book to describe its level-three category, do not do so if your title does not accurately reflect the topic of the book. *Men Are From Mars, Women Are From Venus; What Color Is Your Parachute?;* and *Who Moved My Cheese?* are all great titles, but none of them really describes the book's subject. *Try to keep your description within two to four sentences in length.*

## 2. Elementary and Secondary School Textbooks

The books in this category are designed for use as learning materials in elementary schools, middle schools (also called junior high schools), and high schools. Elementary and secondary school textbooks, commonly called *el-hi books,* include hardcover and softcover textbooks, workbooks, manuals, maps, and other publications intended for classroom use. These titles can be ordered by an individual teacher, a local or regional curriculum committee, or a statewide textbook adoption committee. *Of the twelve categories, is this the most appropriate for your title?*

### Level One

Level one of this category defines the specific grade or grades at which the work is aimed. For example, within elementary schools, you can label a book for use in kindergarten, first grade, second grade, third grade, and so on. In middle schools, the grades may include sixth, seventh, and eighth—although these grades vary from one school district to another. In high schools, level one-categories may cover ninth, tenth, eleventh, and twelve grade. In certain cases, an editor may define a project in terms of its reading level. For instance, a textbook may be described as having a third-grade reading level. In almost all cases, the publisher monitors and adjusts the reading level as necessary. *Select one classification from the following three: (1) elementary school, (2) middle school, or (3) high school. Include the grade level(s) where applicable.*

### Level Two

Level two classifies el-hi texts according to general subject matter. At the elementary school level, this could include art; computer science; health; language arts such as grammar, literature, reading, and writing; mathematics; music; science; and social studies, including current events, economics, geography, history, and government. At

**SAMPLE**
***Economics in Our Times***
by Roger A. Arnold

**Category #2**
*Secondary School Textbook*

**Level One**
*High school*

**Level Two**
*Economics*

**Level Three**
*An introductory text geared toward high school juniors and/or seniors. This book presents all of the basic concepts of economics, including budget and trade deficits, inflation, interest rates, and unemployment. It also explains how economics influences world events, and how it affects our daily lives.*

the middle and high school levels, the classifications could include art; business subjects such as accounting, advertising, finance, and marketing; career training; computer science; English; foreign language; health; history; home economics courses such as family and consumer sciences; mathematics; music; the sciences, such as biology, chemistry, earth science, and physics; technology; and social studies, such as economics, geography, government, and history. *Select one subject classification only.*

Again, you may note some overlap between categories. For instance, mathematics was listed as both a trade book subject and an el-hi text subject. The difference, of course, is that while trade books are designed for the general reader, el-hi books are designed specifically for classroom use.

### Level Three

If your book is designed for elementary school use, level three should define the specific curriculum. For example, your book may cover local history, an integral part of your state's social studies curriculum. Be sure to detail the material in your proposed work. If your book is written for middle or high schools, it should specify the course—trigonometry, for example. Because some course titles do not clearly define the actual topic covered, you should avoid these titles if they do not specify the subject of your work. *Try to keep your description within two to four sentences in length.*

## 3. College Textbooks

These books are created for use in specific college courses—although, in certain cases, they may also be used in advanced high school courses. This category includes hardcover and softcover textbooks, workbooks, manuals, maps, and other publications intended for classroom use. Although college texts are purchased by students, they are chosen by the teacher who is teaching the course, a senior course supervisor, a chairperson, or a department textbook selection committee. *Of the twelve categories, is this the most appropriate for your title?*

## Level One

Level one of this category defines whether the book is designed for a two-year college, a four-year college, both a two-year and a four-year college, or a graduate school. This can get tricky. For example, if your book was created for a two-year college basic core curriculum, it may also fit into some four-year college programs. But since college textbook editors know this already, your level-one category should be "two-year college." On the other hand, if you have written a book for a more advanced two-year college course—one that may also be offered at four-year colleges—you should explain that your book was designed for both two-year and four-year programs.

The same holds true for undergraduate and graduate programs. Usually, these are two very separate marketplaces. However, certain courses straddle the two levels, and if your book is suitable for both, you must clarify this for the publisher.

*Select one classification from the following five: (1) two-year college, (2) four-year college, (3) both two- and four-year colleges, (4) graduate school, or (5) undergraduate and graduate school.*

## Level Two

Level two classifies college texts according to general subject categories. These include anthropology; art; astronomy; biology; business topics such as accounting, finance, and marketing; chemistry; computer science; earth science; English; foreign language; geography; geology; government; health; history; home economics; mathematics; music; physics; political science; psychology; social studies; and sociology, as well as numerous other disciplines. *Select one subject classification only.*

## Level Three

The level-three classification should provide the standard name of the course for which the text is designed. You should also mention whether the book will be designed for a one- or two-semester course. Some courses have rather peculiar names that do not reflect the subject coverage, while others use numbers as designations. Biology of Vertebrates is fine; Biology 223 is not. *Try to keep your description within two to four sentences in length.*

**SAMPLE**

***Microbiology: Principles and Explorations***
by Jacquelyn G. Black

**Category #3**

College Textbook

**Level One**

Four-year college

**Level Two**

Microbiology

**Level Three**

An introductory text for the beginning microbiology student attending a one-semester course. Topics include genetics, viruses, epidemiology, immunology, and environmental biology, as well as other introductory subjects.

## 4. Professional Books

**SAMPLE**

***The English Teacher's Companion***

by Jim Burke and Mary Frances Claggett

**Category #4**

*Professional Book*

**Level One**

*Educational*

**Level Two**

*For both experienced and novice high school English teachers*

**Level Three**

*A teaching guide that presents the foundation for teaching English. It offers practical advice for curriculum planning, effective methods for measuring student progress, and ways to integrate the latest technologies into the classroom.*

Professional books are designed to meet the needs of people who work in a specific profession or technology. This category includes hardcover and softcover workbooks, manuals, guides, dictionaries, directories, and other books intended to improve job performance or provide specialized knowledge. Many of these books may also fall under the reference book category. Professional books are usually higher priced than trade books. These books may be purchased by an individual, or purchased by a company for its employees. They may also be available in specialized bookstores. *Of the twelve categories, is this the most appropriate for your title?*

### Level One

Level one divides the category of professional books into three broad groups and numerous specialty areas. The first of the more general subcategories includes *technical and scientific books.* These titles are directed at scientists, engineers, architects, and other professionals in the areas of technology, engineering, and the sciences. *Medical books* are addressed to medical doctors, nurses, dentists, veterinarians, pharmacists, and other professionals working in the field of health. *Business books* are written for business people, accountants, and managers.

Then, as mentioned, there are many more specific groups. For instance, there are law books written for lawyers, library science books written for librarians, education books written for teachers, and so on. *Select one classification only.*

### Level Two

The level-two classification should provide the name of the specific group the project is directed at within the general field of interest. For example, a professional education book may be intended for an educator teaching a specific grade level; a specialty teacher, such as a teacher of art, science, or special education; or a member of the administrative staff. Try to be as specific as possible when defining your intended audience. *List the appropriate group or groups for your work.*

### Level Three

Level three should define the specific topic of your work. For example, if you have written a professional book for criminal lawyers, what particular subject does the book cover? Jury selection? Plea bargaining? Capital punishment? Do not use the title of your book to explain your subject if your title does not clearly define your topic. *Try to keep your description within two to four sentences in length.*

## 5. Scholarly Books

Although college texts and professional books may be well researched, they are usually not considered to be scholarly books. While a professional book is most often intended to aid the reader in the performance of his or her job, a scholarly book is designed to examine a very narrow topic on an academic level. It is generally written on an advanced reading level that requires the reader to have some prior knowledge of the topic. In addition, most scholarly works are heavily footnoted and referenced. Like professional books, scholarly titles are usually more expensive than trade titles. These books include hardcover and softcover editions, and are purchased by individuals interested in exploring a specific area in depth, or by libraries that specialize in the topic. *Of the twelve categories, is this the most appropriate for your title?*

### Level One

Level-one classifications provide the general name of the profession, occupation, field, or vocation that the book addresses. Writers of scholarly books can draw from literally thousands of diverse subjects, including antiques, architecture, art, astrology, astronomy, biology, business, chemistry, computers, cooking, crafts, engineering, education, environmental science, foreign languages, gardening, health, history, law, mathematics, medicine, metaphysics, military history, military science, music, nature, occult, parapsychology, parenting, performing arts, philosophy, photography, physics, political science, psychology, recreation, religion, sports, stamps, and technology. *Select one subject classification only.*

**SAMPLE**

***Slavery and the American West***
by Michael A. Morrison

**Category #5**

Scholarly Book

**Level One**

History

**Level Two**

For professors of American History

**Level Three**

An examination of slavery in the twelve-year period prior to the outbreak of the American Civil War. Specifically, this book discusses the issue of slavery in the West, where Americans debated whether slaves could be used in the territories of the United States.

### Level Two

The level-two classification should specify the professional specialty or occupation at which the book is directed. If it is a scholarly book on butterflies or butterfly collecting, what type of biologist or butterfly collector does it address? If it is a book on architecture, whom would the book interest? Scholarly books, by their very nature, tend to have limited appeal. The level-two classification should clearly define the specific group or groups who may be interested in knowing about this work. *List the appropriate group or groups for your work.*

### Level Three

The level-three classification pinpoints the specific topic of your work. For example, if you have written a work on butterflies, what group of butterflies does it examine, and why? Do not use the title of your book to explain your subject if the title does not clearly define your topic. *Try to keep your description within two to four sentences in length.*

## 6. Reference Books

A reference book offers its readers facts and information on any number of subjects. Typically used as a resource, rather than a book that is read cover to cover, it provides useful details on specific subjects. The reference books that constitute this category are usually not directed at the general public as are trade reference books, but target a more select group of users. And they are generally among the highest priced titles. These books can be hardcover or softcover, and can take the form of directories, encyclopedias, handbooks, guides, readers, or dictionaries. Many reference books may also fall under the professional book category where they address a profession or trade. But while professional books are primarily sold to individuals, reference books are predominately purchased by libraries and organizations that need these titles as resources. They may also be available in specialized bookstores. *Of the twelve categories, is this the most appropriate for your title?*

### Level One

The level-one classification for reference works provides the general name of the profession, trade, field, or hobby for which the book is designed. Writers of reference books can draw from literally thousands of general categories that cover such diverse areas as antiques, architecture, art, astrology, astronomy, biology, business, chemistry, computers, cooking, crafts, engineering, education, environmental science, foreign languages, gardening, health, history, law, mathematics, medicine, metaphysics, military history, military science, music, nature, occult, parapsychology, parenting, performing arts, philosophy, photography, physics, political science, psychology, publishing, recreation, religion, sports, stamps, and technology. *Select one subject classification that best describes your topic.*

### Level Two

The level-two classification should provide the specific name of the professional trade or specialty at which the book is directed. If it is a reference book on biology, what type of biologist would be interested in using it as a resource? If it is a book on architecture, to whom would the book appeal? In other words, what specific group or groups may be interested in using this book as a reference? *List the appropriate group or groups for your work.*

### Level Three

The level-three classification should define the specific topic of your work and the manner in which the material has been arranged. For example, if you have written a reference work on stamps, what type of stamps does it examine? Is it set up as an A-to-Z encyclopedic listing, or is it arranged by country? Do not use the title of your book to explain your subject if the title does not clearly define your topic. *Try to keep your description within two to four sentences in length.*

**SAMPLE**
*Literary Market Place*
by R.R. Bowker

**Category #6**

Reference Book

**Level One**

Publishing

**Level Two**

For book and magazine editors and publishers, writers, librarians, literary agents, and printers.

**Level Three**

An A-to-Z listing of American and Canadian book publishers, magazine publishers, and literary agents. It is also a resource for a number of editorial services, and provides listings of trade magazines and reference books, as well as industry associations and foundations.

## 7. Religious Trade Books

The books in this category are designed to sell to the religious or

**SAMPLE**
*The God Chasers*
by Tommy Tenney

**Category #7**
Religious Trade Book

**Level One**
Christian adult nonfiction

**Level Two**
Self-Help/Inspirational

**Level Three**
An inspirational book for Christians in search of a personal relationship with God. Using personal accounts of the miraculous, this book guides the reader in using humility and self-examination to "chase after God" and live every day in His presence.

spiritually oriented portion of the general public. There is an overlap between trade books on the subject of religion, found in Category #1, and religious trade books. But the trade books we are referring to in Category #7 are produced by religious publishers rather than secular trade publishers, and are generally for people who have a personal involvement in a specific religion. This category includes paperbacks and hardbacks, large-sized editions such as coffee table titles, medium-sized books the size of standard novels, and small (rack-sized) books such as mass market paperbacks. Like regular trade books, religious trade books are priced to appeal to the general public. These titles are sold through retailers such as general bookstores, religious bookstores, religious article shops, and dot.com companies. *Of the twelve categories, is this the most appropriate for your title?*

## Level One

At level one, religious trade books are divided into the same categories used to classify their secular counterparts. These classifications include religious children's fiction, religious young adult fiction, religious adult fiction, religious children's nonfiction, religious young adult nonfiction, and religious adult nonfiction. In addition, this level should define the specific religion that the book addresses. Thus, at this level, you might describe your work as being Baptist children's fiction, Catholic young adult nonfiction, or Jewish adult nonfiction. Since our book is not focused on fiction, we will concern ourselves only with the nonfiction religious trade book. *Select one classification only from this level. Make sure to include a religious affiliation when appropriate.*

## Level Two

At level two of nonfiction religious trade books, books are grouped specifically within subject categories. These level-two categories reflect the breakdown you would most likely find in religious bookstores. They include art, biography, business, Bible study guides, cooking, counseling, current affairs, devotionals (daily mediations), divorce, education, etiquette, family and single living, healing, health, inspiration, marriage, medicine, metaphysics, miracles, music, parenting, philosophy, prayer, prophecy, psychology, reference, religious architecture, religious history, religious principles, self-help, spirituality, and spiritual living. *You can select up to two classifications for your work.*

### Level Three

While level two provides the general subject category, level three focuses on the specific topic of your work. For example, if you have written a religious history book, your level-three category should clarify what your book is a history of, including the time period covered. Do not use the title of your book if it does not accurately reflect the specific topic of your work. *Amazing Grace, The Battle for God,* and *Conversations With God* are intriguing titles, but they do not identify the subjects addressed in these books. *Try to keep your description within two to four sentences in length.*

## 8. Religious Elementary and Secondary School Textbooks

Books within this category are designed for use as learning materials in religious elementary schools and high schools, as well as in home schooling, much of which is religion-based. Religious elementary and secondary school textbooks, or el-hi books, include hardcover and softcover textbooks, workbooks, manuals, maps, and other publications intended for classroom use. These titles can be ordered by an individual teacher, or by a local or regional curriculum committee. *Of the twelve categories, is this the most appropriate for your title?*

### Level One

Level one of this category defines the specific grade or grades at which the work is aimed. For example, within religious elementary schools, you can designate a book for use in kindergarten, first grade, second grade, third grade, and so on, all the way to eighth grade. For religious high school, level-two categories may include ninth, tenth, eleventh, or twelfth grade. In certain cases, an editor

When scanning the subjects addressed by religious el-hi texts, you may be surprised to see topics such as math and grammar. Do books on such obviously secular topics present a religious point of view? Frequently, they don't. However, texts such as these are often produced by religious publishers to serve the home-schooling market, which is largely religion-based. When parents buy texts for their children, instead of going to one publisher for a book on, say, the Bible, and to another company for a book on grammar or mathematics, they often prefer to purchase all of their texts from one source—a religious publisher who can meet all of their home-schooling needs.

may define a project in terms of its reading level. For instance, a textbook may be described as having a third-grade reading level. In almost all cases, the publisher monitors and adjusts the reading level as necessary.

In addition, this level should state the specific religion that the book addresses. Thus, at this level, you might describe your work as being for a Baptist, Catholic, or Jewish school—whatever your market's religious affiliation may be. *Select one classification from the following two: (1) elementary school or (2) high school. Include the appropriate religious affiliation and grade level(s) where applicable.*

**SAMPLE**
*Coming to God*

**Category #8**

Religious Elementary School Textbook

**Level One**

Catholic elementary school–First grade

**Level Two**

Traditions and teachings of the Catholic Church

**Level Three**

A textbook designed to help first graders come to know and love God. This is done through Bible stories and the story of the Catholic Church, as well as simple prayers that help kids listen and talk to God.

### Level Two

Level two classifies religious el-hi texts according to general subject matter. At the elementary school level, the subjects may include art; Bible studies; health; language arts such as literature, grammar, and writing; mathematics; music; science; and social studies, including current events, history, and government. At the high school level, the classifications may include art; Bible studies; business; English; health; home economics subjects such as family and consumer sciences; mathematics; music; the sciences; and social studies, including economics, government, and history. *Select one subject classification only.*

### Level Three

If your book is designed for elementary school use, level three should define the specific curriculum, such as Christian ethics. If your book is written for middle or high schools, it should specify the course—Family and Marriage, for example. Because some course titles do not clearly define the actual topic covered, you should avoid titles if they do not specify the subject of your work. *Try to keep your description within two to four sentences in length.*

## 9. Religious College Textbooks

These books are created for use in specific religious college courses at either the undergraduate level or the graduate level. Religious college textbooks include hardcover and softcover textbooks, workbooks, manuals, maps, and other publications intended for classroom use. Although purchased by college students, religious college texts are chosen by the teacher who teaches the course, a senior course coordinator, a chairperson, or a department textbook selection committee. *Of the twelve categories, is this the most appropriate for your title?*

### Level One

Level one of this category defines whether the book is designed for undergraduate studies, graduate studies, or both, based on the topic covered. Usually, undergraduate and graduate schools are two very separate marketplaces. However, there are a number of courses offered that may straddle the two levels. In addition, this level should state the specific religion that the book addresses. Thus, you might describe your work as being for a Baptist, Catholic, or Jewish undergraduate program—whatever your market's religious affiliation. *Select one classification from the following three: (1) four-year college, (2) graduate school, or (3) undergraduate and graduate school. Make sure to include the material's religious affiliation when appropriate.*

### Level Two

Level two classifies religious college texts according to general subject categories. These may include art, Bible studies, biology, business, English, health, history, home economics, music, political science, psychology, history, and sociology, as well as numerous other disciplines. *Select one subject classification only.*

### Level Three

The level-three classification should provide the standard name of the course for which the text is designed. You should also mention whether the book is designed for a one- or a two-semester course. Some courses have rather peculiar names that do not reflect the subject coverage, while others use numbers as designations. Comparative Religion is fine; Religion 221 is not. *Try to keep your description within two to four sentences in length.*

**SAMPLE**

***20th Century Theology: God and the World in a Transitional Age***
by Stanley J. Grenz and Roger E. Olson

**Category #9**

Religious College Textbook

**Level One**

Four-year Christian college

**Level Two**

Theology

**Level Three**

*A text designed for a one-semester survey course of the significant theologians and theologies of the twentieth century. The text begins with the Enlightenment, looks at the giants of twentieth-century theology, and studies the influential movements of the time.*

## 10. Religious Professional Books

**SAMPLE**
*Preaching*
by Fred B. Craddock

**Category #10**
Religious Professional Book

**Level One**
Christian

**Level Two**
For ministers

**Level Three**
A practical guide to preparing and delivering sermons. The book emphasizes the Scriptures as the root of good preaching, and explains how to create sermons that are marked by passion as well as instruction.

Religious professional books are designed to meet the needs of people who work in a specific religious profession or job. This category includes hardcover and softcover books, workbooks, manuals, guides, and other books intended to improve job skills or provide specialized knowledge. *Of the twelve categories, is this the most appropriate for your title?*

### Level One

The level-one classification of this category identifies the specific religion that your book addresses. While many books may encompass a wide variety of topics, most can be asigned to a particular religious group, such as Baptist, Christian Science, Greek Orthodox, Jewish, Lutheran, Mormon, Muslim, Presbyterian, Roman Catholic, Seventh-Day Adventist, etc. *List the appropriate religion or religions for your work.*

### Level Two

Within the various houses of worship, there exist numerous positions that require specialized knowledge and training. Each position calls for different skills and a special body of knowledge. Level two specifies the name of the clergyman or layperson for whom the work is designed. For example, your book may address priests, ministers, rabbis, cantors, or deacons. *List the appropriate group or groups for your work.*

### Level Three

Level three should define the specific topic of your work. For example, if you have written a professional book for priests or rabbis, what particular subject does the book address? Is it a guide to writing meaningful sermons? Is it a book on pastoral counseling? Is it a how-to book on developing youth programs? Do not use the title of your book to explain your subject if the title does not clearly define your topic. *Try to keep your description within two to four sentences in length.*

## II. Religious Scholarly Books

A religious scholarly book is designed to examine a very narrow topic on an academic level. It is generally written on a high reading level that requires the reader to have an existing knowledge of the topic. In addition, most religious scholarly works are heavily footnoted and referenced. These books can be either hardcover or softcover, and are purchased by individuals interested in exploring a specific religious area in depth, or by libraries that specialize in the topic. *Of the twelve categories, is this the most appropriate for your title?*

### Level One

Level-one classifications define the religion that the book addresses, be it Baptist, Christian Science, Greek Orthodox, Jewish, Lutheran, Mormon, Muslim, Presbyterian, Roman Catholic, Seventh-Day Adventist, etc. *List the appropriate religion or religions for your work.*

### Level Two

The level-two classification pinpoints the specific name of the professional specialty, occupation, or audience to which the book is directed—clergy, religious scholar, or specialized library. If it is a religious scholarly book on the trial of Saint Joan, what type of reader would it address? If it deals with the life of a saint, to whom would the book appeal? By their very nature, scholarly books of any kind tend to have a limited audience. The level-two classification should provide the specific group or groups that may be interested in knowing about this work. *List the appropriate group or groups for your work.*

### Level Three

Here, you should define the specific topic of your work. For example, if you have written a work on the life of a saint, on what aspect of his or her life have you focused? Do not use the title of your book to explain your subject if the title does not clearly define your topic. *Try to keep your description within two to four sentences in length.*

**SAMPLE**
***An Introduction to the Study of Paul***
by David Horrell

**Category #11**

Religious Scholarly Book

**Level One**

Christian

**Level Two**

For religious scholars

**Level Three**

A scholarly examination of the life of the Apostle Paul. The book traces the development from Saul to Paul, including all key events, and discusses theological doctrines such as atonement, Christology, and Ecclesiology. The main interpretations of Paul are presented and analyzed.

## 12. Religious Reference Books

**SAMPLE**
*Biographical Dictionary of Christian Missions*
Gerald H. Anderson, editor

**Category #12**
Religious Reference Book

**Level One**
Christian

**Level Two**
For students of Christian missions

**Level Three**
Alphabetical entries of 2,400 articles on Christian missions. This reference explores the time period immediately following the New Testament era to the present.

A religious reference book offers its readers facts and information on any number of religious subjects. Typically used as a resource, rather than a book that is read cover to cover, it provides useful details on specific topics. These books can be hardcover or softcover, and can take the form of encyclopedias, handbooks, guides, readers, or dictionaries. Religious reference books are usually very expensive. They are purchased by individuals, religious organizations, and specialized libraries. They may also be available in religious bookstores. *Of the twelve categories, is this the most appropriate for your title?*

### Level One

The level-one classification should define the religion that the book addresses, be it Baptist, Christian Science, Greek Orthodox, Jewish, Lutheran, Mormon, Muslim, Presbyterian, Roman Catholic, Seventh-Day Adventist, etc. In some instances, the book may cover a wide range of different religions. *List the appropriate religion or religions for your work.*

### Level Two

The level-two classification should specify the audience to which the book is directed—clergy, religious scholar, or student of religion. If it is an encyclopedia of important religious dates, who would be interested in using it as a resource? If it is a book on sermons, to whom would the book appeal? *List the appropriate group or groups for your work.*

### Level Three

The level-three classification should define the specific topic of your work and the manner in which the material has been arranged. For example, if your book is a collection of sermons, does it include all types of sermons, or does it focus on sermons that are appropriate only for a specific occasion? Are the sermons arranged according to holiday, or are they arranged by topic? Do not use the title of your book to explain your subject if the title does not clearly define your topic. *Try to keep the description within two to four sentences in length.*

Try to be as objective as possible when writing down the information regarding the category of your work. The more accurate and specific the information, the easier it will be to identify those publishers who are most likely to say "yes" to your proposal. If you have reviewed all twelve main categories and have not found the category into which your book falls, I suggest that you read the "Got Questions?" inset found below. This may provide you with helpful guidance. If, after reading both this chapter and the inset, you feel that the categories that have been defined are too restrictive—that your book defies categorization and is, in fact, for everyone—you may still find a publisher. If you read Rule #1 in Chapter 1, you know that there are exceptions to every rule. However, most editors look for books that fit into a specific category. If you fail to pinpoint that category, you will have significantly decreased your odds of finding an editor interested in acquiring your manuscript.

## Got Questions?

Hopefully, you now have a clear understanding of the Square One Book Classification System. I have found, however, that when I explain this system to an audience, people often have questions. In all fairness, I must admit that it is no easy task to categorize certain books. Not all projects fit neatly into every level of a given category, and some projects simply defy classification. With this in mind, below I present some commonly asked questions about book classification, and supply answers that, in the past, have proven helpful to many authors.

### Can a book fit into more than one category?

The answer is "yes." Although most nonfiction books are published by a company or by a division of a company that specializes in one of the twelve main categories, some of these books could also fit into one or more additional categories.

Consider Stephen R. Covey's book *The Seven Habits of Highly Effective People*. Originally, Covey's title was released as a trade book (Category #1). However, as its popularity increased, it was picked up as required reading in a number of different college business management courses (Category #3). In addition, it sold well to business professionals (Category #4). But while the book did sell well in these two other marketplaces, it was always classified as a trade book.

The fact is that this title could have been published by either a college textbook house or a professional book publisher just as well as a trade house. The book's content and writing style allowed it to fit in all three categories. However, by placing the title with a trade publisher, the author positioned his book for maximum overall success.

Consider two more examples. Let's say you're writing a religious nonfiction book that seems as if it could fit in both the trade category (Category #1) under adult religion, and the religious trade category (Category #7) under adult nonfiction. Or consider a professional directory designed for dentists that seems as appropriately placed in professional books (Category #4) as it does in reference books (Category #6). What could you do in each of these cases? Initially, try to choose the category into which you feel your project best fits, be it trade or religious trade, professional or reference. Later, if your submission package doesn't meet with the success that you hoped for, you can always change your strategy and send your package to publishers in the other category.

Therefore, to reap the benefits of my system, even though your book may have more than one main category, you must at least initially select a *single* category—the one that would best serve your work. You can do this is several ways. First, you might select the category that would best reach your intended reader. Second, you can look at the books currently in print that you consider competition to your own, consider the category of the publisher that produced them, and match your category to theirs. Finally, you can talk to a librarian about your writing plans, and ask her to suggest an appropriate category for your work. And remember that if your initial category choice doesn't lead to success, you can always expand your list of companies to include other publishing categories that are appropriate for your project. It may take a while to find the perfect fit.

## I want my book to be a hardback. Isn't "hardback" a category?

Hardback—a book produced with a case binding and a dust jacket—is very much a category. It is not one of my system's categories, but it is a designation commonly used by publishers, bookstores, and libraries.

In the world of publishing, there are publishers who produce only hardbacks, there are those who produce only paperbacks, and there are those who publish both. If one of your personal goals is to have your book produced as a hardback, you will find that my classification system still works for you. As it turns out, for each of the twelve categories discussed, there are many companies that publish paperback and hardback books.

But even if your heart is set on producing a hardback edition, I suggest that you refrain from mentioning this requirement in your cover letter, as it will diminish your odds of a positive response. Instead, I recommend the following strategy. As you begin choosing your list of publishers, select those firms that publish only hardbacks. (See Chapter 4.) Although this may limit your list of potential publishers, should your work be accepted, your book will definitely be produced as a hardcover edition.

## Shouldn't educational and religious books each occupy a single category?

A number of resources devote only one category to educational books, and one category to religious titles. As you see, I do not. When used as a single heading, these category names indicate the combined revenue produced by each of their market sectors. This is great if you are an economist or investor, but bad if you are an author looking for an appropriate house to review your work. In my system, the categories reflect the way publishing actually works on a daily basis.

## My book doesn't seem to fit into any main category? What should I do?

There will always be a book that does not fit neatly into one of my twelve categories. It would have been easy for me to create a thirteenth category and call it *Miscellaneous;* however, this would have been both wrong and misleading. Publishers may produce very focused books for very small marketplaces, called niche markets, but they never bring out books for a category called *Miscellaneous*.

If you are writing a book that does not fit into my main twelve groups, I would propose that you do the following. Work my three-level category system backwards to arrive at your most appropriate category.

For level three, within two to four sentences, write down what your book is about. Include information on its intended format. Will it be a workbook, a guide, a journal, or a narrative?

For level two, list the group or groups of people who will be using your book. Now, since you are familiar with the book's intended audience—and you should be, considering you are writing a book directed at these folks—consider the system of book distribution that currently reaches this audience. Are reading materials provided directly by a publisher, another type of business, a related-interest organization, or a group of professionals? Are these materials marketed at events, conventions, or meetings? Write down the names of the groups that are responsible for getting this type of information into the hands of your audience.

Finally, to identify the type of publisher for which you are looking—in other words, to define your category—consider the following question: Do these groups actually sell or give away books, as opposed to pamphlets and other handouts? Before you answer this question, do some good, solid research. If the answer is yes—these groups do sell books or give them away—gather the names of all the publishers, businesses, or groups who produce the materials. Then continue to read this book. The names you have gathered can be used to create your rough list of potential publishers, which we will talk about further in the next chapter.

If the answer is no—these groups provide pamphlets or handouts rather than books—it is very possible that there is no established means of reaching your intended audience. In publishing, this is a common problem for certain types of books.

This does not mean that your book will not sell if it gets to the appropriate market. It only means that there are no publishers currently reaching the market for any number of reasons. For instance, the market may be too small, too difficult to reach, or too costly to reach. It could also indicate that it is a very hidden market, out of the scope of most publishers, or that it is a new and emerging market of which few publishers are aware.

If there are no publishers currently selling to your intended market, you must either convince a publisher that this is a market worth pursuing or consider self-publication. (See the "Going It Alone" and "Self-Publication" discussions in Chapter 8.)

## RULE #3

# *Know your book's audience*

All too often, prospective authors tell editors, "My book is written for everyone." Unfortunately, a book that is written for everyone is usually written for no one. If you want to interest an editor in your project, you must have a clear understanding of your intended audience.

## THE IMPORTANCE OF UNDERSTANDING YOUR AUDIENCE

Each of the book categories discussed earlier in the chapter is designed for a specific type of individual. For instance, a trade book is designed for the general reader, either a younger reader or an adult; a professional book is designed for an individual who works in a specific field; and an educational book is designed for a student at a particular level of study.

Publishers—and bookstore buyers, too—know that every book must be designed and marketed for one clearly defined audience. And if you think about it, you'll understand why. You see, a book designed for a professional is not suited for the general reader, who will be intimidated by the technical jargon characteristic of a book geared for people with specialized training. Similarly, while a textbook and a trade book may cover the same subject—the field of genetics, for instance—the textbook is written with a certain reader in mind, and generally contains elements such as summaries and test questions. Such features make the book unappealing to the general reader.

Can a book appeal to more than one audience? As I explain in the inset "Got Questions?," it certainly can. A trade book is sometimes used in a classroom, for instance. But, believe it or not, presenting your work as a "crossover" title will not be in your best interest. And, of course, if your book is written on a very high level and assumes a great deal of knowledge on the part of the reader, it is not suitable for the general reader.

In order for a book to fit into the sales operation of a publishing firm, an editor must know the book's audience from the beginning. If the editor chooses poorly when acquiring a book, disappointing sales may result because the company is simply not set up to penetrate the market appropriately. As a writer who can provide a clear picture of your work's intended audience, you can make it easy for editors to recognize whether your book is a good fit for their house.

## WHAT IS YOUR READER'S PROFILE?

Now that you understand the importance of knowing your book's audience, try to pinpoint the readers that you are trying to reach. What are the characteristics of your intended reader? For example, are you writing for someone who has the reading ability of a ninth grader, or are you addressing a graduate student? Is your topic of greatest interest to males, to females, or to both? Must you supply definitions for all of the technical language used in the text, or will your reader already be familiar with the jargon used in that field? If you have determined your book's category, you should be able to answer these questions. And you should be able to describe your audience to a prospective publisher.

As a writer, you may discover that although you are, perhaps, an expert in your field of study, you are not able to perfectly adjust your writing for your audience. While the quality of your writing is certainly an important factor, a publisher may be willing to help you craft your work so that it conforms to your reader's profile. By showing an editor that you know the audience for whom you are writing, you can help provide the editor with the comfort level that she needs to sign a book on.

## HOW BIG IS YOUR AUDIENCE?

Before most editors select a book for publication, they want to examine two important pieces of information: the size of a book's audience and the past performances of similar titles.

Audience size refers to the number of people potentially interested in a book's subject. For example, if your title focuses on fly-fishing as a hobby, you might tell the editor that, by conservative

Initially, it may seem that the larger the audience, the greater the interest on the part of the publishing house. However, it does not always work that way. Some publishers are equipped to market to large audiences; others are better equipped to market to smaller audiences. The level of interest a publisher shows in a title is usually determined by the publisher's past success in reaching a specific audience. A publishing house that has an established reputation in a particular field can benefit its authors by providing additional details about a book's audience, and by having an established means of reaching potential readers.

## Estimating Audience Size

As explained beginning on page 33, solid information about the size of your book's potential readership can help convince an editor that your project is worth consideration. Fortunately, there are a variety of means by which you can estimate audience size.

Let's consider a book on the care and feeding of cats written for the general reader—a trade book, in other words. In this case, your potential audience is pretty easy to define. It's composed of cat owners. Knowing this, you can begin looking for pertinent statistics.

The Internet is, of course, one good source of information. Begin by connecting to a good search engine, such as Google.com or Britannica.com. If you then type in "pet statistics," various sites will be suggested. One site called "Fun Pet Statistics" provides data gathered by the American Pet Association, the Pet Food Institute, and other related organizations. On this site, you will find, among other things, that 29.1 million homes in the United States have at least one cat as a pet, and that there are 71.8 million pet cats in the United States. So a book designed for cat owners would have quite a substantial market!

Unfortunately, not all statistics can be found by the click of a mouse, and you may not have ready access to the Internet. What other sources are useful? Above, you saw that special organizations often gather statistics on their subject of interest. These organizations can be located through use of the *Encyclopedia of Associations* by Gale Research, a multivolume source found in the reference section of most libraries. Divided by subject, this encyclopedia can guide you to associations that focus on your book's topic. For instance, by looking in the section "Hobby and Avocational Organizations," you will find listings for the American Association of Cat Enthusiasts, as well as many other cat-related groups. Each listing in this source includes addresses and phone numbers. In some cases, e-mail addresses and fax numbers are also supplied.

If you can't get to a library, try contacting a magazine related to your subject. The editorial staff of *Cat Fancy* magazine, for instance, will give you the names and phone numbers of the two organizations that supply their magazine with statistics—namely, the American Humane Association and The Humane Society.

Of course, other books on the same subject may provide you with useful statistics, as may newspaper and magazine articles. Finally, your local librarian may be able to come up with other sources. Once you have gathered the statistics on the size of your audience, you can use this data to demonstrate to publishers that a market exists for your book. (More on this in Chapter 5.)

estimates, there are 7 million fly-fishermen in the United States. The 7-million figure represents the size of your potential readership. Keep in mind that it is important, in this case, to focus on figures for *fly-fishermen only.* The numbers you quote should not include fishermen in general or commercial fishermen.

Additionally, past performances of similar books provide editors with hard sales numbers that can be used to justify the signing of a new book. In some instances, the editor can review internal sales figures supplied by her marketing department. In other situations, the editor can glean information from trade journals, other editors and authors, and sales people. An editor can use these figures to determine whether it is worth her company's time and money to pursue a given project. If past sales were adequately large, the editor will give serious consideration to a similar project.

As the author, although you may not be able to research the sales of competing books, it is definitely in your interest to supply the editor with as much information as possible about your audience. Where can you get the necessary data? The inset "Estimating Audience Size," found on page 34, will clue you in to a number of helpful resources.

## RULE #4

## *Know your marketplace*

At this point, you should know what your category is and who your audience is. Now you need to understand just how your book will reach its intended audience—in other words, the marketplace. Without a clear understanding of where your book is going to sell, you cannot select an appropriate publisher—a publisher who is equipped to promote and distribute your book properly.

### THE IMPORTANCE OF UNDERSTANDING YOUR MARKETPLACE

Allow me to share a story with you. Dr. C. was a biology professor who had written several well-received college-level biology textbooks. In addition to being a good teacher, he was also an excellent writer. He was very anxious to write a book for the general public on genomes, the sets of hereditary factors that make each of us what we are. Considering the interest on Wall Street regarding companies doing genome research, Dr. C. thought that such a book would sell well. He therefore wrote a beautiful trade-oriented book on the subject, a book that in style and format was well suited for the general reader. The publisher with whom he had always worked—a college textbook publisher—jumped at the opportunity to sign on the book.

When it was published, Dr. C's book looked very much like a small paperback textbook. When he asked his editor about getting the book into the hands of the general public, his editor said that they would not have a problem getting the new title into libraries. But when Dr. C. asked about getting it into the bookstore chains, his editor replied that trade sales were handled by a different division of her company. She would be happy to show the book to the trade division, but she doubted that they would handle its marketing since it had originated in the college division.

Many authors mistakenly think that the term marketplace refers to a book's audience. This is understandable, because the term *market*—which is often used as a synonym for marketplace—has two separate meanings. A market can be a place or system through which books are sold to consumers (a marketplace, in other words), or a segment of the population considered buyers for a particular type of book (an audience). For clarity, in this book, we will attempt to use the term *marketplace* only when referring to bookstores, libraries, and other book outlets.

For Dr. C., knowing his book's category and audience were of no use. Being a good writer was of no help. And having a solid connection to a publishing house actually worked against him. As a writer, he needed to know his book's marketplace, as well as the type of publishing company it would take to reach his intended audience.

So, what should you know about marketplaces? You should know that a marketplace is the means through which a publisher is able to sell your book to its audience. If a publisher has no way of accessing the appropriate marketplace for your book, your book will never reach your readers. Just as important, if no marketplace is geared to sell your book, your project will have very little chance of finding an interested commercial publisher. That's why you must know the basics of marketplaces: what they are, what they carry, and how they are reached.

## THE MARKETPLACES

A *marketplace* is simply any place or system that sells books to consumers. As you will see, a marketplace can assume numerous shapes and sizes. In the early part of the twentieth century, the marketplace for books was both limited and uncomplicated. The vast reading audience was generally reached through bookstores and libraries. Publishing firms had salesmen who promoted their companies' lines throughout their territories. Books were then directly sold and distributed by the book publishers to bookstores and libraries. But as time went on, and an ever-growing audience became even more eager to buy books, the number and types of marketplaces increased. Now, any one book may be sold through a host of different outlets.

Let's look at some of the standard marketplaces that serve today's reading public. After reading this section, you will better understand how your particular book can reach its audience.

## Traditional Retail Bookstores

When the publishing industry refers to traditional retail bookstores, it is speaking of stores whose stock is primarily composed of books. Of course, in addition to books, many of these bookstores carry sidelines such as paperweights, book ends, pens, bookmarks, calendars, cards, book lights, videos, and other related items. This marketplace includes chain stores like Barnes & Noble and Borders, as well as independent bookstores.

Most of the books sold in these stores are published by trade publishers. However, retail bookstores may also offer a variety of reference books, professional books, religious trade books, and religious reference books. Their stock includes hardbacks, paperbacks, and mass market paperbacks.

Trade publishers promote their books through sales calls made by either their own sales force or the sales force of a distributor employed by the publisher. They also advertise in trade journals such as *Publishers Weekly*, and through mailings of brochures and seasonal catalogues. A number of the larger trade houses promote their books in newspapers and popular magazines. The stores purchase their books either directly from the publisher or through a distributor.

Unsold books that are held by bookstores can be returned to the distributor and/or ultimately the publisher for full credit, generally for up to one year. This returns policy—which is so different from that used in many other businesses—creates a very risky situation for the publisher.

A number of years ago, terms like distributor, wholesaler, and jobber had very specific meanings in the book business. A *distributor* was a company that inventoried and sold books for publishers, usually on an exclusive basis. Based on their agreement, distributors could sell titles to wholesalers, bookstores, libraries, and nontraditional outlets. A *wholesaler* was a company that inventoried and sold books to bookstores on a nonexclusive basis—sometimes within a local vicinity, sometimes within a regional area, and sometimes on a national basis. A *jobber* was a wholesaler who specialized in selling mass market books to bookstores and supermarkets. Today, in spite of the fact that distributors may still have exclusive agreements with certain publishers, the three terms are used interchangeably.

Specialty retailers have a number of trade organizations that sponsor regional and national book conventions. At these conventions, niche publishers exhibit titles that reflect each group's interests. For example, at the Christian Association of Booksellers convention, representatives of various religious book publishers actively promote their titles. The Religious Booksellers Trade Exhibit is another specialized show. As a writer, you should consider attending such conventions, as they offer an excellent opportunity to meet and learn about publishers who may be interested in your project. (For information on locating appropriate trade shows, see "Other Methods of Finding Publishers" in Chapter 4.)

## Specialized Retail Bookstores

Specialized retail bookstores are stores that primarily sell books focused on a specific subject. Possible areas of interest include Eastern culture; education; engineering; feminism; gay and lesbian lifestyle; medicine; occult; poetry; politics; religion; spiritualism; travel; and more. Often, a store targets a specific audience within one of these areas. For instance, rather than offering books on religion in general, a store will usually focus on Judaic books, Christian books, or a similar category of books. In addition, many of these stores carry sidelines related to the store's specialty. A Christian bookstore may offer rosaries, holy medals, scapulars, chalices, Christian music and videos, and framed pictures of saints, for example. Included in this marketplace are specialty chain stores and independent bookstores.

Most of the books sold in these stores are published by trade publishers. However, these stores may also offer a variety of reference books and professional books, based upon the individual store's focus. Their stock includes hardbacks and paperbacks. Publishers promote their books in this marketplace just as they do in the traditional trade retail marketplace. The stores purchase books either directly from the publisher or through a distributor, and unsold books can be returned to the distributor and/or ultimately the publisher for full credit for usually up to one year.

## Online Retailers

With the emergence of the Internet has come a new way of selling just about anything. E-commerce, as it is known, is composed of Internet stores that allow web browsers to buy products from the comfort of their homes or offices at any time. While there are a number of sites that specialize in books, such as Amazon.com and Barnesandnoble.com, there are literally hundreds of other sites that sell thousands of products, including books. These include such sites as Alldirect.com and Bestbuy.com.

Although a majority of the books sold on these websites are trade books, dot.com companies may also carry a wide variety of reference, professional, scholarly, religious professional, religious scholarly, and religious reference books. Their stock includes hardbacks, paperbacks, and mass market paperbacks.

To date, few trade publishers have advertised their books through website promotion. Instead, they have relied on the media exposure of a title to result in higher Internet sales. Online retailers purchase their inventory directly from the publisher or through a distributor. Most online retailers keep a limited supply of books on hand. At the moment, sales through websites may represent up to 5 percent of a given publisher's sales. Like traditional bookstore retailers, online retailers can return unsold books to the distributor and/or ultimately the publisher for full credit for up to one year.

## Nontraditional Book Retailers

A *nontraditional book retailer* is any specialized retail store that carries books as a sideline. Within this marketplace, you will find gourmet shops carrying cookbooks, museum shops stocking art titles, sporting goods stores selling sports activity books, gift shops displaying gift books, hardware supply warehouses offering how-to guides—and on and on, with new outlets joining the marketplace all the time.

While this overall marketplace has grown by leaps and bounds over the last decade, it is important to understand that this marketplace is, in fact, made up of many separate and distinct submarkets. Each of these marketplaces has its own system of marketing, sales, and distribution. Over the years, the publishers that produce books in these areas have learned to gain access to these various outlets. In most instances, books are sold to retailers on a nonreturnable basis.

When researching publishers for your book, by all means visit any appropriate nontraditional book retailers and look at the books they offer for sale. If, for instance, you are writing a how-to book on gardening, stop by the garden centers in your area and see who publishes the gardening books they stock. Write down the names of *all* the companies, but place an asterisk next to the names of those whose books you find particularly attractive and high in quality. It's very likely that these companies should be on your A List of prospective publishers.

## Mass Market Outlets

Mass market paperbacks are 4½ x 7-inch softcover editions that sometimes are reprints of hardcover trade books, and sometimes are written specifically for paperback publication. While mass market outlets include traditional bookstores, the term *mass market outlets* really refers to book outlets that can be found in high-traffic areas such as airport stores, newsstands, drugstores, and supermarket chains—outlets that can reach the "mass" audience rather than the general bookstore's trade audience.

Few publishers sell their titles directly to mass market outlets. Most books that reach these outlets are sold through wholesalers known commonly as IDs (independent distributors).

Instead of returning unsold mass market books to publishers for credit, IDs rip the covers off the unsold books. They do this because the freight costs involved in returning these inexpensive books to the publisher cannot be recouped, and the publisher cannot resell these books anyway, unlike hardbacks. To keep the IDs in business, the mass market publishers have agreed to accept a verification sheet stating that the covers of the unsold books have been stripped off, and that the remaining inventory has been destroyed. In turn, the unsold inventory is deducted from the publisher's bill. Publishers may have up to 70 percent of their books returned.

## College Bookstores

College bookstores specialize in supplying textbooks and assorted educational materials to college students. Based upon the retail space available to a college bookstore operation, the store may carry no books other than those needed by the students, may carry a limited number of trade books, or may be comparable to a traditional retail bookstore. In addition to books, most carry the usual bookstore sidelines as well as college paraphernalia such as clothing and jewelry. Included in this marketplace are college bookstore chains like Barnes & Noble and Follett, as well as independent stores. While college bookstores order textbooks directly from publishers, the texts used by students are chosen, or adopted, by the teaching staff. These textbooks are nearly all published by college textbook companies. Many of these companies employ college travelers, or sales representatives, that visit college teachers in an effort to win adoptions for their textbooks.

Trade publishers sell their books to college stores in the same way they sell their products to traditional bookstore retailers—through distributors or direct. The variety of titles offered in the traditional bookstore portion of a college store may strongly reflect the programs and interests of the college. For example, a technical college may have more reference and professional books. The stock of college bookstores includes hardbacks, paperbacks, and mass market paperbacks. Unsold college textbooks and trade books can be returned to the publisher for full credit.

## Elementary and Secondary School Textbook Sales

Most elementary and high school (el-hi) publishers employ trained sales representatives who formally present textbooks to school purchasing authorities, including teachers, textbook coordinators, and textbook committees. The sales representatives leave behind samples of the textbooks and any supporting materials, such as teacher's editions, instructor's manuals, and manipulatives, so that the authorities can further examine them. In fact, examination copies are an important promotional tool for publishers of el-hi texts.

Depending on the practices of the state, books may be adopted at the state level or at the district level. Books are sold directly from the publisher to the schools, and usually only nominal discounts are given. Unused books cannot be returned to the publisher.

## Libraries

Books are sold to a wide variety of libraries, including public libraries; state, county, and regional libraries; federally sponsored libraries; educational libraries, such as those found in public schools and colleges; and specialized libraries that serve the needs of specific readers, such as the business community or the music community. Although a public library carries all types of books, including trade books, professional books, and educational publications, the collections of educational and specialized libraries are geared specifically to the needs of their patrons.

Publishers promote their books to libraries via sales calls, catalogues, brochures, and attendance at library conventions and meetings. Libraries are also reached through trade publications such as *Publishers Weekly, Library Journal, School Library Journal, Choice, Booklist,* and *Kirkus Reviews.* Wholesale distributors also often recommend specific titles to libraries based on the profile of the library's patrons. In fact, the majority of library sales are channeled through

How many separate book outlets are out there? Here are the stats on some of the major outlets. In the United States, there are approximately:

- ❑ 3,500 college bookstores
- ❑ 16,000 public libraries
- ❑ 4,000 technical and scientific libraries
- ❑ 3,000 college and university libraries
- ❑ 4,000 religious bookstores
- ❑ 11,000 individual chain and franchise bookstores
- ❑ 14,000 independent bookstores of all types, general and specialty

these distributors, who give larger discounts than those provided by the publishers, and also simplify the ordering process by enabling the library to contact one business rather than a myriad of separate publishing houses.

## Book Clubs

Like publishing houses, book clubs have been undergoing constant consolidation—that is, companies have merged, with one company buying up others. In fact, in 2000, Doubleday Direct and the Book-of-the-Month Club, the two largest clubs in the United States, joined forces to operate under the name Bookspan.

Much has changed since the Literary Guild and Book-of-the-Month Club were launched in the 1920s. Many clubs now cater to special groups of readers, such as those interested in detective novels, history books, classics, cookbooks, and antiques. A wider range of titles is also provided now, enabling the reader to exercise greater freedom of choice. These clubs, which advertise in newspapers and magazines, offer their members substantial savings. In return, members must purchase a minimum number of books within a stated period of time. All clubs contract for rights to the titles they offer, and produce lower-priced editions by using the publisher's plates and/or economizing during production.

## Mail Order

Some books, such as professional and scholarly titles, are widely sold by mail, but are also made available through other channels. Other books, however, have more general appeal, and are specially designed for marketing by mail to the general reader. Mail order publishers such as Reader's Digest, plan and create their own products, and market them to the consumer through attractive brochures, often using the circulation lists of their magazines to reach their audience. Mail order publishing is like book club selling in that it offers popular-interest books. But unlike book clubs, which often produce low-priced editions, mail order publishers often produce fairly high-priced titles or require multiple purchases.

## Special Sales

We have come to the marketplace that is most intriguing of all—at least to me. While the term *special sales* is a catchall phrase, it represents creative and alternative ways for publishers and authors to sell their books to audiences that are beyond the reach of the sales channels that the publishers usually employ. Technically speaking, a special sale refers to the sale of books on a deep discount; on a nonreturnable basis; to a marketplace that does not interfere with any of the marketplaces previously discussed in this chapter. You have probably already seen many books sold on this basis. Some examples include:

- At the end of an infomercial, the host says, "And if you act now, we will include a copy of this beautiful book."
- An ad on the back of a soup can promotes a full-color cookbook that you can purchase by paying a discount price and sending in ten soup can labels.
- A salesman known as a display marketer drops by your office and leaves a book for people to thumb through and use. In a week, he returns to pick up the book and take orders.
- A professional organization sells work-related books to its members at a discount.
- Your bank/investment firm offers you a premium of a new book on retirement if you open up an IRA.
- A consumer's magazine offers you a useful consumer's guide free if you resubscribe to the publication.

For publishers, authors, and book buyers, these are win-win situations. They also open the door for authors to get certain hard-to-distribute books into print. And if an author has the ability to create such sales opportunities, it definitely gets the attention of many editors. I know it gets mine.

## CONCLUSION

The author who approaches an editor with unrealistic ideas regarding her book's category, audience, and marketplace holds up a red flag, and on this flag is clearly printed the words "Bad Risk." But the author who has a clear knowledge of a book's category, who has properly targeted the book's audience, and who understands how and where the book may be sold is viewed by potential publishers as a valuable asset in the publishing process. If you have read this chapter, you have taken an important and fundamental step towards turning your manuscript into a published book. The next chapter will take you further on your journey by explaining the business of publishing and guiding you towards publishers who can help you meet your goals.

CHAPTER 3

# The Business of Publishing

*The writer who sat in front of me was the author of ten published books—a number of which were produced by some of the larger publishing houses. I was definitely impressed, and pleased that he had come by. He was there to pitch his latest book proposal to me. When he finished, I said, "I really appreciate your considering my house as a possible publisher for your book, but why didn't you go back to any of the other publishers you have already worked with?" He explained that although eight of his books had received decent reviews, diminished sales had caused them to be put out of print within two to three years. His two books that were still in print were available only as mass market paperbacks. And in that smaller format, they could not be sold through their most appropriate outlets—those specialty shops for which they were originally designed.*

*When I asked why he had come to us, he replied with a smile, "Well, I visited a few of those specialty shops, and found a lot of your company's books on their shelves. . . . Maybe I should have done that a whole lot sooner."*

*"Wouldn't have been a bad idea," I said.*

In my experience, I have found that the majority of unsolicited manuscript proposals are submitted on a hit-or-miss basis. Most writers—even experienced ones, as my story shows—do not spend the time and effort to research companies before they send in material. On the other hand, the proposals written by those who have done their homework stand out like big neon signs.

After reading Chapter 2, you should have a pretty good idea of your book's category, its audience, and its marketplaces. Now it is time to consider which publishers actually produce your particular category of titles. Before we do this, however, it is important that you have an idea of how the publishing process actually works.

This chapter will provide you with a basic understanding of the nature of publishing. It describes the different types of publishing houses, presents their general editorial structures, and explains the basic criteria they use to review and determine the fate—the acceptance or rejection—of a book proposal. It also points out the advantages and disadvantages of each type of house for prospective authors, and clearly illustrates what happens to a proposal once it is in the hands of a particular publishing company.

## THE COLOR OF BOOKS IS GREEN

In today's business environment, with few exceptions, the primary motivation of a publishing company is to make money—to pay the bills and show a profit. In most instances, editors, based upon their past experiences, believe that the books they sign on will make money for their companies.

Until the middle of the twentieth century, book publishing was dominated by smaller houses that were operated directly by their publisher-owners. The industry itself was made up of individuals who looked upon publishing as an art. Standards for editors and authors were high, and staff advancement usually came after years of apprenticeship. An accountant's advice was important and certainly considered, but not necessarily followed. To a very large extent, book publishers were loyal to their authors and to the people who worked for them.

In 1959, things began to change. This was the year that Random House, the New York City-based trade book publisher founded by Bennett Cerf and Donald Klopfer, went public and offered shareholders an opportunity to own a piece of the pie. It was the first publishing company to do so. And when it did, Wall Street began to focus its attention on the book industry. Suddenly, publishing houses were scrutinized to determine just how big the pie actually was. This close attention to the growth of publishing continued throughout the 1960s. Simultaneously, trade publishing exploded with the advent of highly visible author promotions. Wall Street seemed impressed with the potential.

The 1970s saw a new breed of book publisher. Through the acquisition and consolidation of more and more publishing houses, very large book companies, such as Simon and Schuster, Prentice-Hall, McGraw-Hill, and Random House, began to emerge. Capable of turning out an incredible 500 to 1,000 new titles a year, these firms were ready and able to invest hundreds of thousands of dollars on new projects—a precedent in the book business. Whether part of a larger diverse corporation, part of a media-centered company, or a fully independent entity, these companies changed the face of publishing forever.

While all of this corporate merging and acquisitions was taking place, the overall market for books was growing. Super-sized bookstores began popping up throughout the country. In addition, books were finding their way into a growing number of new, nontraditional markets. No longer were libraries and small bookstores their main outlets. Now books were sold in drugstores, health food markets, airports, supermarkets, gourmet shops, museum stores, and wholesale clubs. In essence, more and more books were being sold everywhere.

Needless to say, the burgeoning book industry and its expanding marketplace gave rise to a new phenomenon—the even bigger *megapublishing company.* Created in the megacorporation mold, these media-driven giants were formed through the steady merger and acquisition of large numbers of well-established publishing houses. Once these houses became part of a megacorporation, they were streamlined in an effort to become more efficient and cost-effective. Under the guiding principle of "economy of size," entire departments were eliminated to avoid duplication of effort. And editorial staffs, although downsized, were expected to produce more.

Billion-dollar megapublishing companies such as the Pearson Group from the United Kingdom, the Thompson Group from Canada, and the Bertlesmann Group from Germany now dominate both the United States and European book markets.

Typically, when a well-known publishing house was acquired by a megapublishing corporation, it was relegated to an *imprint* status, which means it existed in name and logo only. Reduced to a subsidiary or division of the megapublisher, the imprint was now

The first publishing company I worked for was the Charles E. Merrill Publishing Company of Columbus, Ohio. Founded in the early 1900s, the company was originally an independent publisher of elementary school textbooks. When I worked for Charles E. Merrill in the early 1970s, it had been acquired by the Bell & Howell Company and placed under its education division. At that point, it was a publisher of el-hi and college textbooks. In the late 1970s, the Macmillan Publishing Company of New York purchased Charles E. Merrill from Bell & Howell, and changed its name to plain old Merrill Publishing Company. In the mid-1980s, Prentice-Hall purchased Macmillan Education, incorporating its titles and dissolving the imprint. Then Simon & Schuster acquired Prentice-Hall. And recently, the Pearson Group purchased Simon & Schuster Education. Guess it looks like I won't be visiting the old gang again.

responsible for the production of a fixed number of books per selling season—books that fell within a publisher's specific list.

Although profits grew within this type of business environment, old-fashioned loyalty and high editing standards were compromised. Typically, editors were no longer afforded the time they once had to carefully and thoroughly shape manuscripts. In addition, grammatical errors and typos began creeping into the final work. Churning out titles—quantity, not necessarily quality—became the focus.

Along with the emergence of these megahouses came significant breakthroughs in publishing technologies that greatly reduced the time and cost of book production. Computer programs were designed to create typeset pages, prepare photographs for printing, and even color separate images at a fraction of their previous costs. This ability to produce books more economically than ever before gave rise to a large and growing number of small independent publishing firms—some good, some not so good. Whatever the case, these companies represent viable publishing opportunities for authors who are looking to have their work published.

## RULE #5

## *Know the differences between publishing houses*

All publishers are not created equal. And if you intend to find the best company to represent you and your project, it's important for you to be aware of the major differences between them. Most basically, publishing houses are either commercial or noncommercial. The following discussion details the different kinds of publishers that fall under each of these main categories.

### COMMERCIAL PUBLISHING HOUSES

Traditional commercial publishers can be categorized as either large, moderate-sized, or small. Each has its own internal dynamics based upon the company's history, its goals, and the personalities that determine if a book is signed on, as well as how it is produced and marketed. While many publishers have their own distinct company cultures, dictated in great part by corporate ownership, the basic principles underlying their day-to-day operations tend to be universal.

Many writers, especially those who are trying to get their work published for the first time, tend to think only in terms of large publishing houses. This is certainly understandable, considering that the larger firms usually dominate the bestsellers lists. When the average individual reads of multimillion-dollar advances given to best-selling authors, it is generally the larger publishing houses that are behind these big-money offers. By their very nature—and for the sake of their shareholders—large publicly traded publishing houses must be seen continually as important players in the industry.

There are, however, literally hundreds of excellent small and moderate-sized publishing houses that can provide a wonderful home for a writer's book. Many, in fact, may be more appropriate than large firms for publishing certain titles. Without a clear understanding of the wide diversity of existing publishers, writers decrease their odds of landing book contracts. Authors also may limit potential book sales by going to press with a company that is not best suited to promote their work.

Many of the hundreds of small and mid-sized publishing houses may be more appropriate than larger firms for publishing certain titles.

## Large Houses

Typically, it is a publishing house's annual sales that determine its size. To be considered large, this figure is $50 million or more, although some may argue that this number is even higher—upwards of $100 million. Large publishers have highly defined organizational structures in which departmental roles as well as individual accountabilities are clearly established. Through every stage in the creation of a book—from its acquisition and production, to its marketing and promotion—everyone involved knows the responsibilities and parameters of his specific job.

### *Acquiring Manuscripts*

In large publishing houses, each acquiring editor is given a set

## What's In a Name?

Publisher, editor-in-chief, acquisitions editor, copy editor—what do all of these terms mean? Job titles in book publishing mean different things in different companies. Responsibilities of a senior editor, for instance, can be extensive in one house and minimal in another. Generally speaking, however, editorial job titles can be loosely described as follows.

At the top of the chain of command is the **publisher.** In charge of a company or company imprint, the publisher oversees the operation of every department, including editorial, art, marketing, and sales. The **editor-in-chief,** who may also be the publisher in some houses, oversees all aspects of the editorial department, including acquisitions. In some houses, he is also responsible for setting editorial goals and guidelines.

An **acquisitions editor,** sometimes called a **senior editor** or **editorial director,** is responsible for bringing new projects to the company. When he comes across a book proposal that catches his attention and strikes him as marketable—one that he believes will be profitable for the company—he typically presents the proposal to either his department head or an approval committee. This committee, which includes the publisher, editor-in-chief, and, often, marketing and administrative personnel, ultimately decides whether or not it believes the book will find its audience and make money for the company.

A **managing editor** or **production editor** has responsibilities that are largely administrative in nature. In most houses, he oversees the timely coordination between departments—editorial, art, typesetting, and advertising, for instance—to maintain a smooth production process. He makes sure schedules are made and deadlines are met.

In many publishing companies, an **executive editor** is actually an acquisitions editor who spends his time seeking out new projects. In other firms, he is the head of an editorial department, and is responsible for assigning projects and overseeing the work of project editors—**editors, associate editors,** and **junior editors**—the group involved in the actual shaping and organization of the manuscripts.

Once the manuscript has gone through the organizational stage, it is then sent to a **copy editor.** It is this editor's job to make any changes that are necessary for stylistic consistency and grammatical accuracy. He is the one responsible for correcting typographical errors, checking cross-references, and verifying the spelling of proper names and places. He is also accountable for the accuracy of any factual material presented in the manuscript.

Generally an editor-in-training, the **editorial assistant** helps the editors in any way they need him. Depending on a company's specific needs, an editorial assistant's responsibilities can range from making copies of manuscripts and filing, to preparing indexes and proofreading typeset copy.

Once again, editorial job titles and their responsibilities differ from company to company. Large companies tend to be departmentalized, with specific editors responsible for specific jobs. In smaller houses, on the other hand, one or two people may assume several or all of the editorial responsibilities involved in the production of a book.

number of manuscripts he has to sign each year. As mentioned in "What's In a Name" on page 50, this editor presents possible projects to an approval committee. In some companies, he is directly responsible to a department head who oversees the acquisitions process, and who can approve or kill (reject) any project. If a book's estimated production cost exceeds its allotted budget, the editor or department head must seek project approval from a supervisor. Sometimes this process is smooth and direct; in other cases, it is slow and convoluted.

When analyzing a book proposal for possible approval, an acquiring editor considers two basic questions. Will the book sell enough copies to make money for the company? Is the manuscript right for the house? The following is a look at how these criteria are regarded in a large publishing house.

A publisher's *complete list* includes all of the books it owns—both new and old. Its *seasonal list* includes new fall, winter, or spring titles. Published books that are less than nine months old make up a publisher's *frontlist*, while those older than nine months make up its *backlist*.

- ***Will the Book Sell Enough Copies to Make Money for the Company?***

This is the primary question an editor considers when reviewing a manuscript for possible publication. But how, you might wonder, does an editor know if a book will be profitable? Editors are usually given a specific category in which they are expected to find possible titles. Experienced editors know their markets. They are aware of the types of books within their particular categories that have sold well in the past, as well as those that have failed. Conscientious editors keep up with trends in the marketplace. They know the types of books that are hot—that are in demand.

Based in part on personal experience, acquisitions editors are expected to estimate the size of the project's audience and "guesstimate" how many copies will be sold. The editor can then determine the dollar amount any book he signs will earn. As you might imagine, the pressure to come up with realistic numbers is great. The books an editor selects must earn enough money to show a predetermined profit percentage over the course of time. If too many of an editor's choices fail to meet anticipated budgetary projections, he is asked to leave.

- ***Is the Manuscript Right for the House?***

Most acquiring editors in large houses use specific editorial profiles when deciding if a book is right for their particular lists. Does the subject matter fall within the specific category? Is the subject one of interest? What kind of shape is the manuscript in? Will it need significant editing? Is the author of the book credible? In trade houses, a published author with a history of books that sell is highly impressive—especially to the sales department. In professional and educational houses, an author who is recognized as a leader in his or her field is equally impressive.

An editor will also consider if a book's subject matter is too controversial—or not controversial enough. And he will consider if the final format will match the standard format required. For instance, if a proposed book requires color photos throughout, but the list for which the editor is responsible contains only black and white photos, the editor will most likely reject the proposal. Looking at a publisher's book catalogue can help you determine the general profile an acquisitions editor will generally follow when analyzing proposals.

### *How a Manuscript Reaches an Editor's Desk*

An *unsolicited manuscript* is one that an editor has not specifically asked to see. For works of fiction, most large firms have a standard policy of rejecting any manuscript that is not requested or represented by an agent. For works of nonfiction, this is generally the case as well. However, some houses may place unsolicited manuscripts in a *slush pile,* the term traditionally used to describe a stack of unsolicited manuscripts. Once a manuscript has made it to a slush pile, it may be reviewed by someone in editorial—usually an editorial assistant, rather than an editor—who decides if the proposal is worth forwarding to an acquisitions editor for further consideration. As a general rule, however, most manuscripts in a slush pile are eventually rejected.

Having a literary agent vastly improves your chances of getting published by a large house. Trade house editors are incredibly busy. With time at a premium, any manuscript from a familiar source has a better chance of getting reviewed than one that is not.

In most instances, acquisitions editors in large firms rely on their personal networks of literary agents, previously published authors, and other contacts. Many literary agents have cultivated working relationships with editors. They are aware of the topics in which editors are interested, and they pitch appropriate proposals to them. Some agents who do not have relationships with editors (and many of them don't) may send them manuscript proposals blindly, in much the way some writers do. In some houses, such proposals are treated in the same manner as unsolicited manuscripts. In other houses, an editor may review the proposal simply because an agency's name is attached to it. For a closer look at the world of agents in the publishing industry, see "The Role of the Literary Agent" on page 81.

Trade house editors are incredibly busy. Their days are spent attending meetings, filling out paperwork, reviewing proposals, developing manuscripts, and, in many instances, actually editing books directly. Their time is at a premium. This means that any manuscript from a familiar source will have a better chance of getting reviewed than one that is not.

Unlike acquiring editors who work in large trade houses, those in large educational and professional publishing houses are likely to review the unsolicited manuscripts they receive. This is because literary agents represent very few authors of educational and professional books. Editors in these houses also may receive manuscript proposals and ideas from their consulting editors. Generally, *consulting editors* work for publishers on a freelance basis; they are not employees of the company. They are working professionals—experts in their own special fields—who provide valuable information, leads, and insights to editors. An engineer, for example, may offer information to an editor who is working on a book on civil engineering, while a foreign language expert may provide valuable insights to an editor who is preparing a series of language guides.

### *Things to Consider When Working With a Large House*

For some authors, the status of being associated with a large, big-name firm is a reward in itself. For others, however, there are a number of realistic factors to consider when evaluating publishing houses of any size. Keep in mind that when it comes to publishers, bigger—although advantageous in many respects—is not necessarily better.

There are a number of obvious advantages that large publishing houses have to offer. For one thing, large firms usually have experienced sales forces with strong established systems of distribution. They have the financial backing to afford extensive marketing through publicity, advertising, and promotions. They also enjoy well-established connections that allow them to get large quantities of books "out there." And due to their high visibility in the marketplace, large firms are often contacted by people and companies that can offer them special selling opportunities. (See the section on "Special Sales" that begins on page 42.)

Although large publishing companies offer many advantages, from high status to strong systems of distribution, they also may have many drawbacks, such as the allotment of only limited time to the editing of each manuscript.

Another advantage of large publishing houses is that they pay heftier advances to their authors than moderate-sized and small firms. They do this to attract previously published, well-known authors. Contracting a book by a famous or "hot" author can translate into a sizeable return on a company's investment. To some degree, large advances also insure that their authors will provide acceptable manuscripts. This often means that an author may have to obtain the skills of an outside editor or writer to make the work conform to the house editor's standards.

The average author's book, however, does not get the same kind of sales and marketing exposure in a large firm that a famous author's does. Projects not considered priorities are afforded limited exposure and a limited time period in which to perform. If a book initially sells well, additional marketing *may* be added. If it does not produce the necessary sales figures, it is likely to fall between the marketing cracks and disappear very quickly.

A book's sponsoring editor—often the same person who acquired the project—is its overseer. He is responsible for shepherding the project through its various stages of production, each of which involves a different editor who takes care of a specific aspect of the process. However, because of the limited time allotted for editing, many books lack the attention they need and deserve. With editors responsible for turning out a specified number of books for each selling season, each editor has little time to devote to any given manuscript.

Large firms publish books using specific formulas. According to some formulas, approximately 10 percent of a company's new titles must generate enough revenue to pay for its entire list of new books; 20 percent will pay for themselves, plus make a reasonable profit; another 20 percent will just about break even; and the remaining books will lose money. If your book falls within the top 30 percent, it's doing fine. If not, odds are that any royalties you receive will just about cover your advance. Furthermore, in approximately eighteen months from its date of publication, your book will likely be put out of print. Don't expect a large company to give your book a second chance. It goes against the economic principles by which large publishing firms operate.

## Moderate-Sized Houses

Publishing houses with an annual sales volume between $10 and $50 million are considered moderate-sized. Like large commercial firms, they usually have well-defined organizational structures in which departmental and individual responsibilities are clear and specific. Unlike large firms, however, moderate-sized houses do not necessarily follow a standard corporate structure.

Many mid-sized firms have developed their own unique operating systems based upon the marketplaces they serve and/or the people who run them. Often they are managed by one or more individuals as private businesses; run as overgrown family companies; or treated as subsidiaries of other businesses, such as newspaper chains or media conglomerates. So while these moderate-sized companies may give the appearance of standard publishing houses, their methods of operation may vary greatly. As a potential author in search of the right press for your book, be sure to learn as much as you can about the operating practices of the individual firms in which you are interested.

### *Acquiring Manuscripts*

Just as in large houses, an acquisitions editor in a moderate-sized firm is given a fixed budget and a specific number of projects to sign each year. This editor is usually responsible to a department head who oversees the acquisitions process. Typically, the department head has the authority to approve or kill any project. If the project's estimated production cost exceeds its allotted budget, the editor or department head must seek approval from a supervisor, who may, in fact, be the publisher. This process usually runs smoothly because it involves only a few levels of administrative approval.

When an acquisitions editor in a moderate-sized publishing company reviews a book proposal for acceptance, he must base his decision on the same criteria used in a large house. He must consider if the book will sell enough copies to make money for the company, and if the project is right for the house.

- ***Will the Book Sell Enough Copies to Make Money for the Company?***

Just as in large firms, an acquisitions editor of a moderate-sized publishing house is usually responsible for signing on books in a specific category. Knowing his market is critical. To increase his chances of signing on "winning" titles for his company, he must be aware of the type of books within his category that have sold well. He must understand why some books are winners, while others are not.

Like acquiring editors in large companies, those in moderate-sized houses must estimate the size of a book's audience and also predict the number of copies it will sell. Each book is expected to generate enough money to pay for its production cost, plus show a profit. Editors who sign on too many books that do not meet budget projections are at risk of losing their jobs.

**Helpful Hint**

A careful review of a publisher's book catalogue can help you determine the editorial profile used by the company's acquiring editors. This, in turn, can help you decide if the company might be interested in your project.

- ***Is the Manuscript Right for the House?***

Acquiring editors in moderate-sized houses ask the same editorial questions posed in large firms to judge if a proposed book is right for their list. Is the subject of the work within the company's realm of interest? Will the manuscript need significant editing? Is the author of the book credible? Is the subject matter controversial? Will the format of the book fit the list for which it is intended? As mentioned previously, a published author with a string of books that have a history of selling is impressive. An author who is a recognized leader in his or her field is equally impressive. Again, a thoughtful review of a publisher's book catalogue can help you determine the general editorial profile used by the company's acquiring editors.

### *How a Manuscript Reaches an Editor's Desk*

Moderate-sized houses receive many unsolicited manuscripts and submission packages daily. Like large publishers, they will automatically reject works of fiction that have not been requested. However, this policy is often less restrictive for nonfiction. Although some houses may reject works of nonfiction sight unseen, many houses appoint someone in editorial—often an editorial assistant—to scan the proposals and send them to the appropriate acquisitions editor. In these cases, the editor reviews the work and either rejects it immediately or considers it for acceptance.

Mid-sized publishing houses are often more willing than large houses to consider unsolicited book proposals.

In addition to acquiring works of nonfiction through unsolicited proposals, most editors in moderate-sized companies rely on leads from their own contacts in the industry. Previously published authors and literary agents are often good sources of manuscript proposals.

As mentioned earlier, each mid-sized house has its own organizational structure, which can make it easier or more difficult for a first-time author to get his proposal considered. For example, if one or two individuals dictate a rigid editorial policy, this can greatly limit the types of projects an acquisitions editor can suggest for approval. On the other hand, if the company's editorial culture is more liberal, it may be more inclined to take calculated risks on new and interesting projects.

At moderate-sized educational and professional publishing houses, acquiring editors are usually very receptive to reviewing good unsolicited manuscript proposals. Of course, they also rely on their network of contacts for project leads. Many times, an editor may use his network of consulting editors and published authors to get feedback on unsolicited projects he may be considering.

### *Things to Consider When Working With a Moderate-Sized House*

Some mid-sized publishers are very well known in a specific field of publication. This may be an author's draw to certain firms. As with large houses, however, there are a number of factors to consider when evaluating the overall positives and negatives of a moderate-sized company.

Concerning the subject of advances, some moderate-sized houses have been known to pay handsome sums. On the whole, though, advances tend to be on the modest side. Often, depending on the size and quality of its editorial staff, a firm of this size may encourage its editors to work closely with authors, carefully guiding them in shaping their manuscripts. This is a major advantage, as such professional input is likely to result in a more polished final manuscript—one that is competitive in the marketplace. Of course, not all mid-sized houses allow their editors to spend substantial amounts of time with their authors. When investigating publishers for your project, it may be prudent to inquire about their editorial process.

**Helpful Hint**

When investigating publishers for your project, consider asking about each company's editorial process—a process that varies from house to house. For instance, some mid-sized companies work closely with their authors to create high-quality books, while others budget little time for editorial input.

Typically, moderate-sized firms have strong established systems of book distribution. Over time, they have developed the relationships needed to get their books out to the public. And, like large houses, moderate-sized publishers often have high visibility in specific marketplaces, which increases their chances of special selling opportunities.

Some firms of moderate size may have their own in-house sales groups. Others may rely on outside sales forces to represent their titles. Still other houses have both. In such cases, the companies also have someone in-house who acts as an overseer of or liaison to the independent representatives. Some mid-sized publishing firms even use the sales force of large publishers that also carry additional lines. Generally speaking, companies that maintain their own sales forces are likely to give their books the best representation.

Many companies that use outside representatives often lend a hand to encourage sales. They do this through direct mailings, telemarketing, and a variety of other promotional tools—anything that will help their titles stand out. Not all companies, however, put forth this effort. As a potential author, always try to learn how a company sells its books.

Just as in large firms, when books of unknown authors are published in moderate-sized firms, generally they are given limited exposure and limited time to perform. If the book sells well initially, additional marketing *may* be added to further promote their sales. Books that do not sell well, on the other hand, are likely to disappear quickly. Occasionally, but not often, a company will give such titles a second marketing opportunity. This depends on the strength of the company's commitment to a particular book.

Many moderate-sized companies publish books using the same formula employed in large firms. Approximately 10 percent of new titles will generate enough revenue to pay for their entire list of new books; 20 percent will pay for themselves, as well as turn a reasonable profit; 20 percent will just about break even; and the rest will lose money. If your book falls within the top 30 percent, you can expect royalty payments. If it doesn't, odds are that you will not make much more money than your advance. Some mid-sized firms, however, may keep a slow-moving book in print for years. For some authors, this is an important factor.

## Small Houses

Commercial publishing houses with an annual sales volume of $10 million or less are classified as small publishers. While a number of small houses have well-defined organizational structures that spell out individual employee and departmental responsibilities, many others are loosely structured and guided by one or two individuals. By their very nature, small firms rarely follow a standard corporate structure.

In most instances, small presses strongly reflect the vision of their founders. In some cases, former employees of other publishing houses—editors, salespeople, copywriters, marketers, and publishers—establish small companies because they believe they have gained enough knowledge of and expertise in the industry to run a successful business themselves. Other houses are created by special interest groups that want to get their message out to the public. For example, have you ever noticed that when a presidential candidate runs, a book comes out on his or her personal life, political philosophy, and goals? Typically, such books are created by publishing houses that are backed by political interest groups. Some small publishing houses are also formed as hobbies, self-publishing ventures, or even tax write-offs. Motivations for small independent houses are diverse, and it is this very diversity that allows for their wide range of organizational styles, marketing philosophies, and topic coverage.

Today, the term *independent publisher* refers to any publishing house that is managed by its owners, as opposed to being publicly

## The Importance of Shepherding

If your work has been accepted by a publisher, it is important to understand and appreciate the role of the sponsoring editor—the person in charge of overseeing your project through its various stages of production. In many cases, this is the acquisitions editor who initially believed in your book enough to propose it to the company. In other instances, this may be a project editor who has been assigned the job. Of all the people in a publishing house, the sponsoring editor is the person who has real interest in having your book succeed. He is the shepherd, the champion of your book. And it is important to maintain a good working relationship with him.

What happens if this person gets transferred to another department or leaves the company altogether? Suddenly your project will find itself in a precarious situation. More than likely, one of two things will happen. Either it will be assigned to another editor immediately, or it will be temporarily shelved. In either case, your project will no longer be under the watchful eye of the person who first believed in it.

While it's true that you may be limited in controlling the fate of your book at this point, you can still proactively intervene on its behalf. If your book has been transferred to the hands of a new editor, make it your business to contact him. Call and ask to schedule a few minutes of his time to introduce yourself and to discuss a few important aspects of your book. Remember that an editor's time is limited, so be prepared to make your points quickly and professionally. Your objective is to get the new editor to familiarize himself with your book and, hopefully, to form a connection with it.

If you discover that your project has been shelved temporarily, try to contact the person who is responsible for reassigning it. This could be a senior editor or the editor-in-chief. Inquire about the plans for your book, and, again, try to share its obvious assets.

Whatever you do, do not allow yourself to call the editor ten times a day, five days a week. This is the quickest way to alienate yourself from him—or from anyone else involved in the editorial process. Remember to always maintain a modicum of professionalism, and to keep your frustration and worry from overcoming your good sense.

held or part of a large publisher or business entity. While this term also may be used to describe many moderate-sized firms, the true spirit of independent publishing clearly exhibits itself in the form of small presses. Overwhelmingly, small independent publishers are the ones that allow first-time authors to establish themselves as writers. They also provide the forum for authors to break new ground in publishing. For instance, in the late 1950s, then small publisher Viking Press ushered in the "Beat Generation" with Jack Kerouac's *On the Road*—a work that broke away from the traditional rules that writers had followed to that point. The Naval Institute Press was responsible for the publication of *The Hunt for Red October,* Tom Clancy's first novel. John Grisham's first novel, *A Time to Kill,* was picked up by Wynwood Press, and then re-released to become a bestseller after Grisham's second book, *The Firm,* was published. The list goes on and on. What's important to remember is that small publishers are often the risk-takers, the ones that give unknown authors the chance to pursue their visions.

Small publishers are often the risk-takers of the industry—the companies that give unknown authors a chance to pursue their visions.

Small publishing firms are also creatures of their creators. While it is true that they may provide great opportunities for unpublished authors, small houses may reflect not only the strength and vision, but also the shortcomings and weaknesses of the person in charge of the company.

You have already seen the process that large and moderate-sized publishers follow when acquiring new manuscripts. You have also learned of the general advantages and disadvantages of these companies, especially for first-time authors. Now, let's take a look at this same information in terms of small publishing firms.

### *Acquiring Manuscripts*

In small publishing houses, one or two individuals typically choose the manuscripts for publication. In many instances, it is the owner of the press—often the publisher—who makes these decisions. Most small publishing houses work within an established budget when acquiring new projects. Typically, they strive to turn out a specific number of books each year. The discovery of new markets in which to sell books can increase this number dramatically, while, perhaps, an unforeseen cash-flow limitation can lower it.

Naturally, smaller publishing houses have small staffs. Unlike employees of larger companies, who are each responsible for one specific job, those who work in small houses often wear more than one hat. The owner/publisher, for instance, may acquire as well as edit manuscripts and, perhaps, design book covers. Another employee might be in charge of sales and advertising, while the duties of another might include bookkeeping, order-taking, and office management.

As mentioned earlier, the person who acquires manuscripts in a small house is often the owner or publisher, although some firms have a specific acquisitions editor. An acquisitions editor's power varies from firm to firm, but very often, he has the authority to accept or reject projects without first consulting with others. If, however, a project looks as if it might exceed an allotted budget, approval may be required from the publisher. In certain houses, the publisher is always involved in project selections. Since there is direct daily contact between employees in a small house, the acquisitions process is usually a very quick one.

In small houses, whether one, two, or a few people are in charge of choosing projects, the decision is based largely on the same criteria used in larger firms.

- ***Will the Book Sell Enough Copies to Make Money for the Company?***

No matter what the size of the company, a book's potential to generate sales is always considered first. As in larger houses, those who acquire manuscripts in smaller firms are often responsible for finding books that belong within a certain category. They must know the market and marketplaces, and they must keep on top of trends in their respective areas.

In many small houses, estimating the projected sales of each accepted book proposal is often not as formal a responsibility as it is in larger houses. In some small firms, it isn't required at all. Ideally, each project selected should earn enough money to pay for itself and show a profit. If, however, a book does not do as well as expected—if it turns a relatively small profit—the person who acquired it is not likely to lose his job as a result. Of course, too many publishing failures translate into bad news for any company. The missions of a number of small houses, however, allow them to bring out less-profitable quality works. For instance, some small companies produce books on indigenous people, such as Native Americans and the Aborigines of Australia, to insure the preservation of their history and culture. Others produce books to enlighten readers about certain important environmental issues. In such cases, the profit is not the main concern. The need to make the material available is.

- ***Is the Manuscript Right for the House?***

After establishing that a proposal has money-making potential, those who select manuscripts in small firms must consider the same questions that editors of any size firm ask themselves. Is the subject of the work within the company's realm of interest? Is the manuscript in good shape, or does it need significant editing? Is the material covered too controversial, or not controversial enough? Is the author credible? Does the format of the book fit into the standard format used by the company?

The answers to these questions serve as basic guidelines for small publishers. However, small publishers often have the freedom to include projects that do not necessarily fall within these editorial parameters. Let's say that an unsolicited proposal arrives at a small house and excites the publisher. The problem is that the subject matter really doesn't fit into the company's list. If the publisher feels strongly enough about the project, he may decide to take it on and expand into a new market. At large and moderate-sized houses, a decision to expand into a new area of interest is usually handled on a corporate, not an editorial, level. Typically, when a project doesn't fall within a larger company's area, it is rejected immediately. And in the rare event that a project like this *is* considered, it requires review, analysis, and the input of several company employees before a decision is made. This is one of the beauties of small publishing firms—these kinds of decisions are often made by one or two people, and are made in a timely manner.

One of the beauties of small publishing firms is that they often are willing to expand into new markets—to take on projects that do not fit in their established publishing programs.

While larger trade-house editors may go after high-profile best-selling authors, small houses don't. Economic restraints make it hard for small firms to compete for such big names. Small firms, whether commercial, professional, educational, or scholarly in nature, are very happy to work with first-time and lesser-known authors.

## How a Manuscript Reaches an Editor's Desk

Small presses get their share of unsolicited manuscript proposals. For reviewing works of fiction, their policy is more liberal than those of larger presses, which automatically reject unsolicited works. For works of nonfiction, the rule is usually simple—review all proposals that fit the company's list.

For nonfiction trade books, unsolicited proposals that are not addressed to a specific person are likely to be opened by an editorial assistant, and then routinely passed on to the publisher or appropriate editor for review. Of course, in companies without editorial assistants, proposals are likely to be opened and reviewed by the publisher or acquisitions editor immediately.

As most small presses are limited in offering advances—some pay small amounts, while others offer none at all—literary agents tend to shy away from them. In turn, many acquiring editors of small presses stay away from agented nonfiction manuscripts for the same reason. They believe that they can find a similar project that is not represented by an agent.

As mentioned earlier, in small firms, the decision to publish certain titles usually rests on the shoulders of one or two individuals. Because of this, the selection of a project is fairly subjective. A project may be accepted simply because the subject matter is of personal interest to the publisher. Or the decision to acquire a project could be based on a recent conversation that an acquisitions editor had with a book distributor. In many instances, consideration is based on the positive impression made by the author's proposal as presented in his submission package. (More information on the submission package can be found in Chapter 5.)

This "open door policy" for many small houses makes them an appealing choice for authors, especially those who have never been published.

### *Things to Consider When Working With a Small House*

For some authors and their agents, the idea of having a small house publish their work is unthinkable; they know that small firms do not pay huge advances (if they pay any at all); they do not take out full-page ads in *The New York Times* to promote books; and they do not send authors on extensive publicity tours. (Ironically, larger houses probably won't either—especially when the authors are unknown.) Immediately dismissing a small publisher for such reasons is shortsighted and foolish. While it is true that small publishers do not provide some of the benefits that larger companies do, they are capable of offering many others.

Before discussing some of the advantages and disadvantages of small houses, it is important to keep in mind that small companies are different from one another. As explained earlier, each house is a highly personalized operation with its own agenda and system of operation. In most instances, the following information is accurate.

To begin with, most small houses provide their authors with direct lines of communication with the people who are handling their books. In other words, authors are able to speak directly to their editors, public relations personnel, and even the publisher. In larger houses, an outside caller knows the frustration of being shuffled along from extension to extension in search of the right person, only to find himself eventually leaving a voicemail message that is not answered promptly, if at all. It is easier for authors to develop good working relationships with employees at small companies, who can provide them with the information they need.

Small publishers can offer a variety of benefits to the author, from ready access to staff members, to the generous investment of editorial time, to the ability to add new titles to their lists at the last minute.

It is true that some small firms pay no advances, while others may pay modest ones. The reasoning behind this is simple. Rather than tie up their limited funds in the form of advances, small firms choose to use their money as working capital. Unlike larger publishers, small firms spend more time on the development and editing of projects. As a longtime publisher of a small firm, I often had the opportunity to work with authors whose previous books had been published by larger institutions. In nearly every instance, these authors commented on how much more attention their projects were given in small publishing houses, both editorially and promotionally. Without the intense pressure of drop-dead schedules, which are the norm in larger houses, editors are able to invest the extra time in projects where it is required. Companies with greater flexibility in their publication schedules can improve the quality of their projects tremendously.

Once larger publishing houses announce their titles for the upcoming selling season, new titles are rarely added. Not so with most small houses, which have the freedom and ability to add titles to their lists at the last minute. If a small press wants to take on a new project for publication in, say, two months, it has the freedom to do so, even if its distributors have not been notified. A larger firm is more likely to pass on such a project. It is, however, important to keep in mind that adding a new title to an already-announced book list is a good idea only if the book's quick-release date will have an impact in the marketplace—if the book's topic is "hot." Past and present examples of such topics include juicing, channeling, and angels.

A small firm that has been able to establish itself in a niche marketplace over a period of time is likely to have a strong system of book distribution in place. (See the inset "What Is a Niche Market?" on page 67 for more information on this subject.) New, less-established companies have a harder time getting their titles placed in bookstores and other markets. They also have more difficulty getting the attention of reviewers.

Very few small firms have their own sales forces. Few offer direct-mail promotions. Most do not have in-house telemarketing departments. And only a handful provide viable publicity. So how do they sell their books? Some small firms have in-house sales directors, but most rely on outside systems of distribution and sales representatives for their titles. As discussed earlier, an outside sales force can be a group of independent book salespeople who visit accounts on behalf of a company. It can also be an independent book distributor that sells books through its own catalogue and sales representatives. Some small houses utilize the sales force of a larger publisher that carries additional titles. And some rely solely on their own catalogues for sales. As an author, it is important to learn how effective the sales operation is of any small company.

Some small companies sell their titles to very specialized niches, which are relatively easy to reach. Others sell to hidden marketplaces—markets such as charity groups or other nonprofit organizations, who buy outside the traditional channels—that may purchase books to raise funds for their causes. Some firms sell their books through strategically placed ads in newspapers and magazines that target specific audiences. Others work directly with authors to promote sales through such avenues as infomercials, lectures, and demonstrations—wherever and whenever they can.

In order to stay in business, most small companies develop their own personal systems of sales. Some systems work very well, others work marginally well, and some don't work well at all. The financial level of success for a small house, therefore, is determined by just how cash rich or cash poor it is. Traditionally, small houses have limited funding, which tends to reflect in overall sales. Unlike larger houses, they do not produce books on a formula basis. Their approach is much more straightforward—each book must sell to some degree in order for the company to stay in business. A book that has not performed as well as had been expected is not quickly

## *What Is a Niche Market?*

In publishing, a niche market represents a specific category or area of interest. Companies that publish books in one or more specialized areas are considered "niche publishers." Those who cover a wide range of subjects are "general publishers." As discussed in Chapter 2, there are literally hundreds of specialty areas for books. Many of these categories, such as food technology, are fairly permanent and will remain in place for years. Others, such as macramé and fondue cooking, are based on market fads and are short-lived.

Since the early 1990s, a few large general publishers have purchased small niche publishing houses. In some cases, this has allowed the domination of a niche area by large publishers. A number of small niche publishers, however, have managed to maintain their share of the market, and have been able to thrive along with the larger companies.

All publishing companies, no matter what their size, publish books for some type of market. The titles they publish can include a wide range of topics. One company, for example, may publish books ranging from children's stories and cookbooks to political essays and alternative health. When looking at a company's catalogue, one or more common themes—art, travel, foreign language guides, gardening—are usually apparent. A company concentrates on specific areas or niches to maximize the distribution of its titles. When sales representatives visit book buyers at children's bookstores, gourmet shops, or gardening stores, they carry the company's list of titles. This usually allows the salespeople to present a highly focused group of books that appeals to a number of specific customer bases.

The more titles a company has in a particular field and the longer it has been selling them to a specific marketplace, the greater expertise and success the company will have in selling such books. For example, if a particular house has been publishing nursing books for many years and has an extensive list of active titles, it is likely that this company has developed a reputation in the nursing field. The books it releases are likely to be picked up automatically by the existing outlets that sell nursing books.

Conversely, the fewer titles a company has in a specific field, the more difficulty it will have penetrating the existing marketplaces. There are, of course, exceptions to this rule. For instance, if a company has made breaking into a particular market a priority, its first titles, although few, may be aggressively marketed by its salespeople. The track record of a company's sales can indicate how well its efforts with new titles have paid off. It is always a little risky being the first title in a publisher's new category.

put out of print, as is the standard procedure in larger houses. In spite of slow sales, the book will be kept in print for many years.

In most cases, small houses are direct reflections of the individuals who run them. If these people know what they are doing, they can create excellent and exciting opportunities for the writers. On the other hand, those who do not understand how to operate publishing companies correctly can be a source of nightmarish embarrassment for their authors.

## NONCOMMERCIAL PUBLISHING HOUSES

For noncommercial publishing houses, which include university and foundation presses, the "message," not the bottom-line profit, is usually the primary focus.

### University Presses

Affiliated with institutions of higher learning, university presses are primarily not-for-profit publishers of scholarly works—books as well as periodicals—written by professors, scientists, and scholars. Their primary target has always been the academic audience. Recently, however, many university presses have begun to compete with commercial houses by taking on projects of wider appeal and marketing their titles to more general (trade) audiences.

Cambridge and Oxford Universities established the first university presses in England in the early 1500s. In 1869, the first of many university presses in the United States debuted at Cornell University. Most of these businesses were formed to satisfy the university's printing and publishing needs, particularly the publication of faculty members' scholarly works and graduate students' theses. Because of the very limited audiences for their titles, these presses were actually expected to lose money. And they did, year after year. As they received funding from their associated universities, from federal and private grants, and from benefactors, they did not have to depend on a traditional business cash flow to finance their everyday operations. Each university press developed its own special area of interest. Some grew large, while others remained small.

**Helpful Hint**

If you believe a university press might be a good choice for your work, prepare and submit a submission package as described in Chapters 5 and 6. For additional information on university presses, refer to the *MLA Style Manual and Guide to Scholarly Publishing*. Listings of these presses are included in directories such as *Writer's Market*, *Little Magazines & Small Presses*, and *Literary Market Place (LMP)*. Detailed information on these directories is provided in Chapter 4 and the Resource List.

Unfortunately, the economic realities of the 1970s had a profound negative impact on university presses. As many colleges and universities began to see their general operating costs rise steeply, they also saw their funding begin to decline. When they sought to implement cost-cutting measures, the first areas targeted were often the poorly run, fund-depleting university presses. Many institutions simply closed up shop, while others restructured their presses to be run like standard businesses—to make a profit (which was used for the publication of future titles, thus preserving their nonprofit status) or at least break even.

Today, the books published by many university presses run a wide gamut of categories. It is not uncommon, for example, for a single university press to publish titles in areas that range from science and medicine to business and economics to the humanities. Today there are nearly two hundred university presses in the United States, and most are efficiently run businesses.

### *Acquiring Manuscripts*

Acquisitions editors in university presses are also called *sponsoring editors.* It is their job to keep on top of the issues, as well as the leading scholars in a particular field of interest. It is not unusual for a sponsoring editor to attend seminars and professional conferences in search of future authors. This does not mean that you must be a professor to have your book published by a university press. It does, however, mean that your *curriculum vitae* (resumé) will be carefully scrutinized. Your educational background and credentials must show that you are capable of writing the proposed work.

Interestingly, although sponsoring editors in university presses are well educated and familiar with the categories of the books they sign on, not all have degrees in these subjects. In most instances, once an editor has found what he believes to be a possible candidate for the press's list, he will give it to a professional academic *reviewer.* Also called *readers* or *referees,* these reviewers are typically professors who are experts in their fields. If the reviewer believes the manuscript is worthy of publication, the editor will present it to a special board—usually made up of senior professors of the university—for approval.

### *Things to Consider When Working With a University Press*

University presses are committed to publishing works of the highest quality. Typically, the importance of a proposed work takes precedence over its money-making potential.

Keep in mind that most university presses work within tight budgets. Interestingly, they are also competitive with other presses for particular titles. This means that they may offer decent advances to lure desirable authors. Typically, average print runs of titles from a university press are smaller than those of most trade publishers. However, the books are kept in print for longer periods.

## Foundation Presses

Like university presses, listings of foundation/association presses are included in *Writer's Market, Little Magazines & Small Presses,* and the *Literary Market Place (LMP).* The *LMP* has a specific listing of association presses in its subject index.

Like university presses, foundation presses—also known as association presses—are run as not-for-profit corporations. They are often the extensions of established foundations that champion specific causes. Primarily concerned with producing books that highlight their causes, foundation presses rarely concern themselves with making a profit. Most are financed through private sources that are dedicated to the cause represented by the foundation. Staff members of foundation presses generate many of the ideas for their publications. They also welcome and give serious consideration to projects from outside sources that closely reflect the interests of the foundation. Nonfiction writers of specialized subjects that may fall into foundation press categories should consider pursuing this avenue to get their work published.

## OTHER PUBLISHERS

So far, this chapter has presented traditional commercial and noncommercial publishing houses. You may be aware of other types of publishers as well, including vanity presses and electronic publishers (e-publishers). Vanity presses have been around for years, but are unlike the publishers discussed earlier in this chapter. They require substantial monetary investments from authors before publishing their books. As for the burgeoning group of online e-publishers, they are all different. Some may require payment from authors to place their books on the publishers' websites; others may charge to advertise the books online. Both vanity presses and electronic publishers are discussed in detail in Chapter 8.

## SUMMING IT UP

Simple, huh? Well, I know we've covered a lot of information in this chapter; but, in order to see where all of your publishing options lie, it's important for you to know the difference between the various types of publishers.

In Chapter 1, Rule #1 states that every rule has its exceptions. However, you will find that the majority of nonfiction publishers follow the organizational patterns described in this chapter. Armed with this basic information, you can move to the next chapter, which will show you how to begin choosing those publishers that are best suited to your project.

CHAPTER 4

# CHOOSING THE RIGHT PUBLISHER

*I was halfway through my awe-inspiring presentation on "How to Get Your Nonfiction Work Published," when a hand went up in the audience. I asked the gentleman, who seemed to be quite agitated, if he had a question. He did.*

*"Yeah, well, what you're saying sounds fine and good, but what happens when every publisher you've sent your book to rejects it?"*

*I asked him how many publishers he had sent proposals to. "Twenty," he responded emphatically, "Twenty publishers, twenty rejections!"*

*"Well, I know that may seem like a lot, but, in fact, it really isn't." I continued, "Do you know that before writer William Saroyan received his first acceptance, he reportedly had approximately 7,000 rejection letters that measured over thirty inches in height?" I shared other stories of famous writers—George Orwell, Pearl S. Buck, and Stephen King—whose work had been turned down an incredibly high number of times before they connected with the right publishers. I went on, "All things considered, twenty rejections is nothing more than a start, a nice start. . . ."*

Like the gentleman in my opening story, many first-time writers believe that there are only a handful of publishers they can approach with their book proposals. The reality is that there could be literally hundreds of firms from which to choose.

The trick is knowing where to find them, and then zeroing in on those specific publishers that may be interested in your work—those that publish titles in your category and fit other requirements that are important to you. You already know the category or categories into which your book falls, and you also have a solid idea of the different types of publishing houses that exist. Now it's time to zone in on those specific publishers.

This chapter will help you lay the foundation for selecting the best, most appropriate list of publishers for your work. It is a foundation that is laid in two steps. Step One involves an honest assessment of your personal goals in getting published. Once you have a clear picture of your expectations, you will be ready for Step Two—creating that initial list of possible publishers.

## RULE #6

## *Know why you want to be published*

What do you expect to achieve by getting your book in print? What's your motivation? Have you thought about what qualities are really important to you in a publishing house? The following discussion will guide you in analyzing your personal goals for getting published.

### STEP ONE—KNOW WHAT YOU WANT

So let's be honest. What's really driving you to get your work published? The promise of wealth or fame? The desire to get a message to the public? And what are your expectations from a publisher? Big advances and lots of personal attention? Media tours and guest spots on television talk shows? If you have been so busy writing your book that you haven't taken the time to think about these questions, it is time to do so now. Getting in touch with your personal goals and honestly assessing what you expect from a publisher will help you choose the right path for your search. It will lead you to the firms that are most likely to meet your expectations.

## What Are Your Personal Goals?

Every writer in search of getting her work published is driven by different motivations. Status, income, and making a contribution to a specific field are probably the most common. Let's take a closer look at some of these aspirations.

### *I Want a Big-Name Publisher to Publish My Book*

Some writers believe that unless a high-profile company publishes their books, it doesn't count. For them, image is everything. If this is important to you, selecting the names of publishing companies will be very easy. Unfortunately, for most first-time authors, the odds of securing a contract from a big-time publisher are very low. In fact, even writers who have already had a book published will face an uphill battle.

In order to get a big-name publishing house to consider a manuscript, the writer generally has to be represented by a reputable literary agent. The inset on page 76 provides more information on the role of a literary agent.

If you follow the Square One System described in this book, your odds of getting picked up by a well-known publisher will certainly improve. However, this will not necessarily guarantee marketing success, fame, or fortune. It will only mean that the name of the company will appear somewhere on or in your book.

Remember, there are thousands of publishers out there. Some are famous, others not so famous. But just because a publishing house doesn't have a familiar-sounding name doesn't mean it won't do justice to your work. I have been in the publishing industry for over two decades, and I am still running into terrific companies I never realized existed.

While I don't want to discourage you from pursuing the prestige that may be associated with big-name companies, I do encourage you to consider the possibility of contacting other houses. As you do your research, you will come across many fine houses—small and moderate-sized, famous and not-so-famous—that provide solid publishing programs, especially for first-time authors.

### *I Would Like to Make Money*

If you plan on writing a book to get rich on the royalties, it's time for a reality check. This is not to say that it can't happen, but it is impor-

## The Role of the Literary Agent

Primarily, a literary agent is a dealmaker whose main objective is to make a connection with a publisher on an author's behalf. In exchange, she receives a commission—usually 10 to 15 percent of both your advance and your royalties. Good literary agents have connections with acquisitions editors throughout the publishing industry. They also have a finger on the pulse of the book trade, and are aware of the topics in which many publishers and editors are interested. Typically, they are responsible for preparing an author's submission package and knowing the best places to send it. Some agents even lend a hand in shaping and developing manuscripts, making them more commercially appealing.

Should a publisher show interest in an author's work, a literary agent is helpful in negotiating the best possible contract. (After all, the best deal for the author means the best deal for the agent.) Expertise in the area of contract negotiations enables a good agent to troubleshoot any potential weaknesses in terms of the deal. (For more information on literary agents and contracts, see Chapter 7.)

But is it really necessary to engage an agent? For fiction writers, especially those who are interested in having their work represented by moderate-sized or large publishing houses, the answer is yes. The standard policy of these firms calls for the immediate rejection of any unagented manuscript. On the other hand, when it comes to nonfiction, an agent is not always necessary.

Tremendous numbers of first-time authors of nonfiction have been successful in connecting with publishers on their own. (Frankly, because they work on a commission basis, most agents prefer representing previously published authors whose works appeal to large commercial houses—where the big-money deals lie.) Moreover, in the case of educational books or books in small niche areas written by first-time authors, a literary agent may not be worthwhile financially for either party. Most likely, these books won't make enough money to justify the cost of an agent—and agents know this. Agents may be of greater value to nonfiction writers of certain broad subject areas, such as health, cooking, and biographies.

For names of established agents, refer to books such as the *Literary Market Place;* Donya Dickerson's *Guide to Literary Agents;* and Jeff Herman's *Writer's Guide to Book Editors, Publishers, and Literary Agents*. You can also request a membership listing from the Association of Author's Representatives (AAR). For further information on these resources, see the Resource List beginning on page 215.

tant to realize that the average book published in the United States sells approximately 5,000 copies, and the average author rarely sees more money than what is offered in an advance. Savvy writers, however, can find good ways to maximize the income generated by their books. First of all, if authors know their markets, write decent books, and hook up with appropriate publishers, their odds of generating good sales will be enhanced. Remember that a book backed by a large publishing house must sell well initially, producing reasonable profits, or it is likely to find itself out of print very quickly. On the other hand, smaller publishers with strong backlists continue selling their titles for many years. This means that your backlisted title may continue generating income while you concentrate on your next writing project.

The average book published in the United States sells approximately 5,000 copies, and the average author rarely sees more money than what is offered in the advance.

Depending on its marketplace, your book can create opportunities for generating income above and beyond royalties. There are scores of lucrative marketing opportunities in which you can actively participate. Perhaps you can use your book as a vehicle for giving lectures or appearing as a guest speaker. Not only will you get paid for speaking, but in most cases, you can also sell copies of your book to those in attendance.

If you have written a book in which you recommend a certain product or products—for instance, a cookbook that promotes a certain brand of flour; or maybe a book on fishing that recommends a specific brand of lures—contact the companies you mention. Since you have advocated their product, they may be interested in promoting your book.

You can also try making a connection with a company or organization that may have a strong interest in the message your book presents. If, for instance, you have written a book about improving your sales ability, you might try promoting your book to companies with large sales forces. If your book is about taking charge of your life after retirement, you can contact groups associated with senior citizens. And if you've written a book about a specific illness or medical condition, you might contact the organization associated with that particular condition.

Your book may be able to generate literally hundreds of moneymaking opportunities. All you have to do is recognize them. There are some excellent books that can help you determine additional opportunities that are right for you and your work. John Kremer's *1,001 Ways to Market Your Books* is one excellent and informative choice, as is *Publish to Win: Smart Strategies to Sell More Books* by Jerrold R. Jenkins and Anne Stanton. More information on these books and other such titles are found in the Resource List, beginning on page 215.

### *I Want to Make a Contribution*

You have something to say that you believe is significant—something that will make a difference. Your message may involve a specific cause, or a discovery of some sort, or, perhaps, your point of view on a particular subject. No matter what it is, to you, the most important thing is getting your message out.

Let's say you have written a book on the growing epidemic of eating disorders among teenagers in our society. Increasing the public's awareness of this problem is your goal. The message of your book is to encourage society to place less emphasis on "thin is beautiful," and more emphasis on eating healthy. Now all you have to do is find a publisher that is interested and has the capability of reaching your intended audience.

During your research, you might want to start with those companies that have already successfully published titles on similar subjects. Another very effective route is to contact organizations and associations that are affiliated with eating disorders. There are a number of foundation (association) presses that may be interested in publishing your work.

As a publisher, I know that books are powerful tools that can make a difference. In the hands of the right house, your message will get out.

### *I Just Want to Be Published*

Some writers care about nothing more than seeing their work in print—and this is certainly a valid and fairly common reason for wanting to get published. However, if this is your attitude, think about all of the time and effort you have put into writing your book. Shouldn't you consider going to a publisher that can do more than simply put it into book form?

As discussed in Chapter 3, there are many different kinds of publishers out there. If you put forth some basic effort in researching the most appropriate houses for your work, you will increase your chances of seeing your book in print, as well as giving it an opportunity to sell in the appropriate marketplace.

## What Do You Expect From a Publisher?

Now that you have given some thought to what you want to personally accomplish by getting your work into print, you can better pursue those publishers that can help you meet your goals. Of course, just because a publishing house produces books in your category, it is not necessarily the best one to represent your work.

I've heard too many horror stories from authors who, after seeing their books come out, discovered that the publisher did not live up to their expectations. To avoid surprises, think about the following criteria when analyzing publishers. A clear and honest assessment will help you put your expectations into proper perspective.

### ☐ *Publisher's Specialty*

Every publisher specializes in certain markets—some in more than one. Be sure the publishers you place on your list print titles in your subject area. (I will show you how to do this later in the chapter.) This may seem like an obvious consideration, but I must say, it has been my experience that many first-time authors don't realize this.

At my previous company, we published titles in the area of alternative health, yet every week I received proposals for poetry books, children's books, and at least one work of fiction. Obviously, the writers who submitted these submission packages hadn't done their homework. They had wasted both time and money trying to connect with a publisher that was never going to accept their work—not because the work was bad, but because it simply wasn't the right subject for the firm.

While it's true that a publisher's catalogue won't allow you to actually handle or leaf through its books, it can tell a lot about a company. Checking out the book titles and their descriptions will give you a good indication of the publisher's area of interest. The catalogue will also reflect the investment the publisher makes in presenting titles. Is the catalogue attractive and inviting, or dull and unimpressive? A catalogue can tell reams about a company. (For more information on reviewing catalogues, see the inset "Reading a Catalogue Like a Book" on page 138.)

### ☐ *Company Age*

Is it important for you to work with a firm that has been around a number of years, or would you consider working with a younger company? Older companies have track records that you can check for success or failure. Newer companies, on the other hand, may be hungrier for sales. Thus, the age of a company can be worthy of consideration.

### ☐ *Company Size*

It is important to check out the size of any publishing house you may be considering. A quick and easy way to do this, without going into a company's financials, is to find out how many titles a company turns out each year. The fewer books produced, the smaller the company; the more titles, the larger the firm. Will you be satisfied working with a small publisher, or is the status of a large well-known company what you really want? This answer is different for every author. Just keep in mind that there are advantages and disadvantages to each size house, as you saw in Chapter 3.

### ☐ *Quality of Work*

How important is the overall "look" of the finished book to you? Do you expect it to be printed on good-quality paper and have an impressive-looking cover? What about the presentation of the text itself—the typeface used and the page layout? If you have strong feelings about this aspect of the process, be sure to examine the existing works of any prospective publisher. How? The quickest and most direct way is to visit a local bookstore or library and take a look at some of that publisher's existing titles. You can also request a company catalogue, which will give you a good idea about the company and the work it produces.

### ☐ *Marketing and Sales*

Getting your book out there, wherever "there" might be, is an important consideration when looking at publishing houses. What kind of marketing and sales program does the publisher have? Does the company have an in-house sales force to market its books, or does it employ the services of outside salespeople? In addition to promoting its books through catalogues, how else does the company sell its titles? Does it have a distributor? What marketplaces does it reach? Are its books available through Internet bookstores and other online sites? How much money and effort is spent on advertising? Also, consider the number of better sellers a company has within a marketplace. This is usually a reflection of a publisher's sales capabilities.

### ☐ *Publicity*

Everyone expects their book to have some publicity "push" behind it, but few writers have a clear idea as to how this is done. Basically, each publisher has its own methods for promoting its titles. During your research, it is important to ask questions concerning this facet of each company's operation.

Does the company have a designated publicity department? Is it run by one person or a group? Does it have well-established connections with the media? How does it promote its books? Can you expect to help publicize your book through media tours, book signings, or guest spots on radio or television programs? Are books reviewed in appropriate publications? If the company does not have a publicity department, how does it generate exposure for its titles? Is publicity handled through the strategies of its marketing department alone? How heavily does the company rely on its authors to generate their own publicity?

### ☐ *The Offer*

What type of advance or royalty payment do you expect to receive for your book? Not all publishing companies, and especially not smaller ones, offer their authors advances. Keeping in mind that the money offered in an advance will be deducted from future royalties, this may not be an important issue in your search for a publisher. If, on the other hand, you need the immediate income an advance provides, you should consider only those publishers that make such offerings. For more detailed information on the different types of offers that publishing companies make, see Chapter 7, "The Deal."

### ☐ *Company Location*

Is the publisher's geographical location an important factor to you? Perhaps your book has specific "regional appeal" and might be handled best by an area publisher. Or maybe you simply prefer working with a publisher that is located nearby.

Personally, I recommend that if your project is regional in nature, you first check out the publishers within the area related to your work. Otherwise, do not let geography be a determining factor. The choice, of course, is yours.

These criteria should be helpful when assessing publishers. Add your personal requirements and you will find yourself on the right path. Don't skip this important step. An honest evaluation will help you save time and energy. Once you know what you are looking for from a publisher, both personally and professionally, you will be ready to take the next step—creating that initial list.

## STEP TWO—CREATE THE LIST OF PUBLISHERS

Okay, the time has finally come to roll up your sleeves, grab a notebook and pencil, and get ready to do some important groundwork. First, you are going to create a rough list of possible publishers to produce and market your work. Next, you will be narrowing this list to include only those publishers that meet your personal criteria and are most likely to respond positively to your work. I am not going to lie to you—this step requires a decent amount of effort. But by doing your homework here and now, your efforts will be rewarded in the long run.

So how do you begin? You start by compiling an initial rough list, which, depending on the subject of your work, can range anywhere from a few dozen names to a few hundred. It is a list that should include names of publishers only—nothing else. Once this list is established, you will be taking a closer look at the companies to see if they fit your personal criteria. Those that don't will be deleted from the list. Those that do will be placed on a new list along with some basic contact information, including street, e-mail, and website addresses; phone and fax numbers; contact name for submission proposals; area or areas of publication; number of books published annually; year the company was founded; and any other pertinent information you may come across during your search.

### Finding Those Publishers

Where should you begin your quest for the best publishers for your work? Inexperienced unpublished authors may simply turn to *The New York Times* bestseller list, jot down the publishers of the nonfiction titles, and send their book proposals directly to them. Others may take a trip to their local libraries, take a look at the books found in their category, and make a list of the publishers of these books. Good ideas? Well, let's just say that these are minimal starting points at best.

There are many other, much more effective ways for prospective authors to find publishers. It has been my experience that when looking for publishers that meet certain criteria, the most valuable references for providing lists of publishers are the *Literary Market Place, Writer's Market,* and *The International Directory of Little Magazines & Small Presses.*

## Literary Market Place

The *Literary Market Place,* commonly referred to as the *LMP,* is a directory of United States and Canadian book publishers and literary agents, and a resource for a number of editorial services. It also provides listings of trade magazines and reference books, as well as industry associations and foundations. Updated yearly and published in two volumes, the *LMP* is the industry's unofficial bible. Volume 1 of this reference is the one that you—an author in search of a publisher—will find most helpful.

Usually, you will find the most recent *LMP* in the reference section of your local library. It is rather expensive, so using the library's copy should be more than adequate for your needs. An online version is also available at www.literarymarketplace.com; however, you must subscribe in order to take full advantage of this site, and the fee is prohibitive.

Volume 1 of the *LMP* is divided into five sections, each of which is further divided into subsections. For your needs, you will be focusing on the first section—Book Publishers. This section begins with an A-to-Z directory of book publishers that are located in the United States. Each entry provides standard contact information—mailing addresses, phone and fax numbers, e-mail addresses, and websites (where applicable)—as well as the categories published by each firm. In addition, most, but not all, listings include the names of key personnel and information such as the year in which the company was founded, the number of books it publishes annually, and its total number of titles in print.

Wherever applicable, an entry includes the publishing house's divisions, subsidiaries, and/or imprints, which are also cross-referenced and listed individually. Excluded from the *LMP* are "author-subsidized" publishers, also known as vanity presses,

The *LMP* is a comprehensive directory of well-established publishers in the United States and Canada. However, it does not include foreign publishing houses. If you are interested in contacting firms in English-speaking (or non-English-speaking) countries, refer to the *Publishers' International ISBN Directory,* which lists publishers in over two hundred countries. For publishing houses located in English-speaking countries only, the *Writers' and Artists' Yearbook* is an appropriate choice. (For more information on these references, see the Resource List.)

## *Literary Market Place* The Publishing Industry's Bible

Considered the publishing industry's unofficial "bible," the *Literary Market Place*—or *LMP*—includes a comprehensive directory of publishers located in the United States and Canada. Writers in search of the best possible publishers for their work often find this resource a good place to start. The first section of the *LMP* (Volume 1) is divided as follows:

☐ **U.S. Book Publishers.**
A-to-Z directory of U.S. publishers that produce a minimum of three books annually.

- **Geographic Index.**
  U.S. publishers listed by state.
- **Type-of-Publication Index.**
  U.S. publishers listed by type of books they publish.
- **Subject Index.**
  U.S. publishers listed by subjects they publish.

☐ **Imprints, Subsidiaries, and Distributors.**
A-to-Z listing of imprints and subsidiaries, and who owns them, as well as who distributes their books.

☐ **Canadian Book Publishers.**
A-to-Z directory of Canadian publishers that produce a minimum of three books annually.

☐ **Small Presses.**
A-to-Z directory of U.S. and Canadian publishers that produce less than three books annually and are, therefore, not eligible to be listed in the other directories in the first section. Some of these companies are new; others publish unique titles that they want to make known to those who use the *LMP*. All have paid to be listed.

which characteristically charge authors significant fees to get their books into print. (For more information on vanity presses, see Chapter 8.)

After the A-to-Z directory come the *Geographic, Type-of-Publication,* and *Subject Indexes,* which include listings of publishers by name only. As you might have guessed, in the *Geographic Index,* publishers are listed alphabetically by state. This index is useful to authors who are interested in working with publishers in a specific region. In the *Type-of-Publication Index,* companies are listed according to the type of books they print. Categories in this index include, for instance, children's books; directories and references; professional books; general trade books, including hardcover and paperback; scholarly books; and college textbooks. University and association (foundation) presses are also included in this index.

Finally, the *Subject Index* provides an alphabetical listing of over 100 subject categories. Under each subject heading there is a listing of the publishing houses that produce books in that area. Among the companies listed are all types of publishers—trade, professional, college textbook, reference, etc.—but they are not identified as such. A small sampling of these subject categories is provided below. You'll notice that some are general while others are more specific.

- African American Studies
- Advertising
- Animals, Pets
- Antiques
- Astrology, Occult
- Astronomy
- Biological Sciences
- Career Development
- Computer Science
- Cookery
- Crafts, Games, Hobbies
- Criminology
- Disability, Special Needs
- Drama, Theater
- Environmental Studies
- Fashion
- Finance
- Genealogy
- Health, Nutrition
- History
- Law
- Marketing
- Parapsychology
- Photography
- Real Estate
- Religion
- Science (general)
- Theology
- Travel
- Veterinary Science
- Women's Studies

### *Using the LMP to Create a Rough List*

So now you know the *LMP* has these various publisher indexes. That's great. But how do you use them to begin making your list? The best way to explain the process is by using an example. So here's a scenario—you have written a book on how to take professional-looking family portrait photos. It is a book designed for the novice photographer as well as the aspiring professional. In

Chapter 2, you learned to identify this book's category along with its three classification levels. It is broken down in the following way:

***Main Category***

Trade Book

***Level One***

Adult nonfiction

***Level Two***

Photography

***Level Three***

A "how-to" book on taking professional-looking family portrait photos. It is a work geared for the novice photographer as well as the aspiring professional.

With a free afternoon ahead, you make your way to the local library. You walk over to the reference section where you find Volume 1 of the *LMP.* You take it to an empty table and flip it open to the *Subject Index,* which is found in the first section of the book. Thumbing through the categories, you come across two subject headings that apply to your work—Photography and How-To books. You find approximately 130 publishers listed under the Photography heading, and over 300 under the How-To category. Again, only the names of the publishers are listed here—no other information is included. Your first job is to write down the names of those publishers that are common to both lists. You find fifty-five companies, which you place on your rough list.

Next, because your book falls into the category of nonfiction trade, you turn to the *Type-of-Publication Index* and look for the appropriate categories. You find two headings for trade books. One is "General Trade—Hardcover," the other is "Paperback Books—

Trade." As far as you are concerned, it doesn't matter if your work is published in hardcover or paperback. So you take the rough list of publishers you compiled from the *Subject Index* and see which ones are also found in either the "General Trade—Hardcover" or the "Paperback Books—Trade" listing.

After comparing lists, you find that fifty-one of the fifty-five publishers on your rough list are found in one or both of these "trade" categories. (The four remaining publishers on your rough list do not produce trade books. Three are publishers of "professional" books, and one produces "reference" works.)

So now you are left with the names of fifty-one publishers that produce books on photography for the nonfiction trade audience. But at this point, that's all you have—names. You don't know anything about the companies themselves. Your next step? Get more information on the companies to see if they might be the right publishers to represent your work. For this, you would turn to the A-to-Z directory of *U.S. Book Publishers.* After reading through the information provided, you can remove the names of those firms that are not appropriate, and obtain contact information and other pertinent data for the companies that are.

Begin a new list for those companies you believe may be right for your book—the ones you might choose to receive your book proposals. This list should include as much of the following information as possible:

- ☐ Company name.
- ☐ Address.
- ☐ Phone and fax numbers, and e-mail address.
- ☐ Website address.
- ☐ Contact for submission package.
- ☐ Area or areas of publication.
- ☐ Number of books published annually.
- ☐ Year company was founded.
- ☐ Any other pertinent information you may come across during your search.

### Helpful Hint

Be sure to do your homework. Taking the time to research those publishers who may be best suited to represent your work will be energy well spent.

Ideally, this refined list should include anywhere from thirty to forty publishers. You will be referring to this list later on when sending out your submission packages, as explained in Chapters 5 and 6. While it is important to get as much pertinent company information as possible at this point, if certain data is missing, don't sweat it. For instance, if the name of the acquisitions editor is not listed in the reference you are using, don't worry about it—and don't waste any time or energy trying to track down the missing information at this point. You'll be filling in holes and verifying information later on, as detailed in Chapter 6.

The *LMP* is an excellent resource because it lists so many well-established publishers. It does, however, have its limitations. For one thing, it lists only those houses that publish at least three books annually. This means that most new and very small presses are not likely to be included, and, as mentioned earlier, small presses are often the ones most receptive to new authors. As it is primarily a directory, the *LMP* offers only basic statistical data, and few details. Finally, it does not identify the publishers as small, moderate-sized, or large. However, knowing how to analyze the entries, as shown in the samples beginning on page 89, will help you determine company size, editorial interests, and a variety of other relevant facts.

Okay, let's get back to you and your rough list of fifty-one publishers. When checking the companies out in the *LMP's* A-to-Z directory, you find that some entries are short while others are long; some provide lots of information while others offer less. In the following pages, you will find three *LMP* sample entries. Typical of the entries presented in the *LMP,* they are representative of large, moderate-sized, and small publishers that produce works in the area of photography. The information on the right-hand side of each entry appears in the same format as found in the actual *Literary Market Place*. These sample entries have been annotated on the left-hand side with explanatory notes that guide you in pulling out the data you need.

The samples also show how entry information varies from publisher to publisher. After analyzing all of the companies on your list, you will delete some and keep others. By understanding the information presented in the *LMP*, you will be able to better identify those companies that may suit your project best.

## *LMP* SAMPLE ENTRY
### MODERATE-SIZED PUBLISHING COMPANY

| | |
|---|---|
| COMPANY NAME. | **Sunrise Publications** |
| THIS SHOWS THE COMPANY IS A DIVISION OF A LARGER COMPANY. | Division of Sunrise Communications Inc. |
| THIS IS IMPORTANT CONTACT INFORMATION TO INCLUDE IN YOUR LIST. | 35 Frederick St, Fairfield, CT 06430<br>Mailing Address: 35 Frederick St, Fairfield, CT 06430<br>*Tel:* 203-555-3200 *Toll Free Tel:* 800-555-9868 *Fax:* 203-555-3220<br>*E-mail:* info@sunrise.com<br>*Web Site:* www.sunrise.com |
| THESE ARE NAMES OF COMPANY EXECUTIVES. FOR YOUR LIST, YOU WILL WANT THE NAME OF THE ACQUISITIONS EDITOR, BUT NONE IS GIVEN. SELECT THE NEXT LIKELY PERSON. IN THIS CASE, IT WOULD BE THE EDITORIAL ADMINISTRATOR—JESS CARA. LATER ON, YOU WILL BE VERIFYING THAT SHE IS THE PROPER CONTACT. | *Key Personnel*<br>Pres: James F. Ciara<br>Exec VP & Prodn Mgr: Deb Wilson<br>Publisher and CEO: Gabriella Abrams<br>Busn Mgr: Robert Lovelock<br>Edit Administrator: Jess Cara<br>Publicity: Elle D'Amico<br>Intl & Subs Rts: Jason James |
| AGE OF COMPANY. | Founded: 1983 |
| SUBJECTS PUBLISHED. | How-to books on gardening, amateur photography, cooking, home improvements, country living, crafts. |
| ASSIGNED INTERNATIONAL STANDARD BOOK NUMBER(S). | ISBN Prefix(es): 0-945257; 0-866224 |
| ANNUAL NUMBER OF TITLES SHOWS THE SIZE OF THE COMPANY. FIFTY TITLES MEANS THIS IS LIKELY A MODERATE-SIZED FIRM. | Number of titles published annually: 50 Print<br>Total Titles: 400 Print |
| HAS ITS OWN SALES OPERATION AND OUTSIDE DISTRIBUTORS. | *Sales Office:* 35 Frederick St, Fairfield, CT 06430<br>*Distributed by:* The Chrysler Group |
| SELLS ENGLISH-LANGUAGE BOOKS IN FOREIGN MARKETS. | *Foreign Rep(s):* Merrimac Int'l |
| SELLS FOREIGN LANGUAGE RIGHTS. | *Foreign Rights:* Fred Claus Agency |
| THIS INFORMATION IS NOT NECESSARY FOR YOUR INITIAL LIST. | *Advertising Agency:* Sunrise Marketing Services, 35 Frederick St, Fairfield, CT 06430, Michael Masters, *Tel:*203-555-3500 *Fax:* 203-555-3520 *E-mail:* mmasters@aol.com<br>*Billing Address:* 35 Frederick St, Fairfield, CT 06430<br>*Shipping Address:* Merrimac Dist Ctr, 400 Avery Dr, Edison, NJ 08837<br>*Warehouse:* Merrimac Dist Ctr, 400 Avery Dr, Edison, NJ 08837<br>*Distribution Center:* Merrimac Dist Ctr, 400 Avery Dr, Edison, NJ 08837 |

By looking at its subject areas, you can see that Sunrise Publications, detailed in the entry on page 89, publishes "how-to" books on amateur photography. Perfect. This doesn't guarantee that it will take on your project—but it might. With an annual publication of fifty titles, this is most likely a moderate-sized house. That's another good sign for you as a prospective author. Moderate-sized houses often have the desire—as well as the budget—to expand and develop their areas of interest. Final assessment? Sunrise Publications is a "keeper" and belongs on your list.

### *LMP* SAMPLE ENTRY
### SMALL PUBLISHING COMPANY

| | |
|---|---|
| COMPANY NAME. | **Great Southwest Publishers** |
| THIS IS IMPORTANT CONTACT INFORMATION TO INCLUDE IN YOUR LIST. | 3214 Hudson Dr, Phoenix, AZ 85014<br>*Tel:* 602-555-9900 *Toll Free Tel:* 800-555-5990<br>*Fax:* 602-555-9909 |
| THE ONLY EDITOR NAMED IN THIS ENTRY IS MEGGIE ABRAMS. ADD HER NAME TO YOUR LIST. LATER ON, YOU WILL BE VERIFYING THAT SHE IS THE PROPER CONTACT. | *Key Personnel*<br>Pres: Allan McConnach<br>Ed: Meggie Abrams |
| AGE OF COMPANY. | Founded: 1975 |
| SUBJECTS PUBLISHED. | Southwest cookbooks, high-quality photo collections, history. |
| ASSIGNED INTERNATIONAL STANDARD BOOK NUMBER(S). | ISBN Prefix(es): 0-914846; 1-885590 |
| ANNUAL NUMBER OF TITLES SHOWS THE SIZE OF THE COMPANY. FIFTEEN TITLES MEANS THIS IS LIKELY A SMALL FIRM. | Number of titles published annually: 15 Print<br>Total titles: 100 Print |

A simple glance at the entry above and you can quickly eliminate Great Southwest Publishers from your rough list. Why? Because this company produces books of photographs of the Southwest. Your "how-to" book on taking family pictures would be of no interest to this publisher. Sending this company a submission package would be a waste of time, effort, and money.

Infinity International Publishing Group is a large company, publishing 250 books per year. (See page 91.) Looking at its subject areas shows that it publishes books on photography. Unfortunately, photography is a broad term, and this entry doesn't give any

## *LMP* SAMPLE ENTRY
## LARGE PUBLISHING COMPANY

| | |
|---|---|
| COMPANY NAME. | **Infinity International Publishing Group** |
| THIS IS IMPORTANT CONTACT INFORMATION TO INCLUDE IN YOUR LIST. | 2500 Third Ave, Suite 1500, New York, NY 10017<br>*Tel:* 212-555-2300 *Toll Free Tel:* 800-555-2704<br>*Fax:* 212-555-2333<br>*E-mail:* infinity@tac.net<br>*Web Site:* www.infinitybooks.com |
| PLACE BOTH THE VP/SENIOR EDITOR, DARLA STUART, AND THE MANAGING EDITOR, INGRID JUDD, ON YOUR LIST ALONG WITH THEIR TITLES. YOU WILL BE VERIFYING THE PROPER CONTACT LATER ON. | *Key Personnel*<br>Pres & Pub: Albert Will Sonne<br>Exec VP & Assoc Publisher: Tuesday Addams<br>Exec VP & Gen Mgr Rts & Perms: Erica Rubin<br>VP & Sr Ed: Darla Stuart<br>Man Ed: Ingrid Judd<br>Prod Coord: Roslyn Carl<br>Mktg Asst: Joshua Shan Wills |
| AGE OF COMPANY. | Founded: 1980 |
| SUBJECTS PUBLISHED. | General trade books—hardcover and paperbacks; Fiction and nonfiction, history, biography, art and photography, poetry, horticulture, Americana, mysteries. |
| ASSIGNED INTERNATIONAL STANDARD BOOK NUMBER(S). | ISBN Prefix(es): 0-4372; 0-7760 |
| ANNUAL NUMBER OF TITLES SHOWS THE SIZE OF THE COMPANY. WITH 250 TITLES, THIS FIRM IS A LARGE ONE. | Number of titles published annually: 250 Print<br>Total Titles: 3,000 Print |
| INDICATES COMPANY DISTRIBUTES BOOKS FOR OTHER PUBLISHERS. | *Distributor for:* Christiana Press; Green Gables Ltd., Old World News Group; Rhodes Books |
| COMPANY SELLS BOOKS IN FOREIGN MARKETS. | *Foreign Rep(s):* Ashland Southampton (UK); Brightwaters Associates (Europe); Canadian Winston Group (Canada, UK); General Books (Europe, UK); Taylor & Taylor (Asia, South America, UK); Unity Press (Japan, Korea) |
| THIS INFORMATION IS NOT NECESSARY FOR YOUR INITIAL LIST. | *Advertising Agency:* Williams Roth Advertising<br>*Shipping Address:* Infinity International, 77 Kingston Rd, Providence, RI 02904 |

details on the types of photography books it publishes. You are already aware of how difficult it is to get a book proposal accepted by a large publishing house, but you want to give it a try anyway.

In this case, you will keep Infinity International on your list, along with all of its contact information. But before spending the time and effort to send this company your book proposal, it would be wise for you to dig a little deeper. Find out the specific types of photography books this company publishes. One of the best ways to do this is by requesting a copy of its catalogue. You should also visit its website, which is likely to give you the information you need to decide if this company should remain on your list.

After a few hours of checking the fifty-one publishers on your rough list, you have eliminated eleven. According to the information provided in the *LMP,* it was obvious that these eleven publishers were simply not good choices for your work. You now have the names of forty publishers along with their basic contact information. But is this where your investigation should end? It could be; however, further research could prove to be quite valuable. Although the *LMP* is a wonderful reference, I recommended checking other resources, as well. *Writer's Market* and *The International Directory of Little Magazines & Small Presses,* which are discussed below, are excellent choices.

### Writer's Market

Updated yearly, *Writer's Market,* which is available in most libraries and bookstores, is an excellent guide to book publishers, magazine publishers, and literary agents. Although it has fewer listings than the *LMP, Writer's Market* provides more detailed and very useful information for prospective authors.

In addition to providing mailing addresses, phone and fax numbers, and other standard contact information, this guide includes valuable names of acquisitions editors. The annual number of a publisher's titles is listed, as well as the approximate number of manuscripts received. Most entries also indicate the percentage of titles that comes from first-time authors, and the percentage that comes from unagented authors. A company's recently published titles, the type of books it looks for, and its requirements for manuscript submission are also presented in most entries. Many publishers offer their policies on advances and royalty percentages as well.

Publisher listings in this reference, like those in the *LMP,* are also cross-indexed geographically by state and by subject matter. The *Writer's Market* also includes a listing of small presses—those that publish three or fewer titles annually. The most recent edition includes nearly one hundred small publishers. It does not include vanity presses.

### Using the Writer's Market to Search for Publishers

As you did when you created that initial rough list of publishers from the *LMP,* the first place you should turn to in the *Writer's Market* is the *Subject Index.* The subject headings are listed under two main categories—fiction and nonfiction. Naturally, you would look at the nonfiction section and find that, like the *LMP,* the *Writer's Market* lists publishers under Photography, as well as How-To books. Write down the publishers that are common to both lists.

Because you already have a preliminary list of publishers from your work with the *LMP,* you will be using the *Writer's Market* to perhaps expand and refine this list. You will find that most of the same publishers are listed in both books. Check out the entry of any publisher on your list from the *LMP* that is also listed in the *Writer's Market.* It is likely to provide additional and often more pertinent information than what is given in the *LMP.* It may include, perhaps, advance and royalty information, acceptance percentage of projects by first-time authors, and requirements for manuscript proposals. Some entries include a sampling of one or two recently published titles.

Remember the sample *LMP* entry for Sunrise Publications on page 89? On page 94, you can see how the same publisher is presented in *Writer's Market.* Compared with the Sunrise Publications entry in the *LMP,* the *Writer's Market* entry is much more helpful to the prospective author. In fact, it provides the writer with only helpful, pertinent information, such as the names of the proper acquisitions editors. In addition, this entry gives a more detailed look at the types of books the company publishes. It also offers information on submission guidelines and requirements, the annual percentage of books published by first-time writers, and the percentage of manuscripts accepted without agent representation.

While the *LMP* provides basic directory-type data, the *Writer's Market* offers more specific information to prospective authors. Typically, each company entry provides a detailed look at the types of books it publishes. It lists names of acquisitions editors and manuscript submission requirements. In most cases, it also gives the number of books published by first-time writers, as well as the percentage of accepted unagented manuscripts.

**SAMPLE ENTRY**
*WRITER'S MARKET*

**SUNRISE PUBLICATIONS.** 35 Frederick St, Fairfield, CT 06430. (203) 555-3200. Fax: (203) 555-3220. Web site: http://www.sunrise.com. **Acquisitions:** Gary Arthur, editorial administrator; Adam Todd (gardening, home improvements, country living, cooking); Tara Rose (photography, crafts). Estab. 1983. Publishes hardcover and trade paperback originals and reprints. **Publishes 50 titles/year. Receives 350 queries and 150 mss/year. 25% of books from first-time authors; 80% from unagented writers. Pays royalty.** Publishes books within 2 years of acceptance. Reports in 1 month on queries, 3 months on proposals and mss. Book catalogue and ms guidelines free.

🗝 We publish high-quality, illustrated, hands-on, practical nonfiction books for adults.

**Nonfiction:** How-to books in the areas of home crafts, interior decorating, vegetarian cooking, quilting, canning, amateur photography, flower-arranging, gardening. Send Submission with outline and SASE.

**Recent Titles:** *Bonsai Gardening* by J. Smalltree; *Taking Perfect Pet Photos* by Carol Roseby.

Remember, the *Writer's Market* lists a substantial number of small publishers that turn out less than three titles annually. You may run across one, two, or more small publishers that can be added to your list.

## *The International Directory of Little Magazines & Small Presses*

An excellent choice for finding the names of small presses is *The International Directory of Little Magazines & Small Presses*. Starting out as a tiny compilation of small presses in the 1960s, this directory has grown to include over 5,000 small presses and journals. Most entries offer information such as payment rates, proposal requirements, and recent publications. Subject and regional indexes are also included. Copies of this resource are available in libraries and bookstores.

### *Using The International Directory of Little Magazines & Small Presses to Search for Publishers*

As you did when creating that initial rough list of publishers from the *LMP* and *Writer's Market*, the first place you should turn to in

**SAMPLE ENTRY**
***THE INTERNATIONAL DIRECTORY OF LITTLE MAGAZINES & SMALL PRESSES***

**ICU Press.** Leah Jacobs, Senior Editor, PO Box 2445, Los Angeles, CA 90056, 213-555-6776; fax: 213-555-6777. 1983. Nonfiction, how-to art, craft, and photo books. Avg press run 3–5M. Pub'd 4 titles 1999, expects 4 titles 2000, 5 titles 2001. 21 titles listed in the *Small Press Record of Books in Print* (28th ed, 1999-00). Avg. price, paper: $15. Discounts: for resale, 20–40% off; distributor discounts negotiable. 250pp; 6x9. Reporting time: due to volume, we cannot reply unless interested. Publishes less than 1% of manuscripts submitted. Payment: 9% of net. Copyrights for authors. Memberships: Publishers Marketing Association (PMA).

*The International Directory of Little Magazines & Small Presses* is the *Subject Index.* In your search for small publishers that might be a good match for your book on how to take professional-looking family portrait photos, you look under the headings Photography and How-To books. As you did with the other reference books, you find the publishers that are common to both lists, and write down their names only. You find twelve.

Next, flip to the A-to-Z publishers listing and read about those twelve companies you have selected from the *Subject Index.* Although the information in the entries may vary, for the most part, each listing provides the following: name of the acquisitions editor, company address, year company was founded, subject areas published, average print run, number of titles published in the previous year and number expected in the coming year, average copy price, discount schedules, average number of pages in book, average page size, printing method, reporting time on manuscripts, payment or royalty arrangements, rights purchased and/or copyright arrangements, number of titles listed in current edition of *Small Press Record of Books in Print,* and membership in publishing organizations. A sample entry is provided above.

Although the company discussed in the sample entry is very limited in the number of titles it publishes, you feel your book may be of interest to it. However, you would like to learn more about the company first. You place ICU Press on your list, along with the contact information you've pulled out of *Little Magazines & Small Presses.* You plan to call or fax the company and request a catalogue, if one is available. Once the catalogue arives, you'll learn more about the company by scanning its listings.

## Other Methods of Finding Publishers

While the *LMP, Writer's Market*, and *Little Magazines & Small Presses* are superior sources for finding reputable publishers, keep in mind that they offer only those firms that are located in the United States and Canada. If you are interested in finding a publishing house in another English-speaking country, the *Writers' and Artists' Yearbook* is a good place to look. This resource includes listings of publishers in the United States, the United Kingdom, Ireland, Australia, and New Zealand. If you are looking for a comprehensive listing of worldwide publishers in English- and non-English-speaking countries, refer to *Publishers' International ISBN Directory*, which lists over 450,000 publishers in over two hundred countries. (For more information on these international publishing sources, see the Resource List.)

All of these references, while excellent, are not the only means of finding publishers. As mentioned earlier in the chapter, taking a trip to your library or bookstore—especially a superstore—and flipping through the books on your subject will give you names of publishers to investigate. You can also check out the online bookstores like amazon.com or barnesandnoble.com and browse their subject areas of interest. You can get a listing of books in your category, along with their publishers, in most instances.

If the prospective publishers on your list have websites, be sure to visit them. You can learn a lot about a company from these online pages, including a full list of its titles, as well as marketing and distributor information.

Another excellent way to gather information on publishing houses is by attending trade shows. If possible, try to attend Book Expo America (BEA)—the annual trade show for the publishing industry. Publishers, book buyers, booksellers, distributors, authors—just about everyone associated with the book industry is in attendance. Here, you will have the opportunity to meet representatives of many different publishing houses and get a good sense of the types of books their companies produce.

Many editors and marketing representatives attend the BEA, and you might be able to steal a few moments of their time and discuss your project with them. Keep in mind that while your first

### Helpful Hint

Attending trade shows is a great way to collect information on various publishing houses. You can find announcements for upcoming shows in the *Literary Market Place* and *Publishers Weekly*.

instinct may be to approach a company's editors at one of these shows, you might be able to better gauge a company's interest by speaking with someone from the marketing department. In many companies, an editor cannot acquire a book unless the project has the support of marketing. (Remember, in the last chapter, you learned that the number-one question most publishing houses ask before acquiring a book is, "Will it sell enough copies to make money for the company?") And if the people whom you contact do not feel that your project fits into their publishing program, they will often steer you toward a more appropriate house.

In addition to the BEA, there are shows that cater to areas of more specialized interest, such as the religious trade and the health market. Volume 1 of the *Literary Market Place* provides a comprehensive listing of these worldwide industry-related conventions, conferences, and trade shows for the year. *Publishers Weekly,* the book industry's trade magazine, also announces up-and-coming shows. And you can check out the Trade Show News Network (www.tsnn.com)—an Internet site that provides a listing of shows for a number of industries, including book publishing. If you plan to attend a show, be aware that there will be an admission fee, which varies from show to show. You can find out the cost by calling ahead.

## MOVING ON

At this point, you have created a customized list of potential publishers for your work. Not only should these companies be the ones best suited to handle your book's category, they should also meet your personal criteria. If you have taken the time to develop this list carefully, it will increase your odds of getting published.

For now, however, it is time to put the list aside—just for a little while. Your next step will be to turn your attention to preparing that all-important submission package, which you will be sending to the publishers on your list.

# CHAPTER 5

# PREPARING THE PACKAGE

*There it sits on my desk in all its glory—a big brown box. But not just any big brown box. It is a very well wrapped big brown box. I look at the return address, and the name doesn't ring a bell. I survey the box again. It is covered with reinforced nylon strapping tape. I think to myself, "There's got to be an least half a roll invested in this baby." I've seen this before. Mere scissors will not do. I need an X-Acto knife. I go to the art department, retrieve the knife, and return. I am now prepared to do battle.*

*Ten minutes into hacking my way through the wrapping, the outer covering yields. I slit open the top and peer into the box. No! It's filled with Styrofoam peanuts. I put the trash can on my desk and begin to remove the peanuts—first a little at a time, and then by the handful. There, close to the bottom, I see my final objective—a large, thick white envelope. I pick it up, along with a few dozen peanuts that stubbornly cling to the package. The envelope is made of Kevlar, that miracle material that cannot be torn by human hands. I scramble for the scissors. As I cut away the top of the package, I can see more peanuts scattering in all directions. I do not care. I must see what is in the package.*

*I pull out a thick stack of sheets. On top is a cover letter. It starts, "Dear Mr. Shur. I spoke to your assistant and she said to send you my manuscript."*

*"I don't think so," I mutter to myself. I know that my assistant would never request a completed manuscript. Unless this baby is the sequel to "Gone With the Wind," it's history. Finding that it is not the sequel, I place the manuscript on the rejection pile . . . still shaking peanuts off my hands.*

As I have said before, editors are extremely busy people. Their days are filled with a multitude of competing tasks—editorial meetings, production meetings, phone calls with authors, appointments, book projections, and a whole lot more. The author who makes life easy for the editor by submitting a short, to-the-point submission package has increased the odds that his material will be read. If, in addition to this, the writer's material is well written, gives a precise overview of his book, and shows a clear understanding of the book's potential audience, the editor will know he is dealing with an informed author.

This chapter was designed to guide you through the writing of a winning submission package—a package that will invite the editor's attention, give the editor the best possible impression of both you and your book, and provide him with all the information he needs to make an initial decision about your project. You'll learn exactly what should be included and, just as important, you'll discover what should *never* be included. Writing a winning package is probably easier than you think. Editors know what they want. The problem has always been that most authors don't take the time to find out exactly what that is. This chapter will let you in on all our secrets, and help you put together a proposal that will get the best possible results.

## THE GOAL OF THE SUBMISSION PACKAGE

Before you begin work on your submission package, it's important to understand the goal of the material you'll be writing. This goal is really threefold.

First, a winning package is designed to *get read.* That may sound strange, but many submissions are so poorly written, so confusing, or so overwhelming in size that they are destined to be "killed"—rejected, in other words—before the editor even finishes reading the first paragraph. Above all, a winning package is so brief and otherwise so inviting that it maximizes the odds that the acquiring editor will actually read enough of it to learn the merits of the project.

Second, a winning package shows the editor that this is a viable project—a project with potential. It does this by demonstrating that the book addresses a topic in which the reading audience is interested, and by showing that you have the ability to write a marketable book on this topic. An important point to remember is that you are not only selling the idea of the book, but are also selling yourself as the author. Reading your package, the editor will have a chance to assess your writing ability. A good package can convince him that you are credible, and that you have what it takes to produce a good book. On the other hand, if you are unable to organize your thoughts in a one-page letter, the editor will probably feel that you can't handle a three hundred-page manuscript.

Finally, a winning package evokes an interest and, most important, a *positive response* on the part of the editor. If they are interested, most editors will send a form letter, asking for further material. If the editor is sufficiently excited, he might take the time to write a personal letter, send an e-mail, or even make a phone call to discuss the project.

**Helpful Hint**

Always remember that the goal of a submission package is not only to sell the idea of your book, but also to sell *you* as the author. An effective package will convince the editor that you have what it takes to produce a good book.

## THE COMPONENTS OF THE SUBMISSION PACKAGE

A submission package meets its goals through three elements: a cover letter, which is also referred to as a query letter; an annotated table of contents; and an overview of the book. Each of these should be only a page or two in length, so—unless your book involves a long table of contents—your total package should include only about six pages. This may surprise you, because you may have heard that authors are expected to send sample chapters or a prospectus—a long document that includes an overview of the book, an analysis of how the book fits into the marketplace, a review of competing titles, a biography of the author, and an annotated table of contents. But remember that the primary goal of your package is *to be read!* You want to catch the editor's attention in the short amount of time he has to review your material. If you succeed, the editor will ask to see more, and at that time you can send him exactly what he wants, perhaps some sample chapters or a full proposal. If he is overwhelmed by an unexpected stack of material, odds are he will be less likely to want to know more about your project.

A submission package meets its goals through three components: a cover letter, an annotated table of contents, and an overview of the book.

## RULE #7

## *Keep your proposal brief and to the point*

In leafing through reference books like *Writer's Market,* you will find that most publishers request submission packages that are much like the Square One package. In some cases, however, publishers state that they are open to receiving more information—a few sample chapters, for instance. In these instances, should you send the additional material? My advice is to omit the extra material until the publisher receives your package and specifically requests it. The copying and mailing of sample chapters can be time-consuming and expensive, and is not worth the effort unless the editor is truly interested in your project. Don't worry: If the editor wants to see more, he will not hesitate to ask for it.

The remainder of this chapter will explain how to write a great cover letter, a clear annotated table of contents, and a brief but descriptive overview of your work. Throughout, you'll find samples of each of these components. By carefully crafting each portion of your submission package and sending it to the appropriate editor, you will maximize the chance that your package will prompt a positive response.

## The Cover Letter

Because it serves as an introduction to you and your book, the cover letter is the most crucial portion of the submission package.

The cover letter is the most crucial portion of the submission package. As the first part of the package that the editor sees, it serves as an introduction to you and your book. Most cover letters miss some or all of the elements needed to capture the editor's full interest and motivate him to read the remainder of the package. In other cases, the necessary information is there, but is presented so poorly that it casts serious doubts on the author's ability to write. Very few editors will pursue a project further when the cover letter is poorly written. The Square One cover letter is designed to provide all of the information that the editor needs and wants in *four well-organized paragraphs,* which are described on the next few pages. As you read the following, keep in mind that the cover letter should range between one to two pages in length. You'll find sample cover letters on pages 108 through 111.

### *The Salutation and First Paragraph*

Every letter, of course, should begin with a salutation, such as "Dear Mr. Smith." Although a cover letter can begin with "Dear History Editor," "Dear Health Editor," or a similar form of address, I recommend that you use the appropriate editor's name when possible. By using his name at the top of the letter and, more important, on the outside of the package, you will not only make sure that the package gets to the right person, but will also demonstrate that you have done your homework. (More about getting the appropriate editor's name in Chapter 6.)

Below the salutation comes the first paragraph, which is the introductory paragraph. Begin by stating that you are in the process of writing a book entitled such-and-such. *Never* say that you have finished writing the book—even if you have. Why? Most editors want to be able to shape the book to meet the needs of their company's publishing program and to be consistent with house style. If your book has already been written, the editor may feel that too much editorial work will be required to bring it up to par. Just as damaging, he may assume that the manuscript has been floating around for a while, rejected by publisher after publisher. This, of course, will make the book far less appealing. By simply saying that you are *in the process* of writing the book or that you are *currently working* on the book, you will have avoided raising a red flag.

> **Helpful Hint**
>
> Never tell a prospective editor that you have finished writing your book. Most editors want to work with you during the writing process to make sure that the book will meet their company's needs.

The remainder of the first paragraph should include a two- to four-sentence summary of the book that explains what the book is about. At this point, you'll want to refer to the information you gleaned in Chapter 2, where you identified your book's category and broke it down into different levels. How much of the category and level information should be included in this paragraph? The purpose of identifying your book's overall category and—in the case of most books—the first two levels was to help you select the most appropriate publishing houses for your work, to pinpoint the editors who should receive your submission package, and to describe your audience. Therefore, you need not specifically state the general category and the first two levels in this portion of the letter. However, to find the third level of your book, you wrote a few sentences that described its specific topic or, in the case of a textbook, the curriculum or course for which it was designed—which includes your work's specific topic. *This* is the information that should be included in the first paragraph of your letter. At the end of the paragraph, inform the editor that you have enclosed a table of contents and an overview of the book. These, of course, will provide more detail about the book itself. If have not yet read Chapter 2, by all means, go back and read it. The information you gather could make a big difference in your submission package.

### The Second Paragraph

This paragraph is designed to show the editor that you, as a writer, have a reasonably clear idea of the book's audience. As explained in Chapter 2, an author who demonstrates that he understands his book's category and audience is viewed as an asset by the editor—as a partner in the publishing process. Unfortunately, all too many authors show their ignorance of the book world by claiming that their book is for everyone, from the professional to the student to the general reader. A successful author shows the editor that his book has been designed for a specific audience. Again, you might want to refer to the work you did in Chapter 2. Either Level One or Level Two of your book includes the audience for which your work is geared. Try to be as clear and specific as possible. For instance, instead of saying that a travel book is for "an adult audience interested in nonfiction," you might say that it is for "anyone interested in traveling to Europe." The editor will understand that you are referring to a trade audience interested in travel books. By demonstrating that you have identifiable readers in mind, you will provide the editor with the level of security he needs to sign you on as an author.

In this second paragraph, you should, if possible, support the assertion that your book has an audience by giving some idea of the size of your potential readership. In the case of the travel guide, you might say, "Over 10 million Americans visited Europe within the last year." (To learn ways to quantify your audience, see the inset "Estimating Audience Size" on page 34.) You can also mention

#### Helpful Hint

Are you acquainted with someone who is nationally known, or is well known within the field that your book addresses? If so—and if that person would be willing to write a Foreword for your book, or even to write a one- or two-line endorsement for the book's cover—be sure to mention this in the second paragraph of your cover letter. By showing that you can help make your book more marketable, this addition can increase your odds of getting a positive response to your submission package.

the titles of books that are similar to yours, choosing one or two titles that are leaders in the appropriate field. You should then go on to explain how your book is different from or better than its competitors. For instance, your book may be geared for an upscale audience, and may therefore emphasize luxury accommodations and entertainments. Or your book may be geared for the woman traveling alone or for couples looking for a romantic adventure.

Most important, *never say that your book is unique.* Why? Because a unique book has no established marketplace. Many first-time authors don't realize this and emphasize the fact that their book is "like nothing that has ever been done before." But if this type of book has really never been done before, there is probably a reason for that. Editors aren't looking for a unique book; they're looking for a book that fits into an existing category but, hopefully, takes a fresh new approach or is in some way better than its competition. So even if you feel that your book truly is unique, don't say so. Instead, examine it carefully to find the category in which it fits, and then describe the features that differentiate it from its competitors.

Should you actually state your *marketplace*—traditional and travel bookstores, for instance—in your cover letter? If you have done your homework and carefully selected appropriate publishers as explained in Chapter 4, the companies on your list should both know all of the outlets through which your book may be sold and have established means of reaching them. For this reason, in most cases, it is not necessary to identify your book's marketplaces in your letter. However, if you have a difficult-to-reach audience and have found an unusual and effective way of accessing it, it would be wise to highlight this fact.

**Helpful Hint**

*Never* tell an editor that your book is unique. Editors don't want a unique book because such a book has no established marketplace.

### *The Third Paragraph*

The goal of this paragraph is to establish your credibility as the author of your book. Begin by stating your educational background. This would include any colleges you attended, and the undergraduate, graduate, or doctoral degrees you received there. If you did not attend college, simply omit any statement about educational background. It is important not to lie about your educational experience—or about any other experience, for that matter.

However, if you attended college but never actually received a degree, you may say something like, "I attended John Carroll University, where I majored in English."

Remember that the purpose of this paragraph is to show your strongest credentials in terms of the book you are writing. These credentials may be based on a college degree, but they may also be based on work experience or a hobby. Consider, for example, an author of a book on refrigerator repair. Although he may not have attended college, he may have repaired refrigerators for ten years and written a manual for his company that was adopted for use nationwide. This work experience serves as excellent credentials in this case. Similarly, someone who has written a regional cookbook may cite her passion for cooking, and explain that she has collected and tested local recipes for fifteen years. Or perhaps she ran a small restaurant that highlighted local cuisine.

It is important to avoid citing irrelevant accomplishments, however meaningful they may be to you. For instance, the writer of the regional cookbook should not mention that she has been the head of the local PTA for ten years, and the author of the refrigerator repair book should not mention his success in coaching Little League baseball. On the other hand, if he were writing a book on the glories of youth sports, his experience as a coach *would* be appropriate.

Of course, the best credential of all is having had something published, be it a book, a magazine article, or even a local newspaper article. If any of your writings have been published, you should certainly mention this within the third paragraph, as it will show that your work has already been approved by another editor. If you have not been published, consider reworking a chapter from your book into an article and submitting it to a newspaper or magazine. This could greatly strengthen the odds of having your submission package accepted. However, keep in mind that while it is a plus to be published, it is certainly not a prerequisite to having a winning submission package.

### Helpful Hint

Before you begin sending out submission packages, it is important to ask yourself if, considering the nature of your project, you have the background that publishers are likely to demand. Consider a few examples from the area of religious books. A publisher receiving a proposal for a book that examines the importance of religious faith in the life of a particular celebrity would probably not look for any special background on the author's part. But a publisher of Evangelical devotionals would expect its writers to be, at the very least, lay leaders in their respective churches. And a publisher of scholarly books on the Talmud would probably demand that its authors have formal backgrounds in theology. To gauge the type of training and experience that might be expected, scan library and bookstore shelves for books similar to yours, and read the "About the Author" copy. This should help you determine whether publishers are likely to be satisfied by your credentials.

## *The Fourth Paragraph and Close*

The purpose of this concluding paragraph is to wrap up the letter. First, express your hope that the project is of interest to the editor, and offer to send any further material that he may need to make a final decision. Tell the editor that you have enclosed a self-addressed, stamped envelope (SASE) for his convenience, and make him aware that this is a multiple submission—in other words, that you are also sending this package to other publishing houses. Finally, add your complimentary close—"Yours truly," "Sincerely yours," and "Sincerely" are all appropriate—and type your name, placing your handwritten signature above it.

Offering advice on how to end a letter may seem a little strange. However, it's amazing how common it is for publishers to receive letters with bizarre endings and no signatures. So this is just a helpful reminder to wrap up your winning letter with a winning close.

## RULE #8

## *Always send out multiple submissions*

Above, I advised you to tell the editor that you are sending out multiple submissions. Why is this so important? For two reasons, really. First, it is now the usual procedure to send out multiple submissions, so this statement will show your savvy about the submissions process. Second, and just as important, this statement will add a respectful sense of urgency by giving the impression that another editor at another house may snap up your manuscript at any moment. So by including this one simple statement, you will do quite a bit to increase the impact of your letter.

### *Contact Information*

I still find it hard to believe that many authors fail to provide the information the editor needs to contact them by mail, phone, fax, or e-mail. If the submission package is truly outstanding, the editor may try to track down the missing information—but don't count on it! The very fact that this information was omitted is a red flag to the editor, who may then have serious doubts about the writer's commonsense and organizational abilities.

Years ago, an author simply placed his address at the top of the letter. But now that so many methods of contact are available, a number of options are considered acceptable. You can place your address, phone number, and, if available, fax number and e-mail

Don't allow the sample letters in this book to cramp your writing style. While remaining professional and following the recommended structure, feel free to show a little flair and even a little humor, when appropriate.

address at the top of the letter; you can place them beneath your typed name at the end of the letter; or you can work them into the last paragraph of the letter. Of course, if you have stationery that includes all of this information, you needn't retype it in the letter itself. Finally, keep in mind that not every editor is e-mail accessible. Therefore, don't omit your phone number; list every means by which you may be contacted. If the editor is really excited by your submission package, he will want to call you right away!

## Sample Cover Letter #1

44 Berkshire Road
Brightwaters, NY 11747
Phone: (153) 555-1218
Fax: (153) 555-1837
E-mail: erigby@onepot.com

(Current Date)

Gil Grape, Executive Editor
Quick Cuisine Publishers
999 Pesto Street
San Francisco, CA 11937

Dear Mr. Grape:

I am in the process of writing a cookbook entitled *The Beat-the-Clock One-Pot Cookbook.* Written for people who are short on time but still want to eat nutritious, satisfying food, this book will present over 120 recipes for delicious meals, each of which can be prepared in thirty minutes or less. In addition, each meal can be prepared in a *single* pot, pan, or skillet, so that cleanup time is also shortened. Every recipe in the book will be accompanied by complete nutritional information, and will include suggestions for substituting vegetarian ingredients for any meat used in the dish. Best of all, every recipe will be kitchen-tested, and so will have proven appeal. The enclosed table of contents and overview provide more details about the scope and contents of the book, which I expect to be approximately 60,000 words in length.

Although this cookbook can be enjoyed by anyone, including single people and retired couples, it was specifically written for the two-income family, where both parents are out of the house during the day and have only a short time to get dinner on the table at night. As you probably know, more than 75 percent of American families now rely on two incomes. These families too often depend on high-fat fast foods simply because they aren't familiar with the simple techniques that can be used to prepare a meal quickly and easily. Although other books, such as Myrna Stewart's *Meals in Seconds,* have tried to provide easy-to-prepare dishes, the meals usually lack simple kid-appeal. (What child really wants to eat Myrna's Rock Cornish Game Hens in Cointreau?) And none of the leading fast-cooking books uses the one-pot approach—an approach that has revolutionized the way I cook for my own family.

I have been interested in cooking since my student days at the State University of New York at Saratoga. Although SUNY at Saratoga was great, the food served in its cafeteria was truly frightening, so I cooked not only for myself, but also for my roommates. After graduating in 1983 with an MBA in Business, I opened a small restaurant, The Hungry Student, that served home-style foods at prices students could afford. The restaurant flourished until 1987, when I married and started raising a family. That's when I began developing shortcut cooking techniques so that I could continue preparing and eating great meals even while caring for an on-the-go family of five. In 1997, I began teaching cooking in my own kitchen. At first, I taught mostly friends and acquaintances who wanted to learn my techniques for preparing home-style one-pot dishes. Now I teach over twenty classes a week—and I *still* cook for my family every night!

I very much appreciate your taking the time to review my proposal. If this project is of interest to you, please let me know what further materials you would like to see in order to make a decision. A stamped, self-addressed envelope has been provided for your convenience, and I look forward to receiving your response. Please be aware that this is a multiple submission.

Sincerely yours,

Ellen Rigby

Ellen Rigby

## Sample Cover Letter #2

117 Main Street
Florence, ND 11549
Phone: (157) 555-1216
Fax: (157) 555-1738

(Current Date)

Norton Nimrod
Pet Publications
44 Frog Lane
Concord, MA 11735

Dear Mr. Nimrod:

I am currently working on a project entitled *Healthcare for a Healthier Cat.* This book will discuss all of the most common feline health problems, from everyday nuisances like fleas to emergencies such as burns and poisoning, and explain them in easy-to-understand language. It will then look at different methods of treatment, from the conventional treatments usually provided by veterinarians to natural approaches that use herbs, dietary supplements, or homeopathic remedies. Readers can thus choose from among a range of treatments, depending on their preferences and, of course, on the seriousness of the condition. Special cautions are provided when conventional care must be given. However, even in these cases, alternative treatments can often be used to enhance the effects of conventional care. The enclosed table of contents and overview provide more information about the scope and organization of the book, which I believe will run about 160,000 words.

You are probably aware that cats are now the most popular pets in the country. In fact, according to current estimates, 29.1 million of the homes in the United States have at least one cat as a pet. That means that nearly a third of American homes include a feline companion!

As a practicing veterinarian with over twenty-five years' experience, I know that most of these owners are interested in doing all that they can to maintain their cats' health. Yet all too many veterinarians are familiar with only conventional treatments, many of which have harmful side effects or only limited usefulness. And many know of no *preventive* treatments other than standard vaccinations. The cat-care books now on the market reflect this fact, offering little guidance for cat owners who wish to optimize their cats' health through good nutrition, the use of natural remedies, and commonsense measures such as regular grooming. While this book will cover all of the same subjects addressed in other cat-care titles, it will give readers something they have never had before: choice regarding the method of treatment.

Much of my success as a veterinarian has stemmed from my experience in treating animals that could not be helped by conventional medicine alone. After receiving my veterinary degree from the University of Missouri College of Veterinary Medicine in 1989, I joined my father's practice at the Kitty Cat Hospital in Florence, North Dakota. There, I was often struck by conventional medicine's limited success in treating many feline ailments. I therefore began to research alternative treatments, and to use them—alone and in combination with orthodox treatments—in the care of cats. In fact, for the past decade, people have come to my hospital from all over North Dakota because of my unparalleled success in treating disorders as wide-ranging as upper respiratory infections and tooth decay. Because of popular demand, I now write weekly columns on natural cat care for our local newspaper, the *Florence Tribune.* Many of my articles have also appeared in national magazines such as *Cat Fancy* and *Cats.*

It is my hope that *Healthcare for a Healthier Cat* will guide owners in helping their cats live longer, healthier lives. A stamped, self-addressed envelope has been provided in this package, and I look forward to receiving your response to this proposal. I can also be contacted by phone at 800-555-KITTY, or by e mail at kklaus@kittycare.com. Please be aware that this is a multiple submission.

Sincerely,

Kurt Klaus

Kurt Klaus, DVM

## The Annotated Table of Contents

> **Helpful Hint**
>
> An annotated table of contents should be clear but brief. Be sure to provide enough information to show the scope and organization of your book, but not so much that you tax the editor's time and patience.

The second part of the submission package is the annotated table of contents, which is sometimes called an expanded table of contents. As Sample #1 on page 113 demonstrates, in most cases, the annotated table of contents lists the various parts of the book, including the prematter, the actual chapters, and the postmatter. While a standard table of contents lists just the chapter names, in an annotated table of contents, a clear yet concise description of each chapter's coverage is included under the chapter name. (Be aware, though, that you don't have to annotate the sections of the prematter and postmatter.)

Although many books follow the chapter-by-chapter organization shown in Sample #1, some books—most reference works, and a variety of other books, as well—use a different method of organization. Thus, in Sample #2 on page 114, you'll find an annotated table of contents for a book with an encyclopedic format. This book is divided into two parts, with the second part presenting topic discussions arranged in alphabetical order. Since each of these topics is covered in a similar way, you would not want to annotate each topic individually. Therefore, annotations appear only below each *part* title.

Although these two tables of contents are set up somewhat differently, each, in a relatively short number of pages, shows the scope and organization of the book. Even Sample #2, which is two pages in length, would not tax an editor's time and patience. Instead, it allows the editor to quickly scan a list of subjects to assess topic coverage.

If you have not yet written a table of contents for your book—which is likely only if your book is still in the planning stages—doing so will give you an opportunity to assess the organization of your material. If you are, in fact, still researching and planning your book, be sure to take your time in preparing the table of contents, as it can make or break your submission package. Just don't go overboard by writing highly detailed annotations. Remember that, like the other components of the package, the table of contents should be clear but brief. One to three sentences for each chapter or part is perfect.

## Sample Table of Contents #1

**The Beat-the-Clock One-Pot Cookbook**
**Contents**

## Sample Table of Contents #2

**Healthcare for a Healthier Cat**
**Contents**

Diabetes
Diarrhea
Ear discharge
Ear mites
Epilepsy
Eye problems
Feline leukemia
Fever
Fleas
Fractures
Frostbite
Fungal infections
Gastritis
Glaucoma
Hairballs
Head injuries
Heart problems
Heartworms
Heat stroke
Impotence
Incontinence
Infertility
Insect bites and stings
Intestines, blocked
Itchy skin disorders
Jaundice
Kidney diseases
Laryngitis
Lead poisoning
Lice
Liver failure
Lungworms
Mange
Mast cell tumor
Mastitis
Melanoma
Mites
Motion sickness
Nasal discharge
Nerve injuries
Obesity
Osteoporosis
Paralysis
Parasites
Periodontal disease
Pinworms
Pneumonia
Poisoning
Polyps
Rabies
Ringworm
Roundworms
Seizures
Shedding
Sinusitis
Skin disorders
Snake bites
Sneezing
Spider bites
Sunburn
Tapeworms
Tetanus
Ticks
Tonsillitis
Tooth decay
Trichinosis
Tuberculosis
Tumors
Ulcer
Uremic poisoning
Urinary tract infections
Viral diseases
Vomiting
Warts
Weight loss
Whipworms
Wounds
Yellow fat disease

*References*
*Glossary*
*Resources*
*Bibliography for Further Reading*
*Index*

## How to Protect Your Work

When you send out copies of your submission package, you may wonder if any of the editors you're contacting might be so unscrupulous as to steal your idea. Or perhaps this notion won't occur to you until an editor requests sample chapters and you worry if your painstakingly worded text might end up in someone else's book!

If you start to get a little overprotective, you're not alone. The fear that someone, somewhere, will steal or modify your work is a common concern for the writer who is just starting to submit queries and manuscripts to publishing houses. Keep in mind that this rarely if ever happens, simply because an editor is most interested in finding a writer who can produce a marketable book—not just an idea that might someday be developed into a book. But if the possibility of theft remains a concern for you, you'll be glad to know that there are at least three ways of protecting your work.

### Register a Copyright

You may have noticed that every commercially printed book contains a copyright notice on the back of the title page. What you might not realize is that unpublished works can also be copyrighted.

What does a copyright mean? When a copyright is issued in your name by the United States Copyright Office, you will have the legal right to exclusive publication, production, sale, or distribution of your work. In other words, once it is registered, no one else will be able to legally print your work unless you formally grant him or her the right to do so. If anyone does violate your copyright by publishing part or all of your work, the formal copyright registration will speed up any legal battle and avoid complications. And if the work is registered with the copyright office within three months of its appearance in print or before any violation of your rights occurred, you will be awarded the money to pay for any attorney expenses, as well as compensation for the wrongs committed against you.

It is simple to register your copyright with the United States Copyright Office in Washington, DC. And you can register the work at any time—even years after your manuscript is written. First, you will have to fill out an application form, which can be downloaded from the Internet or obtained through the mail. (See the Resource List on page 215 for further information.) You will then send the completed application form, a copy of the manuscript, and a check covering the copyright fee. The office will mail you a certificate of registration once your application has been reviewed and accepted. Be aware that neither the fee nor the manuscript will be returned to you.

One last point should be made. When a copyright is issued in your name, only your actual *words*—not your concept—are protected. It is impossible to copyright a concept, be it the central idea of a book or a unique format or method of presentation.

## Obtain a Notary Public's Stamp

A notary public is a person who has been officially authorized to certify or witness the placing of a signature on a document, and to confirm that the paper was signed on a given date. Every notary has an exclusive ink stamp that contains his or her identification number. Therefore, when you have your work notarized and then, at a later date, someone prints your work without first securing your permission, the notary seal will prove that this work was in your possession on the recorded date.

It's easy to have your work notarized and thus establish visual proof of possession. If you don't already know a notary public, you will be able to find one at a bank, a financial office, or a professional office. Bring with you the manuscript itself, as well as two forms of identification, one of which must include a photo. In the presence of the notary public, place your signature on the first page of each chapter—it is unnecessary to notarize more than this. Then, for a small fee, the notary will stamp, sign, and date each of the signed pages. Keep the notarized documents in a safe place.

## Mail Yourself a Copy of the Work

If notarizing your work sounds like too much fuss, and registering a copyright sounds a bit too time-consuming, another option is available. First, sign and date the manuscript, and seal it securely in an envelope. Then take the package to your local post office and ask the person at the desk to hand-stamp each seam of the envelope or package with an official *dated* post office stamp. Finally, mail the package to your own address. When the package finds its way back to you, it will not only bear the regular postmark, which shows the date it was sent out and the location at which it was mailed, but will also show the stamped envelope seams, which will prove that you did not tamper with the package after receiving it in the mail. To further safeguard your work, you can even send your package via certified mail rather than regular mail. The package will then be given a tracking number and logged in the mailing service's system.

The rationale behind this practice, of course, is that the sealed, postmarked document will serve as visual evidence that the piece of writing was complete and in your possession prior to the postal stamp date. Then, if anyone plagiarizes your work, you will be able to present the package—which, of course, must still be sealed—in a court of law.

## A Final Caution

Any of the three methods described above should allow you to protect your work as you send it out to one or several editors. But do keep one important point in mind: The material you submit should not actually bear a copyright notice or notary seal. Why not let the editor know from the beginning that you've taken steps to safeguard your work? Simply put, such practices are insulting to the editor, as they give the impression that you don't trust his integrity. Perhaps just as important, such practices demonstrate that you lack experience and professionalism. So keep the copyright certificate and the notarized pages in your home records, and send the editor an unmarked copy of your material. That way, you'll both protect your work and project a professional image.

## The Book Overview

> **Helpful Hint**
>
> When writing the overview for your book, keep in mind that the overview very often serves as the basis for the book's introduction. Thus, your overview should be upbeat and enthusiastic, heightening the editor's interest so that he wants to read more.

The book overview is a one- to two-page summary of your book. It is designed to explain clearly and in reasonable detail just what your book is about, and to show why readers would be interested in the title. It demonstrates the scope and thrust of the book, clarifies your point of view, and assures the editor that you can write effectively.

Because there are so many different types of nonfiction books, it is impossible to provide a precise formula for the writing of an overview. It may help you to understand that the overview is very often used as a basis for the book's introduction. Thus, the overview can be viewed as a sort of "hook" that heightens the editor's interest in the book so that he wants to read more. It should be upbeat and enthusiastic, without sounding like an advertising piece. For instance, if the book is a biography, the overview should summarize the life of the subject of the book, emphasizing the high points of his or her life and showing why the subject is so intriguing. If you are creating an overview for a reference book, you can explain what is covered in the book, and why readers would find the book helpful and interesting. By glancing through the introductions of books that are similar to your own, you can get a fairly good idea of what is important to cover in your own overview. Also turn to the sample overviews on pages 119 to 121.

As mentioned above, the overview will serve as a sample of your writing style and your ability to present information. If you can produce two well-written pages, the editor will probably feel that you can produce a satisfactory three hundred-page book. If the editor finds the overview confusing or poorly constructed, he will most likely feel that the finished book will be poorly written.

In the case of trade books—books for the general reader—the overview should reflect the writing style that you will use in the book itself. However, the same is not true of books designed for professionals. Keep in mind that many acquisitions editors of professional books may have only a peripheral knowledge of the field, and may rely on consulting editors—experts in the field—for the editing of actual manuscripts. Therefore, the submission package should be written in an accessible style, without confusing technical lingo. If the editor finds the topic and approach interesting, he will ask for additional material. Subsequent material, such as sample chapters, should then reflect the writing style used in the actual text.

## Sample Overview #1

**The Beat-the-Clock One-Pot Cookbook**
**Overview**

Why does nearly every kitchen in America contain a list of fast-food delivery places? The answer is simple. More than ever before, both men and women are working outside the home, and have little time in which to prepare a delicious, satisfying, and nutritious dinner that will be enjoyed by parents and children alike. *The Beat-the-Clock One-Pot Cookbook* is designed to solve this dilemma with over 120 dishes that can be made in 30 minutes or less, are high in nutrients, and appeal to both parents and kids. Just as important, each dish is prepared in only one item of cookware: one pot, one skillet, or one casserole dish. The result is that these recipes speed up not just prep time and cooking time, but also cleanup time, allowing Mom and Dad to spend less of their evening in the kitchen, and more of it in the family room.

The cookbook begins with a discussion of the basics of fast-and-easy one-pot cooking. Readers will learn about the best cookware to use in one-pot meals, and will be introduced to the simple cooking techniques that guarantee delicious results each and every time. Tips are also provided for choosing the most healthful, most delicious, and fastest-cooking ingredients for one-pot dinners.

Following Chapter 1, each chapter focuses on a specific type of dish. Readers will learn how to make satisfying soups like Twenty-Minute Clam Chowder; pleasing poultry dishes like Spicy Chicken and Rice Casserole; hearty beef dishes like Chile for a Chilly Day; perfect pork dishes like Sweet and Sour Pork and Rice; sensational seafood dishes like Thirty-Minute Paella; and vegetarian delights like Hearty Mushroom Stew. Each recipe includes simple-to-follow step-by-step instructions that can be successfully followed by even the most inexperienced cook, and even the most harried parent. Because of the new emphasis on healthy vegetarian eating, each recipe also includes veggie alternatives to any meat, poultry, or fish used. And for the truly health-conscious reader, each provides a complete nutritional analysis. This helps parents insure that the dishes they serve not only are delicious, but also meet their family's nutritional needs.

It is my hope that *The Beat-the-Clock One-Pot Cookbook* will convince parents and children alike that a homemade meal can be tempting and healthful, and can be prepared quickly and easily. Everyone deserves a hearty home-style dinner. This cookbook will help them enjoy not only a great meal, but also the rest of their evening together.

### Sample Overview #2

**Healthcare for a Healthier Cat**
**Overview**

All cat owners want their cats to live long and healthy lives. Most diligently take their pets to veterinarians for vaccinations and, of course, for treatment whenever their cats show any sign of illness. But most owners aren't aware that, in addition to vaccinations, there are many other ways in which they can help maintain kitty's well-being. They also don't know that when kitty does get sick, there are proven natural treatments that can return him to health without the use of medications or invasive treatments. And they don't know that in still other cases, at-home treatments can supplement the conventional medicine provided by a veterinarian, increasing their cat's comfort and returning him to health all the sooner.

*Healthcare for a Healthier Cat* was designed to help owners maintain and restore their cat's health through a unique approach that combines the best of conventional medicine with herbal medicine, homeopathic remedies, diet, nutritional supplements, massage, and proper grooming. Readers are helped to understand what good feline health is all about, to become aware of the many treatments available, and to make informed healthcare decisions in conjunction with the services of a qualified veterinarian.

Part I of this book discusses the history, theories, and practices of conventional veterinary medicine, herbal medicine, and homeopathy. It also shows how a proper diet, along with carefully chosen vitamin and mineral supplements, can prevent a wide range of feline disorders, and can help correct a variety of health problems. Furthermore, it guides the cat owner in setting up a routine of daily groomings and kitty massage that have been shown to improve feline health and well-being, and to prevent commonplace problems such as hairballs.

Part II of this book is an alphabetical directory of common feline disorders, from abscesses to ear mites to yellow fat disease. Each entry begins with a complete yet easy-to-understand explanation of the problem, its symptoms, and its causes. This is followed by an explanation of treatment options, including recommendations for emergency treatment when appropriate. Readers are guided in determining the best single treatment or combination of treatments for their cats, and are directed to consult a qualified veterinarian when necessary. All of the alternative treatments recommended have been proven effective in clinical studies and anecdotal reports, so that readers can be assured that they are giving their pets the best possible care. Each entry ends with a helpful section on prevention that will aid owners in avoiding this problem in the future.

*Healthcare for a Healthier Cat* ends with useful appendices. These sections explain technical terms used throughout the book; list recommended suppliers of herbal remedies, homeopathic products, and nutritional supplements; and provide a list of further readings for those owners who want to investigate specific health concerns or expand their understanding of complementary medicine.

Many cat-care books discuss feline disorders and tell owners how their veterinarians are likely to treat these problems. *Healthcare for a Healthier Cat* is the first book that provides owners with a real choice in healthcare. This is a reliable source of information that concerned cat owners can turn to time and time again.

## The Self-Addressed Stamped Envelope

As a courtesy to the editor, always include a self-addressed, stamped envelope in your submission package. This will make it easier for the editor to reply to your proposal. Do not, however, expect the editor to send the contents of your package back to you. Anticipate receiving only the editor's reply, be it yes or no. This is another reason to avoid sending sample chapters and the like to an editor who has not yet expressed an interest in your manuscript. The copying and mailing costs are exorbitant, and, most likely, nothing you send out will be returned to you. (For an alternative to stamped, self-addressed envelopes, see the inset on page 123.)

## POLISHING THE PACKAGE

Once you draft the different components of your submission package, you may want to begin sending out queries right away. Keep in mind, though, that you have only one chance to convince each publisher on your list that your book is right for his company. Therefore, it makes sense to take a little extra time and make sure that your package is the best it can be. This involves two steps: checking your material for spelling, grammar, clarity, and flow; and making the materials attractive and professional in appearance. Let's look at each of these in turn.

## Perfecting the Language

As discussed earlier, the goal of your submission package is not just to convince editors that you have chosen a marketable topic and that you have amassed enough material to create a book. It is also vital to demonstrate that you are a writer who can produce copy that is well organized and clear. And, of course, you want to show that you are a careful and conscientious writer—a writer who can and will do any work that is necessary to bring the book to completion. This is best demonstrated by sending a submission package that is as good as it can be.

After you have drafted your cover letter, table of contents, and overview, read through the materials slowly and carefully, checking for spelling, grammar, and organization. Even if everything seems fine to you, run a spell-check on your computer. It's easy to miss mistakes in your own work because after you have read the same material several times, there is a tendency to operate on "automatic." Therefore, the computer may detect errors that you were unable to see. And be aware that although you may think that spelling isn't as important as writing style or content, editors typically don't feel that way. They value careful writing and attention to detail.

After you have polished your writing as much as possible, put the submission package in the drawer of your desk for a day or two. This will place a little distance between you and your work so that the next time you review the material, you can evaluate it a bit more objectively. Correct any further errors that you find.

Finally, consider asking someone else to read through your package and provide you with an appraisal of your work. Ideally, this person should be in the publishing industry. If you know of no such person, try to find someone who has good, solid English skills—someone who is well read, has a good ear for language, and perhaps does some writing of his own. Perhaps most important, this person should be willing and able to provide you with an *honest* response rather than telling you what he thinks you want to hear.

> **Helpful Hint**
>
> Consider asking a friend or coworker to read through your submission package. This person should have good, solid English skills, and should be willing and able to provide you with an honest evaluation of your proposal.

When you hand the material to your "reader," explain that you want him to read the material through for clarity, organization, spelling, and grammar. Explain that the package is *supposed* to be

## "X" Marks the Spot

If you are like most authors, you are more than eager to hear from the editors to whom you have sent your submission package. To make it easier for editors to respond to your queries in a timely manner, consider the option of including in each package a response postcard rather than a self-addressed, stamped envelope. Then, instead of running off a letter, the editor will be able to simply check the appropriate response and drop the card in the outgoing mail bin. And, of course, you will also save a few cents on postage.

Begin your postcard with a general phrase that applies to the submissions process: "Thank you for submitting your proposal. We appreciate your interest in our company." Then follow with a list of options, supplying a check box next to each so that the editor can simply "X" or check the most appropriate reply. You might present the editor with the following choices:

- ☐ We have received your proposal and will contact you soon regarding your project.
- ☐ We like your work and would appreciate your sending us the following additional materials: ______________________.
- ☐ Unfortunately, we cannot publish your book at this time.

If the idea appeals to you, you may choose to add a few comments designed to put a smile on the editor's face—and help get your package noticed, as well. Consider the following:

- ☐ Don't give up your day job.
- ☐ It has Pulitzer written all over it.
- ☐ This is the best damn thing I've read in years.

Before adding any humorous lines to your message, make sure that they are appropriate for your project. If your book is a serious exploration of a shocking social problem, for instance, it would probably be best to maintain a sober tone throughout your package.

Before enclosing the cards, make sure that each one has your address on the front and bears the appropriate postage. Also be aware that you will receive only a response—not your original material.

brief and easy to read; it is not intended to be long or highly technical. And it is supposed to contain just three elements—the cover letter, the annotated table of contents, and the overview. Other than communicating these objectives, try to avoid giving him your "take" on the material. Let him read it through slowly on his own. Then ask him if he finds it clear, logical, well written, and interesting. Also ask him if you have said anything that is unintentionally misleading or offputting. If he has any suggestions, listen to them with an open mind and try to make any necessary changes in your package. Just beware of suggestions that are not in line with your objectives. If your reader tells you, for instance, that you must include a sample chapter, a lengthy market evaluation, or a twenty-page prospectus, thank him politely, but *don't* take his advice.

## Getting the Mechanics Right

**Helpful Hint**

To maximize the readability of your submission package and insure a professional appearance, you'll want to choose 8½-x-11-inch white bond paper; select a basic no-frills typeface; and use a printer that produces letter-quality type.

Once you feel that you have perfected the wording of your submission package, you'll want to make the package as attractive and professional in appearance as possible. This serves two purposes. It makes the copy easy to read, and it shows the editor that you understand what a publishing company expects from a prospective author.

First, choose 8½-x-11-inch paper—preferably a white bond paper. Use 1-inch margins, and type—don't handwrite—all of the submission package materials. If you don't own a typewriter or computer, borrow one from a friend or, if available, use one at your local library.

If you have a choice of typefaces, choose a basic, readable font such as Times Roman, and use 12-point type. Avoid fancy or exotic typefaces, as editors generally don't appreciate hard-to-read copy. For the same reason, don't use a dot-matrix printer. The type should be of letter quality, and should be printed in black.

Start each part of the package—the letter, table of contents, and overview—on a new sheet of paper. Single-space the cover letter, but double-space the table of contents and overview. Number the pages to avoid confusion.

You may feel that the use of standard white paper and a no-frills typeface will result in a boring submission package. It's certainly fine to add a special touch to your package as long as you keep the materials readable and attractive. For instance, over the years, I have received a cover letter for a book on headache relief that had a foil packet of aspirin stapled to its corner; a cover letter for a book on tea that included a gourmet tea bag; and a cover letter for a book on printing that was typed on elegant deckle-edged stationery. Each of these had the desired effect: They attracted my attention and prompted me to spend a few more moments looking over the author's materials. But remember that you want to be

## Ten Common Submission Package Errors

Over the years, I've seen literally hundreds of submission packages. Some of them inspired me to immediately request more information from the author. In other cases, however, I could not send the package to the kill pile quickly enough. Throughout this chapter, I've mentioned several submission package don'ts, but these warnings bear repeating as long as authors keep making the same mistakes. If you avoid the following errors, you will, at the very least, avoid raising a red flag. Here are ten errors that commonly occur in submission packages.

**1 The author claims that his book is unique.** This statement is the kiss of death, because editors don't want a unique book. They want a book that fits into an existing category and meets the needs of an existing audience. At the very best, this statement implies that the author doesn't understand the market for his book. At the very worst, it indicates that the book is, indeed, unique—and therefore either has no audience, or has an audience that is difficult to reach.

**2 The author claims that his book is for *everyone*—professionals, teachers, students, and general readers.** Again, books should be written with a specific audience in mind, be it a trade (general) audience, an educational audience, a professional audience, or a scholarly audience. This is true for a number of reasons. First, educational, professional, and scholarly books all have certain characteristics that are off-putting to the general reader. Professional books, for instance, are written in the jargon of the appropriate profession—a jargon that is unfamiliar to the general reader. Educational books may include review questions and other features that are not usually included in trade books. And scholarly books are often heavily footnoted and referenced. Second, as you learned in Chapter 2, different types of books are marketed in different ways, and are placed in different areas of bookstores. That's why publishing companies demand that every book be designed to suit the needs of a specific audience.

**3 The author states that the book has already been finished.** Few editors want to help an author rework an existing book so that it fits the needs of their particular publishing house. They want to begin guiding the author's work at an early stage, and set it on the right course. Therefore, even if your book is complete right down to the index, tell the editor that you are *in the process* of writing a book.

**4 The author fails to include his address and phone number.** Believe it or not, this silly mistake is made all the time. If the editor doesn't know how to reach you, you can't expect a timely response—or, for that matter, any response at all!

**5 The submission package is sent to the wrong type of publishing house.** Authors have been known to submit their novels to houses that publish only nonfiction; to send their poetry to houses that publish only cookbooks; to send their cookbooks to houses that specialize in romance novels; to send their ideas for coffee-table art books to houses that print mass market paperbacks. To avoid wasting both your time and theirs, do your homework, and send your submission package to the appropriate editor at the appropriate publishing house.

**6 The submission package is the size of *War and Peace*.** This returns me to one of my original points: Editors are busy. They simply don't have the time to wade through a stack of paper, no matter how riveting the material may be. By submitting a package that provides the desired information in a concise manner, you will optimize the chance that your package will, at the very least, be read.

**7 The submission package is triple-wrapped and sealed with packing tape.** As my opening vignette shows, editors usually don't keep power tools in their office. Unless you are dropping your package out of a helicopter, place it in an easy-to-open envelope.

**8 Out of fear that the editor will steal the author's idea, the author only *hints* at the contents of the book.** This may sound incredible, but it does happen. Authors have told me that they have found the cure for a terrible disease, that they have found a foolproof weight-loss technique, and that they have discovered an amazing secret about the Kennedys — but that they cannot tell me what it is unless I agree to publish their book. I think you can guess what my response was. (For tips on protecting your work, see the inset on page 116.)

**9 The author wrongly implies that he has spoken to the editor, and that the editor asked for a copy of his manuscript proposal.** Over the years, I have received countless cover letters that began, "Thank you so much for your interest in my project," or, "Per your request, I am enclosing a manuscript proposal. . . ." These opening lines would be perfectly appropriate—*if* I had ever spoken to the author and actually requested the material. Some authors feel that because editors are so busy, they can be tricked into thinking that they asked for the submission. Don't fool yourself. We're busy but we're not *that* busy, and, in the absence of any prior contact, an opening statement like this is almost guaranteed to put a negative spin on your proposal.

**10 The manuscript proposal is filled with spelling errors, grammatical errors, and awkward sentences.** Happens all the time. Keep in mind that, in addition to selling your expertise in a particular field, you are selling yourself as a *writer*. Therefore, it pays to read over your submission several times, to use the spell-check feature of your computer, and to have others read the material over carefully, looking for problems. The material you are about to send is relatively short, so it shouldn't be too difficult to polish it up. The time you take to make this package the best it can be will definitely pay off.

different in a *good* way—not in a way that will be off-putting to the editor. Don't, for instance, use "zany" stationery or include perishable foods—foods that, very likely, will perish before the editor gets around to opening the package. And don't include a fancy pen or pencil printed with the editor's name. Every time I receive something like this, I feel as if the writer is trying to bribe me—although

I did like a few of the pens. Finally, keep in mind that there is no *requirement* that you add a personal touch to your package. Any editor would rather receive an unremarkable-looking but beautifully composed submission package than one that has an eye-catching appearance but is poorly written.

If you have prepared each component of your submission package with thought and have carefully selected the publishing houses to which you will submit your work, you have greatly increased the chances that your proposal will meet with a positive response. The next chapter presents a proven system of submitting your submission package to selected publishers—a system that will help you minimize costs, capitalize on any feedback you receive, and maximize your chance of success.

## CHAPTER 6

# Using the Square One System

*"Hello, Dr. Bennett. My name is Rudy Shur, and I've just received a copy of your book proposal. I've gone through it, and I like it very much. Could you please send me two sample chapters to review?"*

*"I would be delighted to send them off to you."*

*"Dr. Bennett, may I ask where you learned about my company?"*

*"Of course. I attended the workshop you gave at NYU on getting published."*

*"Why didn't you talk to me about your project there?"*

*"Well, I thought I'd check your company out first before approaching you—as you had discussed."*

*I smiled to myself and thought, "She not only writes well, she listens."*

Chapter 5 guided you through the preparation of the cover letter, annotated table of contents, and book overview. Hopefully, your submission package is now polished to perfection and ready to send to the appropriate publishers. If you are like most writers, you want to immediately mail a copy of your package to each and every company on the list you created in Chapter 4. But, believe it or not, there are several reasons why a mass mailing may not be the best course of action.

Consider what's involved in sending out thirty to forty submission packages all at once. First, the copying and mailing costs

Years ago, editors insisted that writers submit manuscript proposals to one publishing house at a time. They claimed that if they were going to invest the time and money in evaluating a manuscript, the writer *must* allow them the time to review their material on an exclusive basis. If the writer did not, she need never send another proposal to that company. Today, unless an editor has set up an exclusive to review a manuscript ahead of time, it is understood that a writer may contact numerous publishers at the same time.

involved are likely to be sizeable. (For an electronic alternative to using regular mail, see the inset on page 133.) Second, as you'll learn later in the chapter, you'll have to do a little research on each company before you finalize each package. And the task of gathering data on several dozen companies at one time can be overwhelming even to the most motivated of writers. Finally, it's important to keep in mind that although most publishers are likely to respond to your package with form letters, some may provide suggestions for improving the focus, organization, or scope of your book. If your letters are sent out all at once, you will receive this helpful feedback only after all the publishers on your list have been contacted, and therefore will not have the opportunity to fine-tune your package during the submissions process.

The Square One System for query submission is a carefully planned program that guides you in sending out your proposal in groups, with the first group going to those publishers that best meet the criteria you have already established. Therefore, this program can save you time and money by having you first contact the companies you most highly favor. (If the publisher you *really* want to work with immediately sends a positive response, there may be no need to contact the companies at the bottom of your list.) This system also breaks the submissions process into small steps, each of which can be easily managed, and enables you to benefit from any feedback you receive along the way. But most important, the Square One System maximizes your chance not only of getting your manuscript into publication, but of getting it into publication with a company that will work with you to produce a book of which you can be proud. Sound like a tall order? This chapter will show you how it's done—step by step.

## STEP ONE: PRIORITIZE THE PUBLISHERS ON YOUR LIST

In Chapter 4, you formulated your criteria for choosing appropriate publishers for your submission, and composed a list of likely candidates. Unless your book is very specialized in nature, you should have no less than thirty to forty company names on that list. As mentioned above, it is unlikely that all of the publishers are equally appealing. Depending on your criteria, you may, for instance, favor only the smaller publishing houses, the best-known publishing houses, or the houses found in your area of the country. Select the five companies that you feel best meet your criteria, and write the names of these A List companies at the top of a piece of paper. Look at your long list again, and choose the *next* ten companies that appeal to you. Write the names of these B List companies below the A List. Finally, write the names of the remaining companies—the C List—at the bottom of your list. Your prioritized list should, of course, contain all of the company names that appeared on your original list, but should name them in order of preference, with the most promising and desirable companies appearing at the top. In Step Two, you'll work with the first five companies on your list, verifying the information needed to send out your first submission packages.

## STEP TWO: DETERMINE THE CORRECT ADDRESSES & EDITORS

In Chapter 5, I mentioned how important it is to direct your package to a specific editor rather than to the company as a whole or to, for instance, "The History Division." Publishing companies are busy places, and everyone from the receptionist to the publisher usually has more work than she can comfortably handle. For this reason, you cannot assume that the person who opens your package will take the time to forward your proposal to the appropriate editor. To prevent your manuscript from remaining in the so-called slush pile for days, weeks, or months, it is necessary to find the name and title of the appropriate editor and to send the package directly to her. And, of course, to make sure that package reaches that editor, you'll have to find the correct address—the address of the building that actually houses the editorial department and not, for instance, the company's corporate headquarters or warehouse.

When you composed the list of publishers in Chapter 4, you jotted down the appropriate contact information for each publisher, including, of course, the address, phone number, and—to the best of your ability—the name of the editor who should receive your submission package. It's important to understand that even if you feel that your earlier research provided you with exactly the information you need, you must double-check it through a phone call. Why? First, there is a tremendous turnover of staff in the publishing industry, with editors constantly moving from imprint to imprint and company to company. The editor of the juvenile department in January may not be the editor of the juvenile department in March. Just as important, like any company, a publishing house can change its address. So to get the up-to-the-minute information you need, you'll have to place a phone call. And, of course, if your source books were unable to provide you with the name of a likely contact person, a phone call is your best bet.

When your call is answered, remember that you do not want to speak to the editor at this time, as most editors won't discuss a project with an unknown author until they have a submission package in hand. You simply want to ask the person who answers the phone—probably an editorial assistant—if your proposal for, say, a history book should be sent to the address and editor you have noted. If you're in luck, the person you contact will politely provide you with the information you're seeking. However, don't be surprised if she refuses to give you the name of an editor. Many publishing houses are very protective of their editors and try to screen them from unwanted phone calls and unsolicited manuscripts. But don't cross a publishing house off your list simply because the person who picked up the phone is not especially cooperative. Simply verify the address, and direct that particular package to the editor of the appropriate division—the History Editor, Travel Editor, Collectibles Editor, or whatever. Now repeat this process with the other four publishing houses on your A List.

At the end of each phone call, be sure to request a company catalogue. Why? A catalogue can tell you a great deal about the company that produced it, and therefore may be useful later, when you may have to choose which of several companies you want to publish your book. If the person on the phone gives you a choice, ask for the specialty catalogue—in other words, a catalogue that contains only those titles in your area of interest. If a specialty catalogue is not available, ask for a full catalogue and a frontlist catalogue. (For more information on this, see the inset "Reading a Catalogue Like a Book" on page 138.)

## E-Queries—
## A High-Tech Approach to Book Proposals

Your submission package is composed, edited, and corrected, and you're ready to send it off to the carefully selected publishers on your list. But wait! First you have to buy three sheets of stamps, a ream of high-quality white bond paper, and a box of white business envelopes. Or do you?

Although the majority of submission packages are still being sent by mail, a new type of proposal is now available to writers and editors: the e-query, or electronic query. The process of composing the submission package is the same, and the package contains nearly the same elements as usual—a cover letter, annotated table of contents, and overview. But the self-addressed, stamped envelope (SASE) is omitted, and the materials are sent electronically rather than through the postal service.

Are there any advantages to sending e-queries rather than dropping your proposals off at the post office? According to an article in *Writer's Digest* magazine, there are two advantages only: an e-query reaches its destination with greater speed, and the subject line allows you to state the proposed title of your book right at the start—an added feature that may pique a prospective editor's interest. True, the response will also tend to arrive faster simply because it's easier for the editor to respond, but the odds are no greater than usual that this response will be positive. Consider, for a moment, whether you take the letters you receive through e-mail any more seriously than you take those that arrive by regular mail. Probably not. But you may have a greater tendency to read and reply to them quickly.

If you are interested in sending out your submission package over the Internet, first find out if the publishing houses you have targeted welcome e-queries. *Writer's Market* listings often indicate whether electronic proposals are accepted. If you are not sure, by all means place a call to the company and ask about its policy. Some companies are happy to receive electronic queries. Others prefer to review physical submission packages.

Although it's fairly easy to find e-mail addresses through Internet search engines, be aware that you should never send an e-query to a specific editor's personal e-mail address unless you are directed to do so. Many publishers have separate e-mail addresses for submissions, and editors generally don't appreciate your filling their e-mail boxes with proposals that should have been directed elsewhere.

Finally, keep in mind that the rambling, typo-studded paragraphs that are so common in personal e-mail correspondence have no place in e-queries. Despite its high-tech form of delivery, this is a submission package, and—if you hope to impress the publisher with your writing abilities and your professionalism—it must be brief, well written, and error free.

One last point is worth making. If you use e-mail, you've certainly had the experience of receiving letters and other materials that have lost attributes ranging from paragraph breaks to italics. To prevent your e-query from arriving as a jumble of hard-to-read words, be sure to send it as an attachment. This small detail can make a big difference.

## TRACKING CHART

| Publisher/Editor/ Contact Information | Date Catalogue Requested | Date Catalogue Received |
|---|---|---|
| Pet Publications<br>Norton Nimrod, Publisher<br>44 Frog Lane<br>Concord, MA 11735<br>Phone: 212-555-1222, ext. 342<br>Fax: 212-555-1122<br>E-mail: Pets@bks.bks | November 13 | November 26<br>Black and white;<br>boring. |
| Cat Care Publishing Group, Inc.<br>Emma Lo Presti, Executive Editor<br>64 Roy Avenue<br>Spelunk, OR 11943<br>Phone: 639-555-9721<br>Fax: 639-555-2943<br>E-mail: Catcare@bks.bks | November 14 | December 1<br>Full color;<br>well written. |

## STEP THREE: FILL OUT YOUR TRACKING CHART

You now have all the information you need to send your submission package to the first five companies on your list. But instead of rushing out those first packages, take the time to fill in the information on your Tracking Chart. (See above.) At this point, of course, you'll be able to fill out only the first two columns: the publishing company's name, address, and phone number, along with the name and title of the appropriate editor; and the date that you requested the catalogue. As you actually mail out the packages and, later, receive the responses from the publishing houses, though, you can fill in the Date Catalogue Received, Date Package Sent, Date Response Received, Outcome, and Feedback columns.

If you choose to recreate the tracking chart on paper and to write in the information by hand, be sure to leave space between the different entries so that you'll have room to fill in the information as you receive responses and review catalogues. Another

| Date Package Sent | Date Response Received | Outcome (yes/no/maybe) | Feedback |
|---|---|---|---|
| November 20 | December 20 | No | None |
| November 20 | January 2 | Maybe | Like concept. Asked for first 2 chapters. |

option is to create a table in your computer and fill it in as appropriate during the submissions process.

You may wonder why it's desirable to keep track of your mailings and responses. Although you may be one of the lucky authors who immediately receives a positive response from the publisher at the top of your list, chances are that it will take some time to actually go to contract on your book. In the meantime, you'll probably be sending out a lot of letters and receiving a lot of letters and catalogues in return. A conscientiously filled-out Tracking Chart will allow you to quickly check when you sent the submission package out to a particular publisher, when—and if!—you received a catalogue, and when you received a response to your proposal. The data on your sheet may also provide clues about the publishing company itself. For instance, if the catalogue you requested fails to arrive or arrives only after you've made several follow-up phone calls, you will have learned something about the operation of that company. This, like the catalogue itself, will help you select the company with which you ultimately choose to work.

## STEP FOUR: MAIL OUT THE FIRST FIVE SUBMISSION PACKAGES

It's now time to send out submission packages to the five publishing houses at the top of your list! First, finalize the five letters by adding the date; the name and address of the publishing company; and the editor's name and title. (See the sample cover letters on page 108 to 111.) Remember that unless you know the editor, this is no time for informality. The salutation should read "Dear Ms. Smith" or "Dear Mr. Smith," for instance—not "Dear Susan" or "Dear Bob." Do not use the title "Mrs." unless you know that the editor is married and prefers the title "Mrs." to "Ms." And never use the title "Miss"!

Take the time and care to spell both the name of the editor and the name of the publishing company correctly. Remember that spelling counts in every element of a submission package. And while a busy editor may not notice your misspelling of the word "transcendental"—although I wouldn't count on it!—she will certainly notice a misspelling of her own name. I can't tell you how many letters I have received addressed to "Ruby Shore," "Ruddy Schure," or one of my all-time favorites, "Robin Hur." While I didn't toss the packages into the kill pile, these errors certainly didn't assure me that the author was a careful and conscientious writer.

Make a copy of each cover letter, and place it in a file. Then type out the envelopes using the correct editor's name, title, and address. Again, be careful! This is no time to make a careless error. (For more guidelines regarding this final step in sending out submission packages, see "Your Submission Package Checklist" on page 137.) A standard white #10 envelope—one that is $4^1/_8$-x-$9^1/_2$ inches—is just fine. The editor will find it easy to handle, and it will look businesslike. Of course, you will have to fold the letter, table of contents, and overview in thirds, and the self-addressed, stamped envelope in half so that everything will fit into your envelope. If you prefer, you can use a 9-x-12-inch envelope. Although this will increase your mailing costs by a few cents per package, it will make it unnecessary to fold the contents.

I highly recommend that you use regular mail to send out your submission packages. Occasionally, I have received a proposal that was sent via registered mail, overnight mail, or Federal Express. Trust me when I tell you that this is a waste of time and money. Although you may dream of the editor's ripping open the envelope as soon as it is delivered, in truth, it may take her several days or even weeks to get around to reviewing your proposal. The extra time and money you spend to have your package delivered absolutely, positively overnight will probably not be rewarded with a rapid reply. Similarly, I strongly advise against faxing your proposal to the editor so that she can read it "right away." The fact is that she probably won't. And when she does have time to look over the faxed material, she will not be pleased by its messy appearance and indistinct type.

Finally, fill in the Date Package Sent column of your Tracking Chart, and sit back and relax. You deserve it.

## Your Submission Package Checklist

Throughout this chapter and Chapter 5, I present some important submission package do's and don'ts. As you begin mailing your package out to publishing houses, keep in mind all those do's that will help your package invite a positive response. The following checklist was designed to insure that the all-important details will not be forgotten. As you prepare to mail out your packages, be sure that you:

- ☐ Include a cover letter, an annotated table of contents, a book overview, *and* a self-addressed, stamped envelope (SASE) or response postcard (see page 123) in each and every package.
- ☐ Type rather than handwrite all elements of your package.
- ☐ Place the elements of your package in the appropriate order, with the cover letter on top followed by the contents, overview, and SASE.
- ☐ Address both cover letter and envelope to a specific editor by name, or at least to the editor of the appropriate division—the History Editor, for instance. (Make sure to spell the names of both the editor *and* the publishing company correctly!)
- ☐ Make a copy of each cover letter for your files, and fill in your Tracking Chart with all of the appropriate information.
- ☐ Place your materials in a plain envelope—either a #10 business-size envelope or a 9-x-12-inch envelope.
- ☐ Avoid "protecting" your envelope by enclosing it in plastic wrap or sealing it with packing tape. The envelope should be neat in appearance and easy to open.
- ☐ Make sure to use the proper amount of postage—you don't want your package to arrive on the editor's desk marked "Postage Due"—and send your packages on their way.

## Reading a Catalogue Like a Book

Before writing your book, you may have received book catalogues in the mail from time to time. Perhaps you leafed through them to see if they contained anything of interest. What you probably did not realize is that a publishing company's catalogue provides the reader with far more than a listing of its books. As an extension of the company's marketing department, it is a clear reflection of how that company packages and markets its products—not only through its catalogues, but through all its marketing tools.

Depending on the company, it may offer only one catalogue at any given time, or it may produce several, each of which serves a different purpose. Some companies—especially small companies—may produce only a *full catalogue*. This catalogue includes both frontlist titles, which are new releases brought out for the current selling season, and backlist titles, which were published prior to the current season. Most companies offer both a full catalogue and a *frontlist catalogue*—a catalogue that presents only new books. Some companies also offer *specialty catalogues*, which include only the books in a specific area of interest. For instance, a company may produce a health catalogue, which highlights its health titles, or a history catalogue, which features only its history books.

When you receive one or more catalogues from a company, first look at the covers. Are they attractive and enticing, or are they dull and unappealing? Are they printed in full color, or are they black and white? Some companies invest a great deal of time, money, and care in their catalogue covers so that their catalogues will be noticed and read. Others, unfortunately, farm the cover design out and use whatever is given to them—even if the result is unattractive. As a writer, you want your book featured in a catalogue that invites the reader to pick it up and look inside.

Now, open the catalogue and examine its listings. Note whether the interior is printed in black and white or in color, whether the covers of the books are displayed, and whether the format invites you to look further or lulls you to sleep with its ho-hum layout.

Pay special attention to the titles of that company's books. Some publishers work hard to

## STEP FIVE: BE PATIENT!

Now that your first five submission packages have been sent out, you may be tempted to start checking your mail box every day, looking for a response. But, as mentioned earlier, it may take days or weeks for some of the editors to even open your package. So try to cultivate patience during this time. The responses will arrive; they just won't arrive as quickly as you might want them to.

Some authors call each editor a few days after they have sent out their submission packages. They hope that if the editor has choose book titles that are both appropriate and catchy—that both tell the reader what the book is about and engage her interest. Don't underestimate the power of a title. When your book is displayed on the shelf of a bookstore, it is often the title that determines whether the consumer takes the book off the shelf or leaves it there to gather dust. A title can make or break a book.

Now read the book descriptions. The quality and length of these descriptions can vary widely from catalogue to catalogue and from company to company. In the catalogue you're examining, are the descriptions full or skimpy, lively or boring? Do they give you a clear idea of what each book is about, or do they fail to provide any useful information? In other words, do they make you want to order the books, or do they make you want to toss the catalogue into your recycling pile?

Finally, compare the company's presentation of its frontlist books with that of its backlist books. While most companies devote a little more space to a frontlist title than to a backlist book, some nevertheless feature both frontlist and backlist titles in full-color pages, display the book covers of all their titles, and provide well-crafted and intriguing descriptions for every single book. Other companies, unfortunately, give their backlist titles little attention. They may, for instance, merely list their older books in a lackluster black-and-white section, and omit both a photo of the book cover and a description of the book. Why is it so important to analyze the company's treatment of backlist and frontlist titles? Unless your book is of the type that will appeal to readers for only a short period of time—for instance, a book that covers an event such as the bicentennial or the death of a celebrity—you want your work to have as long a life as possible. When a company pays little attention to older titles, sales die quickly. But, as many small publishing companies have shown, continual promotion of an older title can lead to a long life—and a profitable one.

When you have finished reviewing a catalogue, don't forget to note your impressions in your Tracking Chart and to put the catalogues away for safe keeping. You have learned how to "read" a catalogue, and this skill will serve you well as you review the responses to your submission packages and—if you're lucky!—pick and choose among the positive responses and select the company that will provide you with the most rewarding working relationship.

already looked at the package, she will discuss it with them, and that if the editor has *not* yet opened the package, the call will inspire her to do so. I strongly suggest that you avoid making these phone calls. The editor will get to your package as her workload allows, and will probably not appreciate your efforts to hurry her. And if she has already reviewed the package, there is a very good chance that she won't remember your proposal simply because she sees so many of them. Therefore, it is highly unlikely that your call will result in a satisfying and helpful response.

During this waiting period, can you do anything that will increase your chance of getting your book published? You can, of course, begin doing the research needed to send out the second group of proposals. And you can review any catalogues that arrive so that you can start learning more about the publishing companies on your list. (Don't forget to record everything you receive on your Tracking Chart!) If you have not already examined books published by these companies, this would be a good time to visit your local bookstore. Pay particular attention to those books that are in the same category as yours, and examine them as critically as possible. Are the covers attractive? Do the books seem to have been well edited? (In other words, do they read well?) Is the typeset page pleasing to the eye? Are the photos and other illustrations of good quality? Does the publishing company ever highlight its books by arranging for special displays in bookstores? The answers to these questions will tell you a great deal about each of the publishing houses.

I suggest that you wait four weeks before sending out the second wave of submission packages. Hopefully, during that time, you will receive responses to some or all of the initial five packages. Perhaps one of the editors you contacted will even request further material! If so, consider yourself fortunate, and respond in as timely a manner as possible. But don't stop sending out submission packages. I cannot overemphasize the fact that a letter expressing interest in your project is not the same as a signed contract. After seeing the additional material, the editor may decide that the project is not right for her company. And, of course, after learning more about the publishing company, you may decide that you'd be happier working with another house.

If you do not receive a positive response from the first group of editors to whom you have sent proposals, don't be discouraged. Keep in mind that most writers have to contact quite a few publishing companies before they elicit any interest on the part of an editor.

If you do not receive a positive response from this first group of editors, don't be discouraged. Keep in mind that most writers have to contact quite a few publishing companies before they elicit any interest on the part of an editor.

Most of the time, when an editor decides that she is not interested in a project, she responds to the author via a form letter. However, occasionally—and I do mean only occasionally—an editor does provide the author with some feedback on the proposal. For instance, the editor may say that the topic of the book is great, but that the focus is too limited and should be expanded. Or the editor may know of a new development in the field covered by the book, and suggest that you add information on the development to your book. If you are lucky enough to receive feedback such as this, try to consider the editor's recommendations with an open mind. You may decide that they are just what your book needs to make it more marketable—or you may find the suggested changes very unappealing. Whatever your response, I do suggest that you call the editor and thank her for her comments. During your conversation, discuss her letter and ask if she would be interested in the book if you made the recommended alterations. If she answers in the negative, ask if she knows of another publishing company that might be interested in your book. Certainly consider following her advice and revising your submission package before you send out the next group of letters. Perhaps the changes will lead to a more encouraging response from the remaining companies on your list.

## STEP SIX: MAIL OUT THE NEXT TEN SUBMISSION PACKAGES

About four weeks after sending out the first wave of proposals, prepare and send out submission packages to the next ten companies—the B List. Be sure to follow Steps Two, Three, and Four carefully, researching names and addresses, filling out your Tracking Chart, and finalizing each package by adding the appropriate information.

As discussed earlier in the chapter, if you received feedback from any of the editors on the first mailing list, you may want to amend one or more portions of your submission package. If you decide to do so, be sure to take the same care you took when preparing the original package. Read through the new letter, table of contents, and overview, checking for spelling, grammar, punctuation, flow, organization, and style. It should go without saying that any change made in one portion of the package should be reflected, as necessary, in the other components of the package. For example, if an editor suggests that you add a chapter on a cutting-edge development in your field, not just your table of contents but also your cover letter and overview should be revised to highlight the fact that your information is up-to-date and, perhaps, that your book provides information not available in any competing title.

If you feel that you were helped by the comments and suggestions of the friend who read your original submission package, by all means ask that person to also review any subsequent revisions. Don't allow yourself to get sloppy in your rush to mail out the second wave of proposals. And as the catalogues and letters arrive in response to your phone calls and submissions, be sure to keep your Tracking Chart up-to-date.

## STEP SEVEN: MAIL OUT THE REMAINING SUBMISSION PACKAGES

After you mail out the second group of packages, wait about a month. Then repeat all the steps necessary to send out all of the remaining proposals.

What if you already received several positive responses to your earlier packages? Certainly, if you received two or more requests for further material, and if they came from publishing companies that are high on your list, there's no requirement that you continue the submissions process. You may, instead, wish to channel your energies into perfecting the material requested by the editors—sample chapters or a full book proposal, for instance. If these companies continue to respond in a positive manner, you may never have to send out another submission package for your book! And, of course, if the editors decide that your book is not for them, you can always continue the submissions process where you left off.

## STEP EIGHT: REVIEW YOUR RESULTS AND ASSESS YOUR OPTIONS

You have now sent out a number of submission packages—perhaps as many as forty. What are the results of your mailing?

Perhaps you have received a positive response from one or more companies who have reviewed your material and are ready to offer you a contract. If so, congratulations! You now want to turn to the next chapter, "The Deal," and learn about publishing contracts. Like the terms of most contracts, the terms of publishing agreements are negotiable, so you'll want to learn all you can and make the most out of this important document. And if two companies are vying for the opportunity to publish your book, by comparing the two contracts, you may be better able to decide which working relationship would benefit you the most.

What if you have received positive responses to the submissions packages you have sent out? If you have received two or more requests for further material, and they have come from publishing companies that are high on your list, there's no requirement that you continue sending out more packages. You may, instead, wish to channel your energies into perfecting any material requested by the editors.

Perhaps some editors requested further materials, but after receiving sample chapters, they rejected your project. While this is disappointing, it should not make you give up. There may, in fact, be nothing wrong with your book. Perhaps you just haven't found the editor who is willing to give the book a chance. To better understand the reason for the editor's response, give her a call. I know that earlier in the chapter, I warned against calling editors for feedback, as at that stage, the call probably would not yield any helpful information. But once an editor has become sufficiently interested to request further materials, she may be more willing and able to provide you with helpful feedback. And if what she says makes sense to you, you will be able to use it at a guide for reworking your book into a more marketable project.

Of course, you may not have received any positive responses to your proposals. If so, try to analyze the cause of the negative responses. While the Square One System is designed to increase your odds of eliciting a positive response from editors, if there's a problem in the package itself, the system is less likely to work. To help determine if the package may be the problem, see Chapter 8, "When It Doesn't Happen." This chapter is designed not only to guide you in pinpointing your problem, but also to help you rectify it so that you can enjoy more positive results with later submissions. In addition, it looks at a number of proven alternatives, including that of self-publishing.

Perhaps you feel strongly that the package is not the problem. Or perhaps you have already revised your package so that it is more likely to meet the needs of the publishers in which you're interested. What are your options now? First, consider waiting about six months from the time you began the submissions process, and resubmitting the package to the publishers on your original list. If you have received and reviewed these publishers' catalogues, you may even be able to pare down the list to those companies that you feel would best meet your criteria.

You may wonder why an editor who showed no interest in your project several months ago might now view your project in a more positive light. Of course, if you have changed the focus or scope of your book or otherwise altered your package, these changes may have made the book much more marketable. But there is another important element at work here, and that element is *timing.* To a great degree, acquisitions editors seek out books that are in line with their company's publishing program—a program that guides editors to certain types of books in certain areas of interest. These programs change periodically according to consumer interest. And as they change, editors begin looking for books in areas that they may have previously ignored. For example, a decade ago, most books on alternative health—on improving health through supplements, nutrition, traditional remedies, etc.—were produced only by small niche publishers. The larger publishing companies simply were not interested in acquiring such titles. But as the public's demand for information on this topic grew, many major publishers began expanding their own alternative health lists. Now consider a writer of alternative health books who, for her own reasons, prefers to work only with large, well-known publishing houses. Her chances of receiving positive responses from the companies in which she was interested would have changed over time simply because the larger companies changed their programs to embrace this new field.

But editors are affected by far more than just their company's publishing program. Every editor is an individual who is influenced by many factors, from the people she knows to the television shows she watches to the books and magazines she reads. Many times, an editor will simply become excited about a subject because of a story or a bit of information that she heard or read somewhere along the line. (See the inset on page 145.) Then, when a proposal for a book on this topic lands on her desk, she can't move quickly enough to contact the author and request further material. While you may find this a bit maddening—do you have to pray that an editor develops an interest in fly-fishing the day before she receives your submission package?—it does mean that a door that was once closed to you may suddenly open. And the result may be that your book, once rejected out of hand, may suddenly be in great demand.

## Never Underestimate the Power of Timing

In this chapter, I briefly discussed how timing can influence an editor's reception of a manuscript proposal. If you feel inclined to dismiss the importance of this factor, the following story—which is entirely true—will show you how in one instance at least, timing pulled a manuscript proposal from the kill pile and sent it into production.

A few years ago, my executive editor—who, like me, received unsolicited manuscripts—brought a manuscript proposal to my attention. Written by a woman who had experienced so-called mild brain injury as the result of a car accident, the book focused on the problems caused by this little-understood and underdiagnosed problem. Because of her own ordeal, the author—a therapist who now works with other brain-injured victims—had found that many people suffer terrible physical and emotional problems as the result of relatively mild brain damage. Yet they are offered little help by most doctors, who often fail to recognize the seriousness of the condition. In addition to exploring the dilemma faced by brain-injury sufferers, the author offered support and guidance for the victim by exploring conventional medical therapies, alternative therapies, and lifestyle modifications.

Although the subject was certainly an important one and the author seemed well-informed, I realized that the book had a relatively small potential audience, and I felt that those who were affected by this condition would not necessarily seek out a book on the subject. One problem that every publisher has to face is that although a given book may address a real problem, the people affected may not be inclined to look for a solution in a bookstore. Brain-injury victims, in fact, often have trouble reading the written word as a result of their injuries. Therefore, a bookstore might be the least likely place they would turn for help. In addition, in reviewing the proposal, I recognized that the material needed a good deal of work, and at that time, our production schedule was full. Reluctantly, I routed the book to the kill pile.

As fate would have it, a short time later, I received a call from a friend and writer whom I've known for many years. When I inquired about the health of his family, he told me how upset he and his wife were over his son, who had suffered mild brain injuries as the result of an accident. (Was someone trying to tell me something?) Although he had previously held an important job, his son was now unable to work, and had trouble even with everyday tasks. Worse still, the family had been unable to find any doctor or other health-care professional who could offer him help, or who even understood the nature of the problem.

In speaking to my friend, I realized that although the market for this book was indeed small, it profoundly affected more than just the victim. It touched the lives of all the people directly involved with the person who had sustained the injury. There was a real need for this book, and the need would translate into sustainable sales. Eventually, I was able to find a professional writer who was able to work with the author, shaping the manuscript into a book that was clear, easy to use, and truly helpful. I wish I could say that the book became a bestseller, but, as we all knew from the beginning of the project, the potential audience was small. However, the book was able to reach its small audience, and both the author and I had the satisfaction of knowing that we were filling an important need.

Is any other option available to you at this point? Consider putting together an entirely new list of publishing houses and sending your submission package to them. Literally thousands of publishing companies dot the United States, with new ones cropping up all the time, so it's highly unlikely that your initial list of companies included every house that might be interested in your book. Perhaps when you compiled your first list, you did not seriously consider the many small companies that are more likely to accept the works of first-time authors. If so, now is the time to look into these smaller houses. Or perhaps you did not sufficiently hone in on the publishers that focus on books in your particular area of interest. Or maybe your first list *was* put together with a great deal of thought and research, but you simply haven't yet found the editor who is willing to give your book a chance. By choosing thirty or forty new publishers and again following the system outlined in this chapter, you will greatly increase your odds of finding the right publishing house for your project.

Finally, don't give up! Stay positive and keeping working towards your goal. Many authors receive scores of rejection letters before landing a contract. As you have already gathered, this does not mean that you should indiscriminately send out proposals to every publisher large and small, regardless of the company's areas of interest and the quality of its books. (If this book has taught you anything, I hope it's taught you the importance of zeroing in on the publishers that are right for you and your book!) It does, however, mean that it may take longer than you expected to find an editor who appreciates the special merits of your manuscript and has faith in you as an author. By following the Square One System with care, consistency, and perseverance, you will greatly improve your chances of ultimately making contact with the editor who will champion your project and work with you toward the realization of your dream.

## CHAPTER 7

# The Deal

*"About publishers' agreements . . . signing a contract with a publisher is a lot like getting married. If you intend to spend the rest of your life with a person, you better know who that person is and what the rules are for living together. In the same sense, once you sign an agreement with a publisher, you have truly committed your work to that publisher for better or worse. Therefore, you must make sure that you know who your publishing partner is and that you have some say about your living arrangements."*

*—Nathan Keats,*
*Founder of Keats Publishing Company*

Congratulations! Your hard work has paid off. A publisher has responded to your submission package and sample chapters with interest and encouragement, and the much-hoped-for contract has arrived in the mail. But as you slide the contract out of its envelope, your elation quickly turns to anxiety. Printed in small, densely packed type, the multi-page document coldly refers to your treasured book as "the said work." Terms like "indemnities" and "force majeure" send a chill up your spine. As you struggle to interpret the terms of the agreement, you wonder if this contract is the best you can get, or if you could possibly bargain for a larger advance, a higher royalty percentage, or more complimentary copies. Are you expected to negotiate? Should you hire a lawyer or agent to represent you? Should you take a weekend course in contract law?

Most people are intimidated by contracts, and even if you have dealt with contracts in the past when buying a house or leasing a car, a book contract is a very different animal. But there's no need to panic. Most publishing agreements are relatively standard. Although they may vary in length, in the wording used, and in the order in which the topics are covered, all of them cover pretty much the same subjects and offer similar terms. This chapter was designed to explain the standard publishing contract, and to make you aware of the types of terms you are likely to encounter. By the time you finish this chapter, you will have a greater grasp of the rights and responsibilities conferred on you by the agreement, and you will know the warning signs that can alert you to a publisher who may be less than scrupulous in his dealings.

Please be aware that this chapter is *not* intended to provide you with legal advice. If you feel that legal advice is necessary, you should definitely contact a lawyer. In fact, this is one of the first topics I'll cover. (See how careful we have to be in publishing? I've just let you know that anything you do based upon reading the following material is at your own discretion. You have to be *just* as careful in reviewing all matters legal.) But with the help of this chapter, you will be in a better position to figure out the terms of your agreement, and—either alone or with the help of a professional—to ask the most appropriate questions so you can make an informed decision regarding the details of your publishing contract.

## SHOULD YOU HIRE A LAWYER OR A LITERARY AGENT?

Upon receiving their publishing contract, many authors' first question is, "Should I hire a lawyer to review this?" The decision to hire a professional to represent you in negotiations with a publisher is one that is largely based on personal preference. Some authors prefer to manage any negotiations themselves rather than giving a piece of the pie to a lawyer or agent. Others feel that only a lawyer or agent can get them the best possible terms.

If you are not sure whether you want to finalize your contract solo or with professional help, there are a few facts that you should consider. First, while a smart and aggressive lawyer can, to some extent, negotiate profitable changes in the agreement, your lawyer will most likely be able to help you only if he is experienced in negotiating publishing agreements. Ideally, you want to work with an *intellectual property lawyer*—a lawyer who specializes in literary works and their inherent rights. Contracts in other industries are very different from those in publishing, and a lawyer who is unfamiliar with publishing agreements can actually do more harm than good by making unreasonable demands or focusing on the wrong issues. Therefore, although your cousin the lawyer may be a savvy negotiator and may offer to represent you free of charge, he may not be the best choice in this particular instance.

Second, although an experienced literary agent may be capable of getting a larger advance, limiting a publisher's rights, and even assisting you later in the publishing process if, for instance, you need someone to interpret a baffling royalty statement, you must pay a high price for this service. While a lawyer may be compensated with a one-time fee, an agent usually works on commission, garnering 10 to 15 percent of both your advance and your royalties. And these payments are expected for the life of the agreement.

When deciding whether to seek representation, it is important that you take another look at the market for your book. Hopefully, when reading Chapter 2, you spent some time considering the size of your potential audience. If, for instance, your book addresses dog owners interested in dog care, your audience is fairly large. On the other hand, if your audience is comprised of health-care professionals involved in treating a rare ailment, your audience is relatively small. Clearly, the smaller the market, the smaller the possible return. And if the expected return is small, you may rightfully question the wisdom of sharing the profits with someone else.

If you *do* decide to hire someone to represent you in negotiations, keep in mind that in addition to being experienced, your representative should be someone with whom you feel comfortable working. This is particularly important if you use a literary agent, as this person will continue to represent you throughout the life of your contract. Also remember that you should never remove yourself from the bargaining process, leaving the fate of your contract in someone else's hands. Instead, read your contract carefully, and discuss your "wish list" with your representative before

**Helpful Hint**

Before you hire a lawyer or literary agent to represent you in contract negotiations, consider if the royalties you anticipate receiving justify the cost of hiring a professional.

negotiations begin. Let him know exactly what is important to you. You may well care about issues that were of little concern to the authors he worked with previously. Only by developing contract literacy through the reading of this chapter and by staying involved in negotiations will you insure that the terms of your publishing agreement are consistent with your wishes.

## RULE # 9

## *Never sign a publishing agreement without understanding all the terms*

This is a good time to bring up a very important rule—one that bears mentioning even though it should be self-evident. Most of us have been told since childhood that we should always read something before signing it. But when faced with a long-winded document, many of us barely glance at the words before penning in our names. Trust me when I say that you must take the time to plow through the contract that you have received—even if the sight of it makes you want to run for the kitchen and seek comfort in a box of cookies (or a bottle of Scotch). Remember that your contract defines every aspect of your agreement with your publisher. When is your manuscript due? What might cause your book to be taken out of print? Are you expected to take part in a promotional tour? Are you expected to pay for any part of the production process? Your contract spells all of this out. So even if you have hired someone to represent you in negotiations, it is crucial that you read and understand each and every term of the publishing agreement. Whether or not you take the time to read the terms, you will be expected to live by them.

**Helpful Hint**

You will be expected to live by the terms of your publishing agreement. For this reason, it is vital that you read and understand each and every term of your contract.

## THE CONTRACT

Your contract may be five pages or twenty-five pages in length. It may be couched in impenetrable legalese, or it may be worded in relatively plain English. But chances are that much of your contract is "boilerplate"; that is, it follows a formula used throughout the publishing industry, covering the same conditions treated in most publishing agreements. The remainder of this chapter will lead you step by step through a standard publishing contract, explaining the terms and examining the issues to be negotiated.

As you read through the following material, please keep in mind that although most publishing contracts deal with the same subjects, these subjects are discussed under different headings in different contracts. Similarly, the order in which they appear can vary. For ease of understanding, I have tried as much as possible to discuss the various issues in the order in which they appear in *most* contracts, and to choose headings that define the issue being discussed. When possible, I have also indicated the headings under which they may be discussed in your own publishing agreement.

Please note that it is virtually impossible to consider every element that may be included in your contract. Some publishing contracts go on for many pages, detailing every situation that may be encountered in the life of the agreement. My intention is to cover only those terms that are most common and/or most important. Should you encounter terms that you don't understand and that cause you concern, do not hesitate to request clarification from your publisher or from legal counsel. As I said earlier, it is vital that you understand *every* term of your agreement before you sign it.

## Identifying the Parties

Contracts usually begin with an introductory "who's who" paragraph that defines the parties involved through the use of terms that will appear throughout the contract. The writer of the manuscript is referred to as "the Author." The publishing company is referred to as "the Publisher." If the project involves a ghostwriter—a person who performs the actual writing but is not credited as an author—he may be referred to as "the Writer." This introduction also states the tentative title of your manuscript and identifies it as "the Work" or "the said Work." Unlike the clauses that follow it, this introductory paragraph does not usually appear under a formal heading.

## Rights

Before "Internet" became a household word, publishing contracts did not specify which electronic rights were granted to the publisher. Instead, the author simply gave the publisher "all electronic rights." Then, in the last decade of the twentieth century, technological advances led to the development of a variety of electronic marketplaces—and authors found that they had signed away valuable rights. In most instances, courts have held that a contract which specified only the general granting of electronic rights was too vague, and that authors under such contracts do, in fact, still own the electronics rights to their works. Needless to say, publishing agreements now spell out exactly *which* rights are being granted to the publisher.

According to the current Copyright Act, the author is the owner of all rights of the literary work, including the right to publish the work in book form. The author may grant one, several, or all of his rights to the publisher, but such a grant *must* be in writing. Thus, the contract must spell out any rights that the author hands over to the publisher. The various rights that pertain to the publisher's production of, direct use of, and direct sale of the book are generally covered in a section called "Rights" or "Grant of Rights." (For those rights not covered in this section, see "Subsidiary Rights" on page 160.)

One issue defined in this portion of the contract is "the Territory"—the geographical area in which the publisher has the right to sell the book. This territory may include the United States or Canada, North America, or the world.

The contract also generally defines the form of the work to which the publisher's rights extend. For example, it may grant the publisher sole rights to produce the work in book form and/or in electronic data form—tapes, disks, diskettes, databases, networks, CD-ROM, etc. The contract may also specify that the rights include both this edition and future editions, and may state that they extend to hardcover, trade paperback, and/or mass market paperback form. Be aware that if the contract does not specify a form such as hardcover, but does grant rights to print, publish, distribute, and sell "in book form," this means that the grant extends to *all* possible book forms—hardcover, trade paperback, and mass market paperback.

Usually, the contract specifies the language or languages to which the publisher's rights extend. For instance, it may extend the rights to publication and reproduction in the English language only, or it may extend them to "all languages," meaning that the publisher has been granted all translation rights.

Usually, the contract defines the time in which the grant is extended in terms of the copyright, which is in effect for the author's life and fifty years thereafter. For instance, the contract may state that the rights are granted "for the full term of all copyrights and renewals of copyrights." Rarely does the grant extend for less than the term of the copyright.

## The Manuscript

Whether called "Manuscript" or "Manuscript Delivery," this section of the contract spells out the author's obligations regarding the delivery of the completed manuscript to the publisher. The contract specifies the date by which the manuscript must be delivered to the publisher, as well as the length of the manuscript in terms of words. For instance, the contract may state that the manuscript should be "approximately 120,000 words in length"—in other words, about 400 double-spaced *manuscript* pages, or 300 *typeset* pages of a 6-x-9-inch book.

All contracts state that the delivered manuscript must be "acceptable to the Publisher" in content and form. In some cases, they also specify that certain items be included, such as a title page, preface or foreword, table of contents, or computer disk containing the manuscript. If the manuscript is not considered satisfactory by the publisher, the contract may demand that the author rework the problem portion of the manuscript within "a reasonable time." Most publishers reserve the right to either prepare the manuscript at the author's expense or terminate the contract if the author does not provide the company with an acceptable manuscript.

Either within this section or within a section called "Publishing Details," the contract may specify the party that will bear certain costs and complete certain tasks relevant to the completion of the manuscript. For instance, the author may be charged with the responsibility of obtaining written permission to reprint any quotations taken from outside sources, or to use any illustrations or photographs required by the publisher. Some contracts specify that any expenses for such permission will be paid by the publisher. Others state that these permissions will be obtained "at the Author's expense." In the latter case, it is expected that the author will pay for the permissions out of his royalty advance. If the author has to bear the cost of preparing an index, this, too, is specified in the contract.

### Helpful Hint

When calculating manuscript length, keep in mind that the "average" 6-x-9-inch book contains about 400 words per typeset page.

The phrase "at the author's expense" usually refers to an amount of money to be deducted from the author's future book royalties. However, always ask the publisher to specify how such a charge is billed out by the company. You may also ask to put a dollar limit on any specific charge that must come out of your royalty.

## Editing, Proofs, and Publication

The publisher's rights and obligations regarding the editing, typesetting, printing, binding, pricing, and marketing of the book, as well as the author's rights and obligations in this regard, may be addressed under a heading such as "Publishing Details," "Publication," "Editing and Proofs," or simply "Proofs."

The publisher normally reserves the right to copyedit the manuscript in accordance with his house style of punctuation, spelling, capitalization, and usage. In some cases, the contract states that the meaning of the text will not be materially altered during this copyediting. Often, the contract also states that after the manuscript is edited, it will be sent to the author, who will have a chance to make revisions and corrections, but then must return the revised manuscript within a specified period of time. Even when the contract does not include this last statement, it is a standard practice in publishing to submit the edited manuscript to the author for his review and revision.

Years ago, books were typeset using a "hot metal" process. The result of the process was long paper sheets of typeset copy called galleys, or galley proofs. These sheets were proofread by the publisher and author for errors, and then returned to the typesetter for correction—a process that continued until all problems were caught and eliminated. Finally, the long galleys were cut up and pasted onto page-sized paper boards called mechanicals. After being numbered, these page proofs were sent to the publisher and author, and the proofing-correction-proofing cycle resumed until everyone was satisfied.

The contract also normally details the author's rights and obligations regarding the book's *proofs,* the typeset version of the book that is produced after the manuscript has been edited. The author is permitted to review and correct the proofs and "other production materials"—illustrations, for instance. Sometimes, the contract specifies the time period in which the proofs must be returned. The contract may also state that any author's alterations other than corrections of errors made in typesetting will be made "only at the Publisher's discretion," and may be paid for by the author if they are in excess of 10 percent of the cost of typesetting. This last term is usually included to prevent the author from rewriting the book after it has been typeset, and therefore incurring extra costs as well as possible delays.

Normally, the publisher reserves the right to determine what are referred to as the "details of publication"—the format and design of the book; the paper, printing, and binding; the title and price; and the advertising, promotion, and distribution of free copies. Sometimes, the contract specifies the form of the book, whether hardcover or paperback. It also may specify time constraints—for instance, that the edition shall be produced "within 18 months from the date of the Publisher's acceptance of the manuscript." And it may specify the imprint under which the work will be published—provided, of course, that the publishing company is large enough to have imprints.

## The Author's Copies

Either in a section entitled "Author's Copies" or in one called "Publication," the contract may specify the number of copies that will be given to the author free of charge upon the book's publication. Generally, the author is offered fifteen to twenty-five copies, although some authors receive as many as a hundred free books. If the book is to be published in both hardback and softcover editions, the contract may specify that the author will receive *X* number of hardback copies and *X* number of paperback copies.

The contract may also state the discount the author will receive if he chooses to purchase additional copies. Usually a standard trade discount of 40 to 45 percent is given, although an author who wishes to buy a large number of books may be granted a 50-percent discount.

Be aware that if a contract does not spell out what your discount is to be, the publisher may choose to give you only a minimal discount, if any. As an author, make sure you know what the price will be if you choose to purchase copies of your own book.

Today, computers have revolutionized the typesetting process. Electronic copy is imported into a page layout program, which enables the typesetter to compose close-to-finished typeset pages that are already numbered. The pages are printed out—and you have your first set of proofs! Author and publisher still review the copy, but because of the new technology, the process is completed in a fraction of the time—and at a fraction of the cost—of the old system.

## The Author's Promotional Responsibilities

Another subject that may be covered in the contract is the author's responsibility regarding the promotion of the book. For instance, the contract may state that at the publisher's request, the author must participate in a promotional tour of a stated duration—say, two weeks. It may also state that any expenses incurred during such a tour will be paid by the publisher. Publishers who make such stipulations often explain that the author's participation in publicity activities was a "material inducement" to the publisher to enter the agreement. Other publishers, however, do not specify such activities in writing, although they may verbally request—not demand—that the author involve himself in publicity tours, newspaper and television interviews, etc.

If your contract does not address the topic of promotion, and you request such a clause as a means of insuring that your book will, in fact, be promoted, it is unlikely that the publisher will add this term to your agreement. However, this doesn't mean that you shouldn't ask for the clause. By all means, make your wishes known. Then, if your request is denied, ask the publisher for a letter that outlines the proposed marketing program for your title. This will allow you to review the company's promotional plans and to understand the program as it moves forward.

## The Out-of-Print Provision

Under a heading such as "Publishing Details" or "Out of Print Provision," the contract should define the circumstances under which the book will be taken out of print—in other words, will no longer be published by that company. The publisher, for instance, may state that the book will be taken out of print if the book "shall cease to be profitable," if sales fall below a certain number of copies per year, or if the publisher does not reprint the book within a specified time after the existing inventory has been sold. Once the book has been taken out of print, the publisher usually offers the remaining copies to the author at cost—that is, at the unit print cost for each book—or at a specific discount, plus shipping. If the author does not choose to purchase the remaining copies "within a reasonable period of time," the publisher reserves the right to destroy the copies or *remainder* the book—sell it for a price that is below the manufacturing cost.

Generally, the contract specifies that the rights to the book will revert to the author when the book is declared out of print. If your contract does not include this statement, you should make sure that such a provision be added. Remember that if the contract does not specify when a book will be declared out of print, the publisher may retain the rights to the book in spite of the fact that he no longer stocks, markets, or sells it.

## Royalties

Most authors are understandably interested in their *royalties*—the money they will receive based upon the sales of their books. Because this subject is one of both great concern and some complexity, it makes sense to explore it in some detail.

A royalty refers to the money paid to the author for the sale of each book. Royalties can be calculated in two ways. First, they may be based on the *retail price* of the book. This price is easy to determine in the case of trade books, as the retail price is almost always printed on the back of the book. In the case of educational books, however, the retail price is generally not printed on the book, although it can be found in the company's catalogues and brochures. Prices of professional and scholarly books may or may not be printed on the books themselves.

Because customers are not always charged the retail price, royalties are sometimes based on the *net price* of the book, which is the price actually charged by the publisher to the customer. When the book is sold by the company directly to an individual consumer, the net price is usually the same as the retail price of the book. In other cases, however, books are usually discounted. For instance, when books are sold to bookstores, the discount may range from 20 to 40 percent of the retail price. (In other words, the bookstore pays 80 to 60 percent of the retail price.) When sold to distributors, the discount may range from 50 to 60 percent. (The distributor pays 50 to 40 percent of the retail price.)

The concept of paying an author part of a book's profits is relatively new. It was devised by American publishers in the mid-1800s. English poet Elizabeth Barrett Browning was one of the first authors to be offered a royalty for her works by an American publisher. Before that time, publishers simply gave the writer a fixed sum in exchange for all the rights to a book. It is no wonder that so many well-known writers of the past—authors such as James Fenimore Cooper—chose to publish their own works.

When royalties are based on the retail price of the book, they generally range from 5 to 10 percent. (In other words, if the book's retail price is $10.00, the author makes $.50 to $1.00 per copy.) When royalties are based on the net price of the book, they generally range from 5 to 15 percent. (The author receives $.50 to $1.50 per book.) Usually, trade publishers base their sales on the retail price, while educational, professional, and scholarly publishers use the net price.

It is important to be aware that your contract may base your royalties on the retail price in some instances, but on the net price in other instances. For instance, a trade publisher may base royalties on the retail price if the discount given to the customer is less than 50 percent, but switch to a percentage of the net price if the discount is equal to or greater than 50 percent, or if the book sells to an outlet other than a bookstore—to a wholesale club, for instance. In such instances, the contract must spell these terms out.

A number of other variations may be found in a single contract. For instance, the publisher may use a sliding scale so that the royalty increases as sales increase. As an example, the publisher may pay 10 percent of the retail price for the first 5,000 copies sold; 12.5 percent of retail for the next 5,000 copies sold; and 15 percent of retail for any sales in excess of 10,000 copies. The sliding scale may work in two different ways. When computed on an annual basis, the sliding scale begins at ground zero each year. When computed on a cumulative basis, all books sold over the years are included in the calculations.

Depending on the publisher's plans for the book, the section on royalties may include a staggering number of possibilities. The contract may, for instance, list different royalty percentages for hardcover copies, trade paperbacks, mass market paperbacks (sometimes referred to as rack-size paperbacks), large-print hardcover copies, large print paperback copies, audio recordings, and more. The royalty percentage may also vary according to the territory in which the book is sold. For instance, the royalty percentage may be 7 percent for books sold within the United States, but 10 percent for books sold outside the United States.

Some contracts include a section on "holdbacks." This requires some explanation. The publishing industry is unique in that bookstores can send their unsold copies back to the publisher, in which case the money paid for the books is returned to the stores. Because these returns can be large, some publishers hold back between 20 to 60 percent of the royalty payment until a specified date, at which point the balance is sent to the author. Most trade publishers and some educational publishers include a section on holdbacks in their contract. Others simply state that royalties will be paid "on sales, less returns." Because professional and scholarly book companies do not usually allow returns, they may not include such stipulations.

So far, my discussion has assumed that your book has only one author—you. But, of course, many books have two or more authors. In such cases, the contract specifies the royalty split. Again, different contracts handle this differently, usually depending on the degree to which each author has contributed to the finished work. The royalties may be divided evenly among the authors, or one author may receive a greater share than that awarded to the other contributors.

The "Royalty" section of the contract also specifies *when* the publisher will calculate and pay the royalties to the author or authors. Trade book companies generally calculate and pay royalties every six months. Educational, professional, and scholarly publishers generally pay royalties every twelve months.

Your publisher will very likely specify both when your royalties will be reported and when you will receive your actual royalty check. Generally, such reports and payments are promised to arrive within ninety days after the end of each royalty period, although some publishers send royalty payments within sixty days. It is important to note, though, that some contracts specify only when the author will receive the report—*not* when the amount will be paid. The actual payment may arrive months after the end of the royalty period.

## The Advance

Although the advance is usually specified in the "Royalty" section of the contract, it is of such importance to some authors that it merits its own discussion. It has been my experience that some authors are actually more concerned about their advance than they are about the terms of their royalty. Sometimes, this is due to stories they have heard about authors' receiving huge advances. In other cases, the author actually needs the advance in order to live—especially if he must take a leave of absence from his job to finish the manuscript.

It is important to note at the start that an advance is more properly called an *advance against royalties.* In other words, the advance is not additional to the royalty, but is a prepaid portion of future royalties. So, for instance, if you receive an advance of $1,000, this amount will be taken out of any future royalty payments.

Advances are usually paid in installments, with the payment schedule varying from publisher to publisher and according to the size of the advance. For instance, the first portion may be paid on the signing of the contract; the second portion, on the receipt of the first two chapters of the manuscript; and the final portion, on the receipt of the balance of the manuscript. Or half may be paid on receipt of the prematter and the first two chapters; and the other half, on completion of the manuscript. In the case of large advances, payment may be made in as many as ten installments. Still another

### Helpful Hint

Always keep in mind that the advance is not *additional* to the royalty payment, but is a prepaid portion of future royalties. Therefore, any money you receive as an advance will be deducted from your royalty check.

**Helpful Hint**

To avoid future problems, request that your advance be paid out on a nonreturnable basis.

possible payment schedule may give the author the last portion of the advance only upon publication. Most contracts specify that any portion of the manuscript received must be in "satisfactory" form as judged by the publisher before the corresponding portion of the advance is paid.

What happens if a book is put out of print, and the royalties earned by book sales total less than the amount of the advance? Based upon the existing language in the contract, the publisher may have the right to request that the author return the portion of the advance not covered by the sales of the book. While this rarely occurs, *rarely* is not *never.* In order to avoid this problem completely, you can request that the advance be paid out on a nonreturnable basis.

## Subsidiary Rights

The "Subsidiary Rights" section of the contract grants to the publisher certain rights not referred to in the earlier "Rights" portion of the contract. Thus, depending on the "Rights" section, this may include periodical or newspaper publications, either prior to publication of the book (first serial rights) or after publication of the book (second serial rights); condensations and abridgements; book club publications; foreign-language publications; English-language publications not covered in the "Rights" section; reprint editions; motion picture, television, radio, and stage interpretations; audio recordings; electronic recordings; public reading rights; and Braille, large-type, and other editions for the handicapped.

In the case of each of these rights, the contract specifies the allocation of the money received by the publisher from the granting of these rights to third parties. In the case of those forms of the work with which the publishing company does not involve itself, the proceeds are usually shared with the author in a fifty-fifty or sixty-forty split. However, in the case of those forms in which the company does involve itself—if, for instance, the publisher owns an audio books company that produces an audio recording of the work—the split is likely to be based upon the standard royalty in that business.

The "Subsidiary Rights" section of the contract may also detail the allocation of any money received by the publisher for premium sales. This occurs when a business or organization wishes to purchase a large number of copies for the purpose of providing the book free of charge or at a discounted rate to its customers or members. For instance, a bank might purchase a book on retirement, have it customized so that the cover bears the name of the bank, and then present it to every customer who opens an IRA. In such a case, the publisher would make a special low-cost run of the book, using inexpensive paper and customizing it as desired, and sell the book to the bank at a low price. In other cases, the premium might be taken out of existing inventory rather than a special run, but would still involve a bulk sale of the book at a large discount. In the case of premium sales, the author generally receives a royalty of 5 to 10 percent of the amount received by the publisher.

## Revisions

Some books become out of date in whole or in part as time passes. For instance, a restaurant guide will become out of date as old restaurants close, move, or change their names, and new restaurants open. As a result, some contracts specify that the author must revise the work if the publisher considers it necessary and in the best interests of the work. If the author does not prepare a revision "within a reasonable time"—either because he refuses to do so or because he is deceased—the publisher can have the revision prepared by another party, charge the cost against the author's royalties, and add the name of the person who revised the work to the authorship.

## Accounting

Either under the heading "Accounting" or a heading such as "Royalty Statements and Payments," all publishing contracts include certain details about the publisher's records on the contracted book. In general, the publisher agrees to keep records of payments due the author, and to send statements of such payments to the author at times specified in the agreement. The contract may further detail exactly what these statements must include—for instance, the number of copies sold, the list price, the royalty rate, and the amount of royalties.

Most contracts also state that the author or a representative of the author has the right to examine the publisher's records for the book during normal business hours at the author's expense. The contract may or may not specify how often such an audit may be performed. If an error of 5 percent or more is found in the publisher's favor respecting a royalty statement, the money must be promptly paid to the author, and the publisher must contribute to or cover the cost of the examination. It should be noted that if the author or the author's representative accuses the publisher of underpaying the author, the publishing company can take issue with the author's interpretation of the accounting records. Thus, accusations of underpayment don't necessarily result in additional royalties for the author.

## Warranty and Indemnification

The publisher must rely upon the author to produce an original work that has never before been published. So in the "Warranties" or "Warranty and Indemnification" section of the contract, the author guarantees that he is the sole proprietor of the work—in other words, that he did not plagiarize material from other sources—except in those instances in which he quoted material with written permission of the copyright owner. (For more on this, see "The Manuscript" on page 153.) The author may further guarantee that he has the full power to enter into this agreement and grant those rights granted within the contract; that the work does not contain any material that is libelous or that violates any right of privacy; and that no formula, recipe, or instruction contained in the work would injure either the reader or others.

**Helpful Hint**

Most publishers have an insurance policy that covers the company if it is sued for libel, copyright infringement, or invasion of privacy. To make sure that you are protected, request the addition of a clause which states that if any action is brought against you, you will be covered by the publisher's insurance policy.

Either in the same section of the contract or in a separate "Indemnities" section, the author usually indemnifies the publisher—that is, protects him—from any loss, damage, or expense that may be incurred if the author is, in fact, accused of breaching any of his warranties. It is worth noting, though, that most publishers have an omissions and errors insurance policy that covers the company if it is sued for libel, copyright infringement, or invasion of privacy. To make sure that you are properly protected, you should request the addition of a clause which formally states that if any action is brought against you, you will be covered by the publisher's insurance policy.

## Reserved Rights

Many publishing contracts include a "Reserved Rights" paragraph, which simply states that any rights not granted to the publisher in the agreement are reserved by the author, but that the author will respect the rights granted to the publisher within the contract. While it may seem a little strange that this clause does not simply spell out the rights to which it is referring, the clause does actually serve a purpose.

As you learned earlier in the chapter, in a standard publishing contract, the author grants the publisher the specific rights in which a publisher is usually interested—the rights to sell paperback and hardback editions of the book, for instance. But, according to this clause, should a new area of rights emerge—think CD-ROMs and electronic books—this new area will be controlled by the author.

## Competitive Material

Under the heading "Non-Competition" or "Competitive Material," authors must agree that as long as the publishing agreement remains in effect, they will not prepare or cause to be prepared any work that is on the same subject, directed at the same audience, and treated in the same manner, *if* the new work would conflict with or lessen the sales of the present work. This does not mean that the author can never write a book on the subject addressed by his current work. However, it does mean that he cannot write a book on the same subject if it would compete with the work under contract. Consider, for instance, a music expert who writes a book entitled *Music Appreciation* for use in a college course. If he wrote another music appreciation book—a book called *Understanding Music,* for instance—he would be acting in violation of his contract. However, if he wrote a book on the history of music, on music theory, or on the life of Mozart, he would not be violating the terms of the agreement, as the new book would in no way compete with the contracted book.

## Copyright

Sometimes within the "Rights" section of the contract, and sometimes within a special "Copyright" section, the publisher is charged with the responsibility of registering the book for United States copyright. In most cases, the contract states that the copyright will be taken out in the name of the author, who is the owner of the work. In the case of textbooks, however, the copyright is sometimes registered in the name of the publisher. Occasionally, even a non-text is registered in the name of the publisher. The contract may specify that the publisher will print a copyright notice in every copy of the book. Since doing so is standard practice, however, the omission of such a statement should not be viewed as a problem.

Sometimes the publishing agreement also specifies that in the event of any infringement of the work, the publisher "may employ such remedies as it deems advisable." The contract may even specify whether the author, the publisher, or both the author and the publishing house will pay for any such litigation. In such cases, it will also state how any recovered funds will be divided between the various parties.

## Option

Some contracts give the publisher an option to acquire the author's next book before it is offered to another publishing house. This is referred to as the right of first refusal. Usually, the publisher is given a specified amount of time—thirty days, for instance—in which to examine the new manuscript and determine whether he wishes to acquire it. If he does not offer to publish it within the period specified, the author may show it to other parties and sign a contract with the publisher of his choice. The author may also offer it to other parties if the publisher *does* wish to produce the book, but the author and publisher are unable to agree on financial terms within a stated period of time.

Sometimes this clause gives the first publisher the opportunity to match the terms offered by another publisher competing for the next book. If the first company does offer the same terms, that company is entitled to the publication rights.

## Rights of Termination

Some contracts include separate sections that spell out the circumstances in which the author and publisher can terminate the publishing agreement. For instance, if the publisher does not publish the work within a specified time, or if the work is out of print and the author sends the publisher a written request for a reversion (return) of rights, the contract may state that the publisher must return all rights granted initially to the publisher to the author.

On the other hand, the publisher may have the right to cancel the agreement—and, therefore, not publish the work—if the author does not deliver the manuscript by the specified date, if a requested revision is not submitted within the time specified, or if the manuscript or revision is not judged to be acceptable by the publisher. The contract may further state that under such circumstances, the publisher has the right to recover any advances already paid to the author under the agreement.

## Proceedings

Under a heading such as "Proceedings," "Arbitration," or "Applicable Law," the contract may specify that any major problem or disagreement relating to the contract, or to a breech of the contract, will be settled in a specific manner, through legal proceedings or arbitration, and in a specific location—usually in the city or state in which the publishing company is located. For instance, the contract may specify that any legal proceedings will be governed by the laws of a particular state and be venued—in other words, take place—in that state. Or it may specify that any controversy or claim shall be settled by arbitration in the specified state. In the latter case, the contract may also state who shall bear the costs of the arbitration.

Because the financial resources of a publisher are generally greater than those of an author, publishers usually prefer to resolve differences in a court of law if they cannot resolve them through direct negotiation. For the same reason, in most cases, it is in the author's interest to choose arbitration rather than legal proceedings as a remedy.

### Helpful Hint

Be sure to note how any contract-related disagreement between you and your publisher will be settled. As an author, it will be to your advantage if differences can be resolved through arbitration rather than a court of law.

## Benefit

> **Helpful Hint**
>
> If you have a coauthor or several coauthors, and you believe that your book will be available for a long time through successive revisions, you and your coauthors should work out an appropriate arrangement for handling your book in the future. By arranging things correctly now, you may save yourself or your heirs a great many problems.

A publishing contract usually states that should the publishing company be sold or acquired, the terms of the agreement will continue to apply to the new company or its successor. It may further specify that if the author is deceased, the terms of the contract will apply to the author's executors, administrators, or assigns (anyone to whom the author legally transfers the rights to the book). If there is more than one author, the surviving author will have the authority to revise the book at the publisher's request without the consent of the estate of the deceased author. Note that the surviving author or authors will *not* receive the royalties of the deceased author—only the power to revise the work.

If you have a coauthor or several coauthors, and you believe that your book will be available for a long time through successive revisions, you and your coauthors should work out an appropriate arrangement for handling your book in the future. By arranging things correctly now, you may save yourself or your heirs a great many problems. For instance, you might decide that upon the death of a coauthor, the publishing rights of the deceased author will revert to the remaining authors. Or you might decide that authors who do not participate in the revision of a future edition will have their royalty percentages reduced at that time. If, on the other hand, there is little likelihood your book will be endlessly revised or be kept in print for the next fifty years, the standard terms should be more than adequate.

## Bankruptcy

This clause has always caused me a great deal of concern. First, I hate to see the words "publisher" and "bankruptcy" in the same sentence. More important if you're an author, I don't think that this clause holds much weight.

The bankruptcy clause itself is relatively straightforward. It states that if a publisher becomes insolvent and petitions for or goes into bankruptcy, all rights to the book will revert to the author. Who could argue with that? Unfortunately, a great many people can and do.

From what I have seen over the years, when a publisher declares bankruptcy, all of his contracts are viewed by the court as company assets. As such, the rights granted in these contracts cannot be reverted to the authors no matter *what* the bankruptcy clause states. Usually, if a buyer can be found for the publisher, the rights to the books are transferred to the buyer. If the company goes under reorganization—that is, if it remains as a working company with all contracts in place—it is protected under the bankruptcy laws. For authors, this means that the bankruptcy clause is unenforceable.

So why have a bankruptcy clause at all? I have discussed this question with numerous agents and attorneys, and all have cited the same reason: It makes authors feel more secure.

If you want this clause in your agreement for a greater feeling of security, fine. However, if you want actual protection in the event of company bankruptcy, consider another option. One excellent clue that a company is having financial difficulties is its failure to send out royalty checks. By incorporating a clear statement under the "Royalty" clause or the "Rights of Termination" clause that provides for the reversion of rights if the publisher does not make timely royalty payments, you may be able to protect the rights to your book. However, if the publisher seeks relief from the bankruptcy court before the appropriate reversion procedure is concluded, even this may not work.

Although the standard bankruptcy clause may make you *feel* more secure, be aware that it will provide little actual protection in the event that your publisher declares bankruptcy.

When all is said and done, the standard bankruptcy clause won't harm you. But it may not help you, either.

## Force Majeure

Many publishing contracts include a section on a so-called *force majeure*—an unexpected event that cannot be controlled. In such a section, the contract usually states that the failure of the publisher to publish or reissue the work will not be considered a breech of the agreement or give rise to termination if it is caused by events that are beyond the publisher's control. These events may include restrictions imposed by governmental agencies, labor disputes, and the inability to obtain the materials necessary for the book's manufacture. In such a case, the publication of the work would simply be postponed until the events no longer posed a problem.

## THE NEGOTIATIONS

Hopefully, you now understand most or all of the terms of your contract. If you have any questions about the meaning of any portion of the publishing agreement, do not hesitate to speak to the editor or publisher with whom you've been dealing. He should be able to explain any and all of the terms to your satisfaction. And, of course, if you are working with an agent or a lawyer, he will be able to interpret the contract for you.

You may, at this point, find the terms of your agreement satisfactory, or you may wish to change some of them. The following discussion explores the negotiations process. Be aware that it is beyond the scope of this book to look at every possible contract term and then discuss if and how it might be changed. Rather, I

### Know the Warning Signs

Hopefully, you will be satisfied with the terms of your contract, or you will be able to negotiate better terms—at least regarding the issues that are most important to you. Remember, though, that any contract is only as good as the parties who sign it. How will you know whether the publisher you're dealing with will honor the terms of your contract and treat you honestly and fairly? While there's no surefire method of gauging the character of a company, there are certain warning signs that should alert you to a possible problem. You may want to contact a lawyer or resume your search for a reputable publishing company if:

- ☐ The contract is so full of legalese and so convoluted in wording that it is impossible to understand without the help of a lawyer.
- ☐ When you ask the publisher or acquisitions editor for clarification of some of the terms of the contract, he never gives you a straight answer.
- ☐ When you attempt to negotiate the terms of the contract, you find that there is no give and take on the part of the publisher.
- ☐ Other authors who have worked with this publishing company report that the publisher is late with royalty payments, or that he rarely makes good on verbal promises regarding marketing or other aspects of the publishing process.
- ☐ The contract states that the author will pay the publisher for one or several aspects of the publishing process. This is a bad sign *unless* the payment is expected to come out of the royalty advance—a practice that is acceptable and used by many legitimate companies. Any company that expects the author to pay for editing, typesetting, printing, or warehousing may be a vanity press masquerading as a commercial publisher.

hope to provide you with some insight into the "dance" of negotiations, as well as a closer look at a few important terms that are of interest to many authors. For a more detailed look at publishing agreements, refer to Martin P. Levin's *Be Your Own Literary Agent,* which includes a term-by-term review of a standard book contract, or *Kirsch's Guide to the Book Contract* by Jonathan Kirsch, a detailed clause-by-clause guide to the publishing agreement.

## What Terms Can Be Negotiated?

Once you understand all the terms of your contract, you may recognize a fact that is well-known in the industry: Most contracts are weighted on the side of the publisher. The reasons for this are pretty clear. First, it is the publisher who actually creates the contract. Second, it is the publisher who invests the money and time needed to edit, typeset, print, bind, warehouse, ship, and market the book. Naturally, the publisher therefore feels that he deserves the lion's share of the profits.

On the other hand, it is also true that *most* terms are not set in stone. Virtually any term—from the territory in which the grants apply to the subsidiary rights—can be amended. As a publisher, I have never been insulted by an author's request to change a term of the contract. However, there are certain points that for me are *not* negotiable. And over the years, in my experience with other authors and publishers, I have found that every publisher has certain points on which he stands firm. Which terms *are* negotiable in your case? You will have to find this out through discussions with your publisher.

Before beginning negotiations, I suggest that you determine which points are most important to you. Perhaps you will have to take a leave of absence from your job to complete the manuscript, and therefore need an advance of a certain size. Or perhaps you want a discount given to a particular group or institution that will purchase copies of your book. Once you decide the specific changes you would like to make, you will be better focused and more likely to get what you want—as long as the terms you wish to amend are among those that the publisher is willing to change, and as long as your requests aren't truly outrageous. In any case, don't be afraid to

**Helpful Hint**

Before beginning contract negotiations, determine which points are most important to you. This will help you maintain focus during the negotiations process.

at least request those changes that are important to you. The worst your publisher can say is "no."

**Helpful Hint**

Don't be afraid to at least *request* those contract changes that are most important to you. The worst your publisher can say is "no."

While most publishers do expect some give and take and do allow for a period of negotiations, be aware that negotiations don't always have a happy ending. If you insist upon changing a specific term, and if the publisher is equally determined to leave that term as written, that term may prove to be a deal breaker. Similarly, if the negotiations drag on too long, the contract may be withdrawn. But if you and your publisher can't agree on the terms of the contract, this may be the best outcome.

## Important Bargaining Points

Throughout my years of publishing experience, I have found that the contract terms which authors seek to change vary radically from person to person. One author may refuse to extend the publisher's rights beyond the United States. Another one may demand a greater number of author's copies. But in addition to any special concerns such as these, most authors are very interested in three issues: advances, royalties, and subsidiary rights. Let's look at each of these in turn.

### *Advances*

**Helpful Hint**

Keep in mind that large advances are the exception rather than the rule, and are usually given to known authors.

Everyone has heard stories about authors' receiving outrageously large advances. But it is important to remember that large advances are the exception rather than the rule, and are usually given to known authors. Standard advances—if any can be said to be "standard"—range between $2,000 and $25,000. And some authors get no advances at all.

What dictates the amount of the advance? Many factors come into play, including the policies of that particular publishing company, the company's strength of interest in your manuscript, the size of the market for which your book is intended, and your need for money in order to complete the manuscript. For instance, if the potential audience for your book is small, it would not make sense for the publisher to offer a large advance, as the sales will never pay for that advance.

If you are dissatisfied with the amount of your advance, by all means, discuss it with your publisher. But in addition to considering the factors mentioned above, keep in mind that while your advance may provide you with ready income, this income is not additional to the royalties. Rather, it is a prepaid portion of the royalties that your book will eventually earn, and will be deducted from your royalties.

## *Royalties*

Royalties are another issue that, quite understandably, is of interest to most authors. As explained earlier in the chapter, standard royalty percentages range from 5 to 10 percent of the retail price, and from 5 to 15 percent of the net price. While this may appear satisfactory on the surface—especially if your contract specifies 10 percent of retail!—you do want to watch out for a common pitfall of many contracts. Earlier in the chapter, I explained that some contracts reduce the royalty amount when the discount given to the customer is equal to or greater than 50 percent. What these contracts do not state—and what the publisher who offers such a contract is not likely to explain—is that most books are not sold directly to the bookstore, but are sold through distributors *at discounts of 50 to 60 percent.* Thus, most of the royalties you collect are likely to be based on the smaller percentage listed in such a contract, rather than the more generous percentage.

What can you do to avoid such a pitfall? Now that you're aware of this potential problem, by all means request that the percentage and the basis for the percentage (net or retail) remain the same based upon discounts up to *60 percent,* not 50 percent. This is a point worth negotiating for, as it will have a marked effect on any earnings you enjoy from the sales of your book.

## *Subsidiary Rights*

As discussed earlier in the chapter, subsidiary rights are those rights derived from the literary work other than the primary right to publish the work. These rights are a common point of negotiation. Many authors want to retain various subsidiary rights, from the right to publish their book in a foreign language to the right to movie adaptations of the work.

Helpful Hint

If you are thinking of retaining one or more subsidiary rights, consider if you will be able to sell them on your own. If not, it may be in your best interest to grant these rights to your publisher.

If you wish to retain one or more of the subsidiary rights, consider if you are truly able to sell them on your own. If these rights are granted to the publisher, he will be committed to presenting your work to interested parties. Many publishers have personnel devoted only to selling subsidiary rights. And, of course, your publisher will divide any resulting proceeds with you as detailed in your contract. But if you retain these rights for yourself, your publisher will not have a vested interested in contacting such parties, leaving you to your own devices—unless, of course, you employ a literary agent to represent you in this regard.

I would be remiss if I didn't mention that some publishers are better equipped than others to find parties interested in buying various subsidiary rights. If you are considering retaining any rights, be sure to explore your publisher's abilities in this regard.

Let's say, for instance, that you want to retain the rights to foreign-language editions. Ask your publisher about his track record in selling foreign rights. Are his books internationally distributed? Are his books represented by agents in foreign countries? Does he attend the Frankfurt Book Fair and the London Book Fair—two shows at which publishers often make contacts with publishers from other countries? Does he attend BookExpo America (BEA), another show at which foreign rights may be sold? By asking questions about your area of interest, you will be able to judge who can best represent you in the selling of subsidiary rights.

## If More Than One Company Offers You a Contract

If two companies are interested in publishing your book, you are in an excellent position to compare contract terms and to use the publishers' interest in your project as a bargaining tool. Naturally, you should begin by comparing the terms of the two agreements so that you can see if one is more attractive than the other. Then list the changes you would like made to each contract, and present your requests to the respective publishers.

What if publisher #1 makes only a few modifications, while publisher #2 agrees to make virtually all of the requested changes?

Your initial response may be to sign the second contract, as that publisher seems most willing to work with you and give you what you want, whether it is additional author's copies or a greater share of the royalties. But don't forget the personal criteria you established in Chapter 4. Does one of these company's meet your criteria better than the other? If so, you may be happier working with that

## Is This Publisher Right for You?

Throughout this book, I have emphasized the importance of seeking out a publisher who will meet your personal criteria as established in Chapter 4, produce a high-quality book, market your book aggressively, and deal with you fairly and honestly. In reality, you may be offered a contract by only one company. But if you are lucky enough to elicit the interest of more than one publisher, the following steps may help you choose the one that will provide you with the most rewarding relationship.

- [ ] Request and review the publisher's catalogues to see how the company markets its books. (For tips on assessing catalogues, see page 138.)

- [ ] Examine the publisher's books—especially those books that are in the same category as your own. Be critical, and look for specific things. Are the covers of the books inviting? Are the titles catchy and clever? Is the typeset page appealing? Are the illustrations of good quality? Unless your goal is simply to get your book into publication, you want a company that will produce an attractive, high-quality edition. Any books already published by the company will give you a fairly good idea of how your own work will be treated.

- [ ] Ask the publisher who distributes his books in the relevant market. Also ask him how many sales representatives the company employs, how many books the company has produced in that category, and how many copies have been sold of each title. The answers to these questions—and to any other questions that occur to you during your conversation—will indicate how aggressively the company will market your book, and how much success they have enjoyed in the appropriate marketplace.

- [ ] Ask to speak to two or three of the authors who have published their books with this company. If the publishing company is reputable, your publisher will gladly give you the names and numbers of some of his authors. You will then be able to ask these authors about their experiences with the company. Has the publisher made good on his verbal agreements? Has the author's book been effectively marketed? Was the editing of good quality? Have the royalties been paid on time? Although the publisher will probably choose those authors with whom he feels he has the best relationship, the authors will nevertheless provide you with helpful insights. (Some of these insights might surprise the publisher if he heard them!) And, of course, if the publisher refuses to put you in touch with his authors, you will have a pretty good idea of how he's treating them.

company even if it means sacrificing a few free copies of the book. In addition, one company may have a more aggressive and effective marketing department than the other, or may produce more attractive—and, therefore, more marketable—books. (See the inset on page 173 for additional means of evaluating a publishing company.) Clearly, if company #1 has the ability to sell far more books than company #2, it may be to your advantage to work with the first company even if the royalty percentage it offers is less generous than that offered by the other firm.

Of course, you might be able to "encourage" company #1 to offer more liberal terms by making it known that another company is interested in your project and is more than willing to give you what you want. This may motivate the first publisher to make some of the requested changes in your contract. But, again, you should not necessarily choose the company that offers the largest advance or the highest percentage of subsidiary rights fees. Always look beyond the cold terms of the publishing agreement, and try to determine which company would, overall, provide you with the most satisfying and profitable working relationship.

In its most basic form, a contract spells out your rights and responsibilities as an author, and the company's rights and responsibilities as the publisher of your work. Hopefully, this chapter has provided you with an understanding of your responsibilities, and will help you negotiate for those rights that are most important to you. Of course, a contract is only as good as the people who sign it, and it would be naïve to think that there are only good publishers out there. But if you have done your homework, and have examined not only the publisher's contract, but also the quality of his product and the spirit with which he has dealt with other authors, you have taken an important step in reducing the problems that can occur in the author-publisher relationship. Now the real work will begin as you and your editor seek to polish your manuscript and make it the best it can be. If you and your publisher have dealt honestly and openly with each other throughout the negotiations, you have paved the way for honest, open, and *effective* communications throughout the editorial process. The result should be a printed book of which both you and he can be proud.

## CHAPTER 8

# When It Doesn't Happen

*Our editorial board has met and decided that your project does not fit into . . .*

*Presently our plate is full, and we cannot . . .*

*Although your idea may have merit, I doubt our program is suited . . .*

*Thank you so much; however, at this time . . .*

*Because we cannot find a place on our list . . .*

*We are sorry to respond with a form letter, but . . .*

—*Publishers' annoying rejection lines*

The aim of this book is to show you how to select the right publishers and increase your odds of getting your work in print. But the fact is that sometimes it doesn't happen as quickly as you would like. And sometimes it doesn't happen at all.

In a famous scene from the 1972 movie *The Godfather,* Michael Corleone and his brother Sonny discuss a brutal action that had to be taken. "It's not personal, Sonny," Michael reminds his brother. "It's strictly business." Ideally, this is the way rejection letters should be viewed. The editor is not passing judgment on you as a person, and may not even be passing judgment on you as a writer. A rejection letter may simply mean that at this time, the publisher is not interested in a book on this subject. Having said this, let me quickly add the following: If in response to your submission package, you have received only rejection letters, it's pretty hard *not* to take it personally. And it's pretty hard not to feel bad.

What can you do to lift your spirits? First, think about all the now well-known authors who were rejected time after time before they got their first break. John Le Carré, George Orwell, H.G. Wells, Pearl S. Buck, and Chaim Potok all received letters of rejection for works that later became famous. (See the inset on page 178 for a few choice excerpts from these letters.) In fact, almost every major modern-day author has received his or her share of rejection letters. So you're in good company.

Second—and most important—take steps to accurately diagnose where the problem may lie. In earlier chapters, we discussed a few possible roadblocks to success. For instance, you know that by failing to target the right publishers, you can significantly decrease your chance of finding an interested editor, and may even totally sabotage your efforts. And you know that a poor submission package can also prevent you from reaching your goal. Your topic, your timing, and your approach may also be "off."

If the task of diagnosing the problem, let alone fixing it, seems a bit overwhelming, take a deep breath and relax. This chapter was designed to help you analyze where the problem may exist, and then choose the course of action that is most likely to get your book into print. It will also provide you with some intriguing possibilities, including that of self-publication. In fact, you may be amazed by the options available to you—options that will allow you to reach your goal of seeing your work move from manuscript to printed book.

## IDENTIFYING THE PROBLEM

Short of a concerted plot to stop you from getting your work published, there are only a few basic reasons why manuscripts get rejected: the topic, the approach, the timing, the choice of publishers, the submission package, or some combination of these. Let's first briefly consider each of these possibilities so that you will be in a better position to pinpoint your problem. Later in the chapter, we'll look at what you can do to overcome these roadblocks.

## Your Topic

Your choice of topics can greatly influence your chances of getting published. If you have chosen a subject that has a very limited or difficult-to-reach audience, you may have created a project that is simply too hard to sell to a commercial press. On the other hand, if you have selected a topic that *everybody* is writing about, titles like yours may have already saturated the marketplace. Publishers may be reluctant to put out any more books on the subject—at this time, at least. Finally, if you have presented your topic in a manner that is unclear or that fails to demonstrate the project's marketability, you have definitely reduced your odds of being picked up.

There is yet another consideration when it comes to your choice of topics. Every once in a while, I receive a manuscript proposal on a topic that I personally think is a little out there or just plain over-the-top. Who, I wonder, would ever want to buy such a book? Sometimes the topic is so outrageous that I reject the proposal after reading only the first paragraph of the cover letter. In other cases, even if the topic is a little outside my normal editorial pursuits, I do finish reading the letter, if only to discover the audience whom the writer imagines she is addressing. What kind of reaction do you think editors are having when they read your proposal? While your topic may seem viable to you—and perhaps even "hot"—an editor may have quite a different reaction.

In addition to the topic of your work, there are other reasons why your manuscript may get rejected. These include poor choice of publishers, your approach, bad timing, or a poorly written submissions package.

## Your Approach

Let's assume that the topic of your book is solid, with a good size audience and a very reachable marketplace. Still, you are not getting any nibbles. The problem may center on the way you have decided to present or explore your topic—in other words, on your approach.

For instance, let's say that you are an expert on knitting, and have produced an 800-page guide to knitting geared for the general audience. Knitting is a topic that is always of interest to a segment of the population, so the topic may very well be marketable. However, in this case, the length of the manuscript is likely to be a deterrent to the editor, as the average reader simply wouldn't want

## Welcome to the Club

It's easy to allow rejection letters to make you doubt your worth, as well as your ability to get your book into publication. To gain perspective, and to enjoy some much-needed laughter, spend an afternoon leafing through *Pushcart's Complete Rotten Reviews and Rejections*. This book includes hundreds of scathing comments directed at authors whose works are now regarded with respect and, in some cases, with reverence. As you read the following remarks—all culled from rejection letters—think of the joy that the reading public would have missed if these writers had meekly accepted the editors' comments as gospel instead of continuing their search for the right publisher.

*Mastering the Art of French Cooking*
by Julia Child, Simone Beck,
and Louisette Bertholle, 1961

. . . It is a big, expensive cookbook of elaborate information and might well prove formidable to the American housewife. She might easily clip one of these recipes out of a magazine but be frightened by the book as a whole.

*The Spy Who Came In From the Cold*
by John Le Carré, 1963

You're welcome to Le Carré—he hasn't got any future.

*Animal Farm*
by George Orwell, 1945

It is impossible to sell animal stories in the U.S.A.

*The Good Earth*
by Pearl S. Buck, 1931

Regret the American public is not interested in anything on China.

*The Chosen*
by Chaim Potok, 1967

. . . too long, too static, too repetitious, too ponderous and a long list of other negative "toos" . . . he has no novelistic sense whatever . . . most of the time it is solidly, monumentally boring.

*The Time Machine*
by H.G. Wells, 1895

It is not interesting enough for the general reader and not thorough enough for the scientific reader.

*And to Think That I Saw It on Mulberry Street*
by Dr. Seuss, 1937

. . . too different from other juveniles on the market to warrant its selling.

*Kon-Tiki*
by Thor Heyerdahl, 1952

The idea of men adrift on a raft does have a certain appeal, but for the most part this is a long, solemn and tedious Pacific voyage.

such an overwhelmingly large—and most likely expensive—book. Or perhaps your approach involves a huge number of illustrations that would have to be supplied by the publisher. This, too, would be a problem, as it would require a sizeable investment of money on the part of the publishing company. Or perhaps your book is geared only for the expert knitter who has already mastered the craft, and fails to provide information for the person who wants to learn the basic stitches. Here, again, your approach may have caused a problem—this time, by narrowing the potential audience too much to justify the cost of producing the book.

## Timing

Closely related to the problem of topic is that of timing. When I talk about timing, I am referring to the specific time an editor receives your submission. This topic was first explored in Chapter 6. (See page 144.) But if you have not yet found a publisher who's interested in your proposal, the subject is well worth revisiting.

Timing can be everything. Your proposal can be wonderful, and the publisher you submit it to may be the perfect house to bring it out. Then one week before you send in your proposal, the house may sign an agreement with another author for a similar project. Odds are you will never know of the earlier project. All you will know is that "the perfect house" said no. This is bad timing.

Consider another scenario. The topic of your book is a little quirky or unfamiliar to most people, but you feel that it is ready to explode in the marketplace. You tell the editor how this subject is going to be really "hot," but the editor doesn't agree. Being ahead of a trend may result in continuous rejections from editors who don't share your vision. This, too, is bad timing.

Or imagine that an editor rejects your manuscript because the house isn't looking for a book on that subject. Two months later, at an editorial meeting, there is a radical shift in editorial direction that might now make your project a prime target for publication. The editor vaguely remembers receiving your proposal some time earlier, but cannot locate a copy of the rejection letter, and so is unable to contact you. Sound bizarre? Things just like this happen all the time. You may have a great idea for a book, but if your timing is off, it is not going to happen.

## Your Choice of Publishers

There are a couple of problems that are related to the choice of publishers. Let's first assume that you sent your proposal to appropriate houses—companies that produce the type of book you are writing, and that are willing to consider unsolicited manuscripts. Why hasn't your book been snapped up? If no other problems exist—if your approach, topic, and other elements are all what they should be—it may just be that you haven't yet found the editor who will find your proposal exciting and intriguing.

On the other hand, you may have unintentionally targeted inappropriate publishers. For instance, although your topic may be perfect for small publishers that operate in a specific region of the country, you may have targeted only major New York houses because you want your book produced by a company with "a name." If you have followed your heart's desire—or anything else—instead of following the advice provided in Chapters 3 and 4, you may have virtually guaranteed a stream of rejection letters.

## Your Submission Package

Let us assume that your topic is fine, your timing is not a problem, your approach is flawless, and you carefully selected the publishing houses to which you mailed off your submission package. Nevertheless, either no one asked for further materials, or one or more editors did request materials, but no one followed up with a contract.

Now it's time to take a step back and consider if the problem may be with your submission package. Most likely, if your manuscript is being held back by a problem found within the submission package itself or within any follow-up materials you sent, you should be looking for at least one of two possibilities. Either the writing of the submission package or of the materials sent subsequently is lacking in necessary quality, or you have not identified the audience and marketplace for your book in a way that favorably impressed the editors. Let's look at each of these in turn.

### *Writing Quality*

As discussed in Chapter 5, "Preparing the Package," your submission package not only provides a summary of your book, but also serves as a sample of your writing style and your ability to present information. A number of writing-related problems can turn an editor off, but the problems that are most likely to cause an editor to reject a proposal are poor grammar, lack of clarity, and lack of organization. Any of these difficulties signals the needs for hours of rewriting by a capable editor. And in an industry in which the bottom line is all important, few if any publishers are interested in a manuscript that requires such an investment of time and money.

### *Painting the Right Picture*

If your submission package does not provide the editor with the information for which she is looking, there is little chance that your proposal is going to make her sit up and take notice. Perhaps your proposal does not adequately identify your topic, your approach, your audience, or your marketplace. You may be very aware of all

## How to Profit From Rejection

If you're lucky, at least one of the rejection letters you received was not a form letter, but actually mentioned the reason for the rejection. Perhaps an editor noted that the proposed book would be overwhelming in size to the average reader. Or perhaps after you had sent a chapter of your crafts book to an interested editor, she informed you that the directions were unclear. This is not to suggest that the editor's evaluation was necessarily correct. Every editor is a human being, after all, and if the inset on page 178 proves anything, it proves that editors can be wrong. However, if an editor has taken the time to note her impression of your project, it would be foolish not to take a long, hard look at your materials. Then, if the editor's criticism does make sense to you, you can move on to making any necessary revisions.

If none of the editors shared her thoughts with you, you may be tempted to call some of them up and ask the reason for their rejections. While this may seem like a simple, commonsense approach, as I explained in Chapter 6, your calls are not likely to yield helpful answers. Most acquisitions editors sift through so many queries on a daily basis that they will probably not be able to even remember your proposal, much less offer useful comments and suggestions. On the other hand, if an editor was sufficiently impressed by your submission package to request further materials, and if she sent a rejection letter only after reviewing those materials, it would make sense to give her a call, as she may now be both willing and able to provide you with the feedback that you seek.

of these factors, but simply have failed to point them out to the person on the receiving end of your package. Perhaps you excluded certain pertinent facts, such as how the publisher might gain access to a hard-to-reach audience. Or perhaps you overstated certain points. I don't know how many proposals over the years have stated, "I'm sure that if you publish my book, you will sell a million copies." I love that one. It usually indicates that the author knows very little about publishing.

Your book may be on an important topic that has a sizeable audience. You may have chosen a wonderfully effective approach to the topic. And your timing may be right on the mark. But if your package doesn't convey these facts to the editor, it's possible that no one will ever know just how great your book is.

> **Helpful Hint**
>
> When assessing your submissions package, keep in mind that although your book may be on a relevant topic that has a sizeable audience, if your package doesn't convey these facts to the editor, she won't be likely to give your work a chance.

## Strategies for Pinpointing the Problem

You now know there are a handful of problems that may be holding your project back. The possibilities include your topic, your approach, your timing, your choice of publishers, and your submission package. During your reading of the above discussions, you may have identified the problem. If you're still in the dark, though, there are a number of things you can do to pinpoint the flaws in your project.

### *Look for Clues in Your Rejection Letters*

If you're lucky, you may be able to glean some clues from your rejection letters. True, most of them—perhaps all of them—will be form letters. But occasionally, an editor takes the time to mention the reason for the rejection. If one of the letters states that the topic matter is too specialized, that the approach is too scholarly, or that another problem exists, by all means, take notice. (See the inset on page 181 for more details on this strategy.)

### *Enlist Some Help*

If your rejection letters failed to provide any clues, consider showing your submission package to one or two people who you feel can be both discriminating and honest. Ask them for their opinion, and try to consider their comments with an open mind. You might want to provide them with a list of the pitfalls we've just discussed, and ask them if they believe that any of these may be holding your project back.

If you took the advice presented in Chapter 5, you have already shown your submission package to one person. This time, try to choose different people so that you can get a new perspective. As before, it would be helpful if your reviewers had solid English skills. Someone with a background in teaching English would be a particularly good choice, as English teachers are used to providing constructive criticism on writing, and might be more likely than others to offer you a candid appraisal of your work. It would also be a plus if the readers were familiar with your topic. If the subject of your book is related to your work, an intelligent and trusted coworker might be an ideal candidate.

If your chosen reviewers have not provided you with the answers you're searching for, you may want to look outside your circle of friends and acquaintances. Writers' groups and writers' workshops can be found throughout the United States. Through these groups, you may be able to find other writers who can look at your work objectively and offer valuable criticism. Similarly, writing courses can put you in touch with other writers and, perhaps more important, with instructors who are both able and willing to critique your work. Objective advice such as this may be exactly what you need to pinpoint problems in both your proposal and your actual manuscript. (More information on these resources is provided later in the chapter.)

Involvement in a writers' group or workshop will put you in touch with other writers who can look at your work objectively and offer valuable criticism.

### *Examine the Competition*

If the cause of your problem still eludes you, you may want to carefully examine published books that are similar to yours in subject and focus. Be discriminating, and choose only those books that you feel are clear and informative, paying special attention to titles that are especially popular. Your goal is to note the differences between your own book and other books on the same subject. Compare the material covered; the tone and level of the writing; the viewpoint of the author; the organization of the material; and any special features such as illustrations, tables, boxed insets, and case histories. If you find marked differences—if other books on the topic are written on a less technical level, provide more basic information on the topic, or cover a narrower or broader range of topics, for instance—you may have located the source of your problem.

What if you can't find any books that are similar to yours? If your search has turned up no books on the same topic, that alone may indicate a problem. I have made no secret of the fact that editors are simply not interested in unique books. They want books designed for an existing category and an eager audience. On the other hand, your search may have turned up dozens and dozens of similar books. You now know that you've chosen a subject of interest. However, the glut of competing books may mean that the market is already saturated with books like yours. This, too, is not good.

### How Much Are You Willing to Change?

Before I move on to suggest ways of remedying any problem found, I want to point out that it is not necessarily in your best interest to do anything and everything to get your book into publication. Perhaps you were inspired to write your book by the very fact that you have a new and different viewpoint of the topic being discussed. Perhaps you have experienced success in the classroom by using a revolutionary approach to your topic. If this is the case, you certainly would not meet your personal goals by catering to popular opinion. But you should seriously question if the uniqueness of your book is a necessary and essential component of the work, or if it is an expendable feature that may be keeping you from getting published.

As just mentioned, editors are not looking for something that has never been done before. They are looking for a book that fits into an existing category, that has an existing and accessible audience, and that meets the needs of that audience in established ways. Your book may prove to be the exception—a work that is accepted by both professionals and laymen, or that successfully "breaks the mold" of standard titles in that field. Chances are, though, that if

## Troubleshooting Checklist

This chapter examines various problems that may be keeping your proposed book from exciting the interest of an acquisitions editor. Earlier chapters, such as Chapter 5, warned of other possible problems—problems related to the submissions process as a whole. The following checklist was designed to help you consider a wide variety of potential roadblocks to success. Before you decide that you have done the best you can possibly do to "sell" your book, ask yourself the following questions:

- [ ] Did I target the right publishers?
- [ ] Did I send my submission packages to specific named editors?
- [ ] Did I target an existing audience?
- [ ] Did I identify the category into which my book fits?
- [ ] Did I choose a topic with audience appeal?
- [ ] Did I select an effective approach?
- [ ] Is the level of my writing appropriate for the intended audience?
- [ ] Is my writing grammatically correct?
- [ ] Is my writing clear and well organized?
- [ ] How does my proposed book compare with other books on the same subject?

you insist on a truly unique approach, you will greatly decrease your odds of finding an editor who is willing to champion your project.

## SOLVING THE PROBLEM

Hopefully, you have now identified the problem that potentially is standing between you and a publishing contract. Your next step is to revise your materials in a way that will make your project more attractive to the targeted publishers. Depending on the nature of the problem, on your skills, and on the time you are able to devote to your proposal, you may be able to solve any problems alone, or you may want to enlist the help of others.

### Going It Alone

Regardless of your writing skills, you will probably be able to make many types of changes on your own, without the help of either a more experienced writer or further training. Let's look at some of the problems discussed earlier in the chapter, and see the types of action you can take to remove any roadblocks to success.

### Topic

The solution to a topic-related problem will depend on the exact difficulty caused by your topic. If, for instance, you feel that your topic may be limiting your audience, and therefore may not be considered sufficiently profitable for a commercial press, consider refocusing on the nonprofits—the university and foundation presses. These houses are more likely to accept a book that has a relatively small audience.

If there appear to be too many books on your subject, try waiting six months or even longer, and then resubmitting your proposal to the publishers on your original list. As time passes, many of the other books on the subject will disappear from the marketplace, possibly leaving room for yours. (For more about this strategy, see "Timing," on page 187.)

Finally, reread your cover letter. What do you think the editor's reaction will be? Is the topic of your book clearly spelled out? Have you avoided making your topic seem outlandish? Have you provided enough details about the book's audience and its intended marketplace to show that the book would, indeed, be marketable? By showing that your book has an existing and accessible audience, you may stimulate interest in the subject matter of your project.

### Approach

If you have decided that the flaw in your proposal lies in your approach to your topic, you may very well be able to rework your cover letter, table of contents, and overview so that they reflect a new and more marketable approach. For a moment, let's return to the knitting book mentioned earlier in the chapter. If you have determined that the book is simply too long, it should be an easy matter to revise the submission package so that the stated size of the proposed book is more in line with the needs of the marketplace. At the same time, you may need to eliminate one or more chapters or sections from the table of contents to allow for the reduced length. (Admittedly, if the book has already been written, you will have a more daunting task ahead of you once the project has been accepted.) Similarly, if you have concluded that your book should be more useful to the novice knitter, it would be easy to add a chapter called "The Basics" to your table of contents, and to revise the cover letter and overview to emphasize the book's benefits to those readers who have yet to master the nuts and bolts of the craft.

Other problems, too, may be solved through fairly simple modifications of the submission package. Let's say that you have developed a new way to teach art appreciation to college students, and that your proposed book mirrors your revolutionary approach. If you feel that the unusual teaching method is preventing publishers from accepting your book, it might be beneficial to actually *highlight* your approach in your cover letter. Use the letter to explain that your book is designed for a trend that is just beginning to gain acceptance, and that it will meet the changing needs of the educational market. Editors, who are aware of the rapidly changing nature of the marketplace, are likely to understand and appreciate a presentation such as this. They may even be excited by the prospect of championing a book that is on the cutting edge of the field.

Finally, if you suspect that your approach is the problem, but you're not sure what type of approach would be a *better* choice, consider adding a line to your cover letter stating that you are amenable to changing your approach if necessary. Of course, this is a good option only if you are not married to your approach, but are truly willing to make any change necessary to get your book into print.

If you believe that the potential problem standing between you and a publishing contract lies in your approach to the topic, you may be able to rework your cover letter, table of contents, and overview to reflect a new and more marketable approach. If you are not sure what type of approach would be a better choice, but you are amenable to changing it if necessary, consider stating this in your cover letter.

## *Timing*

Timing is a unique problem in that you cannot solve it by changing your table of contents, reworking your cover letter, or taking a new approach, because the problem isn't in the proposal or the project. What you can do is adopt one of the strategies suggested earlier, under "Topic." Simply wait six months, and send out another set of submission packages to all of the publishers on your original list. You can begin your cover letter by stating that this is a resubmission, and that you hope the editor will reconsider your project in light of changing editorial needs.

Does this strategy work? Based on experience, resubmissions do hit their marks—not always, but enough times to make this a worthwhile option. Within six months, a company's ownership can change hands, editors may be replaced, editorial programs can be modified, new topics can catch on—dozens of things can happen to turn your project into a strong candidate for publication. Resubmitting your material will keep bad timing down to minimum.

### *Your Choice of Publishers*

If your problem is related to your choice of publishers, there are a couple of solutions you should consider. If you feel that the publishers on your original list were, in fact, appropriate, keep in mind that you have probably sent out your proposal to only about thirty publishers, while there are *thousands* of book publishers in the United States. That's why within Chapter 6, I suggest that if you don't find an interested editor among those on your first list, you put together another list of companies. If you haven't already done so, give this strategy a try. This time, consider expanding your list to include companies that may in some general way touch on your book's topic, but do not seem to cover the topic specifically. By basing your selection on more liberal criteria, you can probably find *an additional hundred publishers* who may show interest in your book.

**Helpful Hint**

If you have focused on North American publishers up to this point, consider expanding your list by adding publishers from English-speaking foreign countries. Look for listings of these publishers in the *Publishers' International ISBN Directory* and the *Writers' & Artists' Yearbook.* (See the Resource List on page 215.)

After you have put together your new list of publishers, go back to Chapter 6 and use the Square One System to send out submission packages to these new companies. Perhaps your new list contains an editor—and, remember, it takes only one!—who will appreciate your project and personally guide it through the editorial process, all the way to publication.

What if you suspect that you did not, in fact, select the best publishing houses for your original list? Chapter 3, "The Business of Publishing," and Chapter 4, "Choosing the Right Publisher," will guide you to the most appropriate companies for your project. This time around, though, you may have to be a little more careful or a bit more realistic in your selection, and closely consider each company before adding it to your list.

### *Your Submission Package*

Depending on your skills, you may be able to solve various problems with your submission package once these problems have been identified. For instance, although you may not initially have recognized that your writing contains too many technical terms or that poor organization has made your book overview confusing rather than illuminating, now that you have found the problem, you may be more than capable of restating your proposal in plainer English or of revamping the organization of your overview. And once you realize that your cover letter or overview fail to clearly describe your topic, audience, or approach, you may be able to easily integrate the missing information in your package. However, if these tasks are currently beyond your reach, if you suspect that your grammar or general writing skills are weak, or if you are unable to invest the time needed to bring your proposal and manuscript up to par, you may benefit from outside help. The following discussion will guide you to a variety of resources that may be able to provide just the guidance and support that you need.

## Finding Training, Support, and Other Assistance

If you have decided that you need help in revamping your submission package and/or your manuscript, you will be glad to know that a variety of options are available. Some are designed to get your skills up to speed, while others involve finding a skilled individual who is capable of performing the rewrite for you.

### *Writing Classes, Groups, Conferences, and Workshops*

Earlier in the chapter, I mentioned how writing courses, writers' groups, and writers' workshops may put you in touch with people who have the judgment needed to critique your submission package. These same groups and courses may also help you hone your writing skills.

If you have determined that your grammar skills are in need of improvement, a grammar course at a local college will be your best bet. These courses, which generally take you step by step through a

If you wish to improve your grammar or develop your writing skills, consider taking a class. Most colleges and adult education curriculums offer writing classes and courses in basic grammar.

grammar workbook, cover a variety of important topics such as parallelism, tense, and verb and noun agreement—areas that baffle many writers. Just as important, most teachers are happy to address any specific questions that you have, and may also be willing to read through your proposal and offer constructive criticism. Night courses are usually available, and some colleges have continuing education programs designed specifically for adults.

If you wish to develop your ability to organize material and to express yourself clearly in writing, you should consider taking a writing course, also available at most colleges. In a good writing class, you will learn to arrange words to form a structured whole. Your writing will then be submitted for criticism to your teacher and, possibly, your classmates. Afterwards, you will rewrite your work, taking any comments and suggestions into account. You may also be asked to offer constructive criticism of your fellow students' writing—a process that will help you sharpen your ability to identify strengths and weaknesses. Although some of the focus of a traditional writing class may be on elements of fiction such as plot and dialogue, you will also learn about structure, transition, and other topics relevant to nonfiction writing. Contact those colleges and adult study programs near you and see what they have to offer. And keep in mind that, like any instruction, a writing class will give you only as much as you put in, so be prepared to work hard if you are serious about improving your skills.

## Read, Read, Read!

Writing classes, conferences, and workshops can do much to make you a better writer. And, of course, it's important to keep writing, as any skill improves with practice. But as every professional writer knows, another great way to develop your writing abilities is to read. Read everything you can get your hands on—books, magazines, and newspapers. Read good books so that you acquire an ear for clear, polished writing. Read bad books so that you can learn to identify—and avoid—writing pitfalls. Take the time to notice how writers handle introductions and conclusions; how they explain difficult-to-understand terms and concepts; how they use subheadings; and how they move from one subject to another. For the rest of your life, the time you invest in reading will pay you back every time you sit down to write.

Involvement in a writers' group can provide you with the support of people who have objectives similar to your own, and are eager to share writings, tips, and encouragement. To find a local group that is being formed or is trying to fill a chair, check advertisements in local newspapers; scan school bulletins and writers' websites; and read coffee house, bookstore, and library posting boards. Allow yourself to be picky, and don't hesitate to leave a group that you feel isn't giving you the help and support you want. For a writing group to be productive, the members have to get along well, trust one another, care about one another, and be compatible in intelligence and focus. It may take some time to find a group that can provide you with the constructive criticism that you need, and that includes writers of nonfiction as well as fiction.

Yet another option is to join an online writing group. These groups don't foster the camaraderie and trust that "in-person" groups might, but if you don't have the time or opportunity to attend such a group, an online group is a good alternative. The Internet Writing Workshop has a group specially devoted to nonfiction writing. (See the Resource List on page 215.)

You might also wish to consider attending writers' conferences and workshops. Depending on their focus and format, these gatherings can provide you with tips on writing through workshops, discussions, and one-on-one tutorials; insights into the publishing world; and encouragement from both peers and professionals, including book editors and literary agents. Some writers have even been able to forge useful relationships with editors and agents at such events. Anne Rice, for instance, presented the manuscript for her first novel to an editor from Knopf who was lecturing at a writers' conference. The editor was so impressed by her work that he submitted it to his publishing house for consideration, resulting in the publication of Rice's *Interview With the Vampire.*

If you are looking for a local workshop or conference, flip through regional magazines and newspapers, and contact your local and state arts councils; your Town Hall; and your local schools, libraries, and community centers. For instance, YMCAs across the country sponsor YMCA National Writer's Voice Centers. These centers host a variety of events, including workshops and writing camps.

Perhaps you would like to combine your training with a trip to another part of the country. Fortunately, hundreds of writers' conferences and workshops are held throughout the United States every year. A number of gatherings are listed in the *Literary Market Place (LMP),* which devotes an entire section to writers' conferences and workshops. Also look through the ads and events listings in magazines such as *Writer's Digest* and *The Writer,* and explore books like *The Complete Guide to Writers' Groups, Conferences, and Workshops* by Eileen Malone. And, of course, the Internet can provide you with listings of numerous writers' gatherings. Simply use the search engine of your choice to look for "writers conferences."

## Working With a Ghostwriter

If for any reason you feel that you cannot rework your submission package and/or your manuscript as necessary, you have another great option—a ghostwriter. A ghostwriter can organize your ideas, thoughts, and writings into a readable book. You will provide the knowledge of the subject—be it cooking, music, art, law, or whatever—and your ghostwriter will provide the writing. A talented ghostwriter can even "mimic" your writing voice. Your name will still appear alone as author of the book. The ghostwriter will not be credited as an author. She will, however, be compensated through a flat fee and/or a percentage of the royalties, depending on your arrangement.

Where can you find a competent ghostwriter? Begin by talking to the people around you. Perhaps one of them knows an experienced ghost. Writers' workshops and conferences are other good places to find candidates for the job. (Don't forget that the teachers of most writing courses are themselves writers, and may be interested in your project!) The "Editorial Services" section of the *LMP* lists companies that provide ghostwriting. Finally, magazines like *The Writer* and *Writer's Digest* contain numerous advertisements of people who are willing to edit or rewrite your manuscript.

Whether a ghost has been highly recommended by a friend or was located through an ad, you'll want to do your homework and make sure that she is a skilled writer. Ask the ghost about her background. What kinds of books has she written? Has she been published? Ask to see some of her work, and read it critically. If in doubt, ask other people to read it, too. Finally, make sure that this is a person with whom you can work. Collaboration can be a positive experience. It can also be instructive. Your own writing may improve as you see what your ghost does with your material. But collaboration can also be a nightmare if you don't choose your writer carefully. You and your ghost should be able to work well together.

### Helpful Hint

If you decide to work with a skilled ghostwriter or coauthor, be sure that the person is someone with whom you can work well. Collaboration with a partner can be a positive experience, but it can also be a nightmare if the two of you don't get along.

### *Collaborating With a Coauthor*

If you need help in the writing or the rewriting of your submission package and manuscript, another good option may be a coauthor. What's the difference between a ghostwriter and a coauthor? Both are collaborators, but a ghostwriter is not credited as an author, while a coauthor is. Your coauthor may get equal billing, or may have a byline such as "as told to" or "with." And, of course, your coauthor will get a share of the royalties.

The working arrangements of coauthors vary widely according to the skills of the two people. Sometimes, each coauthor writes different sections of the book, with each working on the areas in which she has expertise. Sometimes, though, one does the research and provides the information, while the other does the lion's share of the writing. If writing is a problem for you, the latter arrangement may best fill your needs.

If you don't already know someone with whom you feel you can collaborate, you may be able to find a competent coauthor just as you would find a ghostwriter—through workshops, conferences, recommendations, and ads. If you would prefer someone with expertise in your subject, try contacting a club related to that subject, or get in touch with the author of an existing book or article on the same topic. Again, before signing this person on, make sure that she has the necessary skills, and that the two of you can get along.

## OTHER OPTIONS

Perhaps, despite your best efforts to rework material, your book has not been published. Or perhaps you feel that it would not be in your best interest to change your work to meet the needs of a commercial publisher. Not every author wants or needs to get her work edited and produced by a standard commercial, scholarly, or university press. Maybe your objective is to simply get your book into print. As you will soon see, this is still a very realizable goal.

## Vanity Presses

A vanity press—also called an author-subsidized publisher, a subsidy publisher, an author-investment publisher, and a cooperative publisher—requires the author to pay for the cost of production and distribution. Usually, the fees charged by a vanity press are high. For the 5,000-copy printing that is normally considered a minimum run by these presses, the publisher may charge as much as $35,000, and sometimes more. For this fee, the company will typeset, print, and bind your book, and may even edit it. Generally, they will also warehouse half of the print run. And some vanity presses may offer to market your book. Most will send copies of your book to reviewers. Typically, the royalties are large—usually about 40 percent of the retail price.

What's wrong with this picture? Perhaps nothing. However, you should be aware that vanity presses make their money through the fees they charge their authors, and not from the income made via book sales. Therefore, they have no great commitment either to produce a quality product or to market that product. As a result, many vanity presses only claim to edit manuscripts, and, in reality, do no editing at all or perform only the most superficial of edits. According to *Writer's Digest* magazine, most also do not deliver the promotion they promise. And when books do get sent to reviewers, the reviewers are generally not enthusiastic about them simply because they have been produced by a company known to willingly publish any book, good or bad. In fact, vanity press books rarely return even a fourth of the author's investment. In addition, most bookstores won't carry titles produced by a vanity press, and if you later send the printed book to a regular publisher in hopes of having it acquired, the editor probably won't seriously consider the title.

Considering the poor track record of vanity presses as a whole, as well as their negative image in the publishing world, should vanity presses ever be considered a viable option? If your goal is to simply get your book into print, and if you have the necessary money and the necessary storage space, a vanity press might be a good choice, as it will take the entire production process off your hands. Approach these presses with your eyes open, though, and investigate each company thoroughly. First, ask to see the company's existing books to determine if the quality is up to your standards. Then ask to see its catalogues and brochures so that you can find out how—and if!—your book will be marketed. Perhaps most important, ask for the names and numbers of some of the company's authors, and question these authors closely to see if the press actually provides the advertised services.

The *LMP* and *Writer's Market* do not list vanity presses. However, you can find ads for these presses in magazines such as *The Writer* and *Writer's Digest.* Do not look for the words "vanity press," as this term is never used in ads. Instead, find a publisher who directs his ad "To the author . . ." or who states that "Manuscripts of all types are wanted. . . ." In other cases, a vanity press may advertise a "subsidy publishing program," or one that offers to "edit, design, illustrate, print, and store your book" regardless of the genre, and all for "easy installment payments." Another avenue of research is the Internet. Simply perform a search for "subsidy presses." If a vanity press is what you're looking for, you should be able to find one with very little trouble.

## Self-Publication

Although the uninitiated often think that *self-publishing* and *vanity publishing* are one and the same, in truth, there's a big difference between the two. While a vanity house takes care of the whole publication process—albeit, for a hefty fee—in a self-publishing program, you literally do everything yourself. You edit the book or hire someone else to do the editing for you; design the layout and either typeset the text or hire a typesetter to do so; proofread and correct the copy; design the cover or arrange to have it professionally designed; arrange to have the book printed and bound; warehouse the finished book; and even do your own marketing and publicity. You then sell your book to individuals, bookstores, libraries, or other outlets. Finally, you do your own billing and collections.

Although self-publishing involves a lot of effort, it is a great option for a writer who can't find an interested publisher, isn't amenable to making the changes requested by a commercial publishing house, or simply has an entrepreneurial spirit and wants to take on the challenge.

While this may sound overwhelming, history has shown that self-publishing is a great option for an author who wants to get his book into print; who either can't find an interested publisher or refuses to make the changes requested by a commercial publishing house; and who has an entrepreneurial spirit. Why do most people prefer it to vanity publishing? First, self-publishing is an old and honorable practice. William Blake, Washington Irving, Walt Whitman, and Mark Twain were all self-publishers. Well-known books that began as self-published titles include classics such as *Robert's Rules of Order* and *Bartlett's Familiar Quotations,* and blockbuster hits such as *The Prince of Tides* and *What Color Is Your Parachute?* So self-publishing does not involve the stigma associated with vanity publication. This means that once your book is in print, you will have a good chance of getting it into bookstores; of getting it reviewed; and—if you can eventually show a solid record of sales success—of having it acquired by an established publishing house.

Second, self-publishing is usually much less expensive than publication through a vanity press. Thanks to computers and laser printers, authors can get their books and promotional pieces ready for printing without the numerous costly production steps that used to be necessary. Then, many small-run printers will print as few as 200 to 500 copies of the book—a far cry from the 5,000-book run demanded by most vanity presses. Naturally, prices change all the time, and your own costs will depend partly on the manufacturers with whom you deal. But, in general, authors who shop for the best prices can save thousands of dollars by choosing self-publication over vanity publication.

This is not to say that self-publishing is right for everyone. As stated earlier, you do need entrepreneurial zeal and some business savvy. At the very least, you will have to find an affordable and reliable short-run printer. You will probably also have to find someone to design the cover of your book. Then, unless you are producing your work only for friends and family, you will have to arrange for your book's distribution, and you will have to market and publicize your book. And you will have to set yourself up as a business—either a sole proprietorship, a partnership, or a corporation. (To further examine if self-publishing is right for you, see the inset on page 198.)

If you are interested in publishing your own book, it is essential to thoroughly investigate the self-publishing option before you make any commitments. A number of books can familiarize you with self-publishing and provide you with valuable tips. For starters, take a look at *How to Get Happily Published* by Judith Appelbaum, which devotes several chapters to this topic, and *The Self-Publishing Manual* by Dan Poynter, which is regarded as a leader in the field. Another book that is bound to be of help is that bible of the publishing world, the *Literary Market Place.* The "Book Manufacturing Section" of the *LMP* includes listings of typing and word-processing services, art services, and printing and binding services. Many of the printers specialize in short-run book manufacturing, and the majority of entries state the company's minimum run, which, in some cases, is as small as two hundred books.

You can learn a great deal about producing, marketing, and selling your book by joining one or two trade groups: the Publisher's Marketing Association (PMA) or the Small Publishers Association of North America (SPAN). Founded in 1983, PMA has a membership of three thousand-plus United States and international publishers—including many self-publishers. Created in 1996, SPAN has a membership of over one thousand publishers. And, again, this includes many self-publishers.

Through their individual newsletters, publications, and services, the PMA and SPAN can guide you to reputable typesetters, printers, editors, and more; inform you of worthwhile publishing fairs, seminars, and workshops; and otherwise provide you with the information you need to be a successful player in the publishing world. (See the Resource List for further details.)

### Helpful Hint

If you have chosen the option of self-publication, I offer one rule: Print only as many books as you really need. Don't base your decision on what you hope to sell, but consider only the sales that you can count on. To this number, add a few extra copies for promotion. Even if this strategy results in a higher cost per printed book, it will help you avoid the problem of storing hundreds—perhaps thousands—of excess copies. Remember that you can always print more books if you run out.

## Electronic Publishing

When most writers dream of getting their books into publication, they think of *physical* books published by traditional "brick-and-mortar" companies—books that will appear in displays at their local bookstore or, at the very least, can be presented to friends and family. But times have changed, and if you can revise your notion of a book to include works that exist not as physical volumes but as electronic publications, you will find that another option is available. You can see your work published as an e-book. Just keep in

## Is Self-Publishing Right for You?

If you have given up hopes of finding an established publisher for your book—or if you are too independent-minded to cater to the demands of a commercial publishing house—self-publishing may allow you to get your book into print without making any compromises. But, as discussed on page 196, self-publishing isn't for everyone. When you commit to self-publishing a book, you are really starting your own business. To see if you have what it takes, ask yourself the following questions:

- ☐ Is the publication of my book of such importance to me that I am willing to invest both thousands of dollars and countless hours of time?
- ☐ Am I willing to accept the fact that I may never again see the money that I invest?
- ☐ Am I willing to investigate typesetters, printers, and other manufacturers and services to find companies that can give me what I need for a reasonable price?
- ☐ Am I thick-skinned enough to face the possibility that bookstores may refuse to carry my book?
- ☐ Am I thick-skinned enough to face the possibility that the media may ignore or criticize my book?
- ☐ Will I really do the homework necessary to learn about book distribution, publicity, and marketing?
- ☐ Once my book is published, will I really spend the hours necessary to distribute, publicize, and market my book?
- ☐ Do I have the motivation and self-confidence it takes to continue to promote my book despite any rejections and setbacks?

It's not easy, but if you answered "yes" to most of these questions, self-publishing may be just what you're looking for.

mind that while the world of e-publishing is growing by leaps and bounds, and definitely offers a seductive alternative, it is a bit more complicated than you might think.

### *How Do E-Publishers Operate?*

In a nutshell, e-publishers convert existing bound books or unpublished original works into electronic formats that can be downloaded by Internet users. The e-publishers then sell these e-books from their websites or through other Internet sites. Sounds good so far.

Over the past few years, the better financed e-publishers have concentrated their efforts on securing the electronic rights of books that have already been published as printed works. The companies rely on the track records of these works to generate Internet sales.

But while sales are growing, they are still very limited, and most of these e-publishers continue to lose money.

Along with these electronic "reprint" publishers have emerged e-companies that produce only original works—books that have never been printed on paper. Some of these e-publishers operate like traditional publishing companies. They review manuscripts, edit the books they sign, and market their titles as best they can. They underwrite their own costs and pay their authors royalties. Unfortunately, these companies are few in number, and for the most part, they are unprofitable.

The fastest growing sector of e-publishers is comprised of vanity e-publishers—although these companies, of course, do not call themselves vanity publishers. Vanity e-publishers sign authors up, convert the manuscripts to the appropriate electronic format, and provide a place on their site for the e-books to be reviewed and sold. They even pay a royalty on works sold. What they do *not* provide is editorial guidance and editing. They make their money by charging authors a small monthly fee for placing their books on their website. In many instances, they require a minimum one-year commitment from the author. Not surprisingly, a number of these e-companies are showing a profit—not from selling e-books, but from selling the use of their sites to authors.

Now that you have a better understanding of what's out there on the web, what are your e-options? With few exceptions, the electronic "reprint" firms deal only with the rights departments of traditional publishing houses, and with the literary agents of authors whose books have been published the old-fashioned way. So if you are a first-time author, you have virtually no chance of landing on the website of one of these companies.

On the other hand, those e-publishers that are the real deal—that operate like traditional publishing houses—should definitely be considered a solid option. As a general rule, they pay little, if any, money in advances. However, because they do not have to invest in storage and inventory or worry about returns, they do pay nice royalty percentages—from 24 to 75 percent of the retail price. If this type of e-company seems like a good alternative to you, just make sure to determine the type of e-publisher you are dealing with before making any submissions.

Now, we turn to the vanity e-publisher. If your goal is simply to make your book available to others, this is a reasonable option. It is certainly cheaper than going to a regular vanity press. And once your book has been made available as an e-publication, you can consider approaching traditional publishing houses, and telling them that your work has been picked up by an e-publisher. Keep in mind, though, that if the editor knows that the e-publisher is a vanity operation, this will probably work against you.

### *Where to Find an E-Publisher*

If you are interested in making your book available in electronic form, your first step, naturally, is to locate some e-publishers, a task that can be performed in at least two ways. The most obvious approach is to perform an Internet search for "e-book publishers" through your favorite search engine. Unfortunately, this would result in a large listing of all sorts of e-publishers. Another and perhaps better tactic is to visit the website of the Association of Electronic Publishers (AEP). (See the Resource List.) This member-run organization seeks to insure that certain standards are met among its participating publishers. The association's website provides a list of its member e-publishers, along with complete contact information and a list of genres produced by each company.

## *POD—Print on Demand*

As technology continues to change the way business is done, many e-publishers not only make books available in electronic form, but offer another service as well. Using a process called print on demand (POD), these publishers can produce one bound book at a time, and fill orders as they come in.

Currently, you sign onto the Internet, go to the site of the e-publisher, and choose a title from the publisher's catalogue of books. The e-publisher keeps no physical inventory of the title on hand. Instead, she contacts her POD printing source, who is able to download an electronic version of the title, print and bind one copy, and send it off to you, the customer. In approximately one week from the time you placed your order, you receive your book. And everyone is happy.

When you think about it, POD may be the wave of the future.

Once you have put together your list of potential publishers, visit each company's website and review it critically, noting the relative ease with which you can navigate the site and locate submission and ordering information. If a publisher looks good to you, order a book from the company and note how it handles the order. Was your order confirmed? Was it filled promptly? Was the book—whether downloaded or on disk—easy to read? Your answers will tell you a great deal about the company's operation and about the ease with which readers will be able to access your work.

Of course, you'll want to check the formats in which the books are made available by each e-publisher. Some can be downloaded, and some are produced on disks. Some can be read on your computer, while others require a "reader." And some, but not all, companies make their books available through online bookstores. Obviously, there is a variety of factors—including the contract—that may make one company more appealing than another.

Once you choose a publisher, you'll find that the submissions process used in e-publishing is similar to that used in traditional publishing houses. You will very likely be asked to submit a cover letter, an outline, an overview, and a few sample chapters. As indicated earlier, some publishers are likely to accept your manuscript regardless of its subject matter or quality, while others are likely to be more selective. With a little luck, your book will soon be made available to its potential audience—and you will join the growing ranks of e-authors.

## A New Topic, A New Book

If vanity publishing sounds too risky, self-publishing requires more time and money than you care to invest, and e-publishing is a bit too high-tech for your taste, there is yet another way in which you can enter the world of publishing—a way that you have probably not yet considered. Simply put the manuscript for your old book away, and begin a new one. Why might you have greater success with your new project than with your current work? For starters, this time you will carefully choose a topic that has proven to be marketable. In addition, this time you will make less of an investment in time and money by initially writing only a submission

There's an added bonus to writing an entirely new project. If the second book is accepted for publication, doors will start opening for you. Your new status as a published author might increase the chance of getting your *first* book published!

package, instead of the full manuscript that you may have prepared for your first book. The unexpected bonus of this new enterprise may be that if your second book is accepted by a publisher and does well in the marketplace, doors will open to you, and you will have a greater chance of getting your *first* book into publication!

How can you choose a marketable topic? While, of course, there is no way of selecting a subject that will guarantee acceptance by the publishing world, there are a number of things you can do to increase your odds substantially.

First, consider the category of books in which you have an interest. (See Chapter 2 if you have any questions about categories.) Are you, for instance, interested in writing a how-to book for the trade? A professional book aimed at a particular group? A textbook for high-school students? A religious trade book? Each category has its own bestsellers, as well as books that enjoy steady, if not spectacular, sales. Research your category with an eye to finding what sells and what doesn't. A variety of resources can help you in your investigation. For instance, if books in your category would be sold in a general bookstore, visit one and look at the wide assortment of nonfiction books that are enjoying success. Don't hesitate to talk to the bookstore manager, who is certain to be aware of sales trends. To research other categories of books, visit religious bookstores, gift shops and other specialty stores, college bookstores, stores that cater to professionals in a certain field—you get the idea.

Your local librarian may also be able to clue you into what's hot and what's not, as may a visit to Internet sites such as barnesandnoble.com and amazon.com. And don't forget trade magazines. A magazine in your field of interest may advertise a selection of popular books. And, of course, *Publishers Weekly*—the trade journal for the publishing industry—often provides informative articles on current book trends in various categories.

If you read Chapter 2, you may remember the inset "Estimating Audience Size," which guides you in assessing the size of your potential readership. (See page 34.) Before settling on a topic, estimate the size of your book's audience. This may help confirm that the subject is a winning one—or that you should keep on looking.

Once you have chosen a topic for your next project, you can start defining and researching your audience. Definitely look at other books on the subject—especially any books that have enjoyed healthy sales—and make decisions regarding approach and topic coverage. Then go back to the earlier chapters of this book so that you can target the most appropriate publishers and write a strong and persuasive submission package. If you've researched your topic and you know it has audience appeal, the odds are now on your side that your new project will find a home.

You've now come to the end of this chapter, and perhaps you are still not sure what the problem is and what you want to do about it. Is it you? Is it them? Is it the project? Should you revamp your old proposal, or start an entirely new book? If your path is not clear to you at this point—if, in fact, you'd rather hide under the covers and not take any path at all—I have a suggestion. Put this book away, put the project away, and let both sit for a few weeks. Then, once you've had some time to relax and gain some perspective, come back to this chapter and reread it. You may discover that this chapter does hold an option that will work for you.

On the other hand, you may now be excited about one or more of the possibilities presented in this chapter. In that case, don't be afraid to go for your dream. When I first started my own publishing company, I had several publishing people tell me exactly why I could not succeed: I didn't have enough capital (which I didn't); I didn't have enough experience (which I thought I did); and, of course, I couldn't compete against the bigger, more established companies (which was nonsense). Guess what? I proved them wrong by believing in myself and working toward my goal. I hope that this chapter will help you do the same.

# Conclusion

*"A professional writer is an amateur who didn't quit."*

*—Richard Bach*

There are milestones that we remember throughout our lives—graduations, marriages, births, and deaths. For some, it is seeing their book in print for the first time. Consider the moment when a young Hemingway, Steinbeck, Steele, Rice, or Grisham held copies of their newly published first book. For each, it must have been a wonderfully exhilarating experience.

Unfortunately, for the majority of people who dream of writing, it will remain a dream. However, the fact that you've come to the end of this book indicates that you have the drive you need to reach your goal—unless you're cheating, in which case, I suggest you get back to the chapter you were on.

It is not always easy to get a book published. The publishing process can sometimes be quite confusing, not to mention a little intimidating. Too often, the smoke and mirrors of the industry obscure the view of the budding writer. If someone has something worthwhile to say, I think that they should have an opportunity to say it. In this book, I have tried to provide you with both a working knowledge of the industry, and a system that enables you to implement this knowledge and get your work in print. While this book focuses on the publication of nonfiction books, I am keenly aware that the term "nonfiction" covers an extremely wide variety of subjects. I hope that in my efforts to shed some light on the publishing process, I have addressed your particular needs and questions—or at least have directed you to resources that can provide the answers you are looking for.

I firmly believe that if you have a good proposal, have targeted a reasonable market, and have produced decent copy, my system will work, and work well. Use your passion for your project to fuel your efforts. One way or another, as I have discussed in a number of chapters, you can make it happen.

In Chapter 1, I talked about Rule #1: There are always exceptions to the rule. Sometimes luck *does* play an important role. Sometimes it even plays a significant part in making a book a bestseller. But to a great degree, I believe that we make our own luck. You can make your own luck by setting up a course of action and following it with intelligence and perseverance. And remember not to get confused by the exceptions. These are the false road signs that will have you traveling in the wrong direction, with very little to show for it but frustration and a lot of unnecessary expense.

I'd like to share a secret. As a publisher of nonfiction books for over twenty years, I have been involved in the publication of over a thousand titles. And I *still* get a kick out of seeing one of my author's books roll off the press. In the not-too-distant future, I hope that you have an opportunity to experience the joy of seeing your own book in print. Till then, I look forward to seeing you in the bookstore, one way or another.

One last thought: Even though this book has been edited and printed, it is still a work in progress. It will be updated and revised as needed. In order to make sure we meet your needs, we would like to know what you think. Therefore, should you have any comments or suggestions you would like to offer, please write to:

Att: NF Department
Square One Publishers
16 First Street
Garden City Park, New York 11040

# GLOSSARY

All words that appear in *italic type* are defined within the glossary.

**acquisitions editor.** The person in a publishing house who has the job of acquiring new books. This person may not have the actual title of acquisitions editor, but instead have a title such as senior editor, *executive editor,* submissions editor, or *publisher.*

**advance.** Money paid to the author in advance of publication. Sometimes described as an "advance against royalties," the advance is actually a prepaid portion of the money that will be earned from future *royalties* on book and *subsidiary rights* sales.

**association press.** See *foundation press.*

**author-subsidized publisher.** See *vanity press.*

**author's copies.** Copies of the author's work given to him or her free of charge directly after publication. The number of author's copies is generally stated in the publishing contract.

**backlist.** A publisher's *titles* that were published more than nine months ago, but are still in print and available from the company. See also *frontlist; complete list; seasonal list.*

**bestseller.** Traditionally, any book that has sold over 50,000 copies in one year.

**brick-and-mortar publisher.** Any publisher that produces books in a physical—hardbound or paperback—edition. The term is commonly used to differentiate an *e-publisher* from a traditional print-on-paper publisher.

**business books.** A subcategory of *professional books* designed to meet the needs of business people, accountants, and managers.

**category.** A division of books into which a work falls because of its subject matter and intended audience. Book categories differ somewhat based upon their intended use. Therefore, library categories differ from bookstore categories, and both differ from publishing categories.

The Square One Book Classification System is specifically based upon the needs of editors. It is comprised of twelve categories, including: trade books, elementary and secondary school textbooks, college textbooks, professional books, scholarly books, reference books, religious trade books, religious elementary and secondary school textbooks, religious college textbooks, religious professional books, religious scholarly books, and religious reference books.

**complete list.** All of a publisher's *titles*, old and new, that are still in print and available from the company. See also *backlist; frontlist; seasonal list.*

**consulting editor.** An expert in a specific field who works for a publisher on a freelance basis, providing valuable information, insights, and leads. Consulting editors are most often used in educational publishing.

**copy editor.** The person in a publishing house who is responsible for making manuscript changes necessary for stylistic consistency; for correcting spelling, grammar, and typographical errors; and for fact checking.

**copyright.** The legal overall right granted to an author or publisher for ownership of a written work. Under this ownership comes a number of specific rights, including the exclusive rights to print, sell, distribute, and translate a literary work.

**cover letter.** A short letter written to an acquiring editor to spark his or her interest in the author's book. This is also called a query letter.

**distributor.** A company that inventories and sells the books of one or more publishers to bookstores, libraries, and nontraditional outlets on an exclusive or nonexclusive basis. Although the terms formerly meant different things, the words distributor, jobber, and wholesaler are now used interchangeably. See also *independent distributor.*

**editor.** The person in a publishing house who actually shapes a manuscript by making necessary changes in format, organization, coverage, focus, and reading level. See also *acquisitions editor; copy editor; editorial assistant; managing editor; sponsoring editor.*

**editorial assistant.** The person in a publishing house who helps the *editors* by making photocopies, filing, proofreading, indexing, and performing similar tasks. The editorial assistant may also review manuscripts in the *slush pile* to see if they may be appropriate for the publishing house.

**editor-in-chief.** The person in a publishing house who oversees acquisitions and editorial operations, and may set editorial goals. In some houses, the *publisher* may perform the functions of an editor-in-chief.

**educational books.** Books designed to meet the needs of either the elementary and high school (*el-hi*) market or the college market.

**el-hi books.** Books designed to meet the needs of the elementary and high school market.

**e-publisher.** A publisher that produces, distributes, and/or sells electronic versions of books to customers via the Internet. See also *brick-and-mortar publisher.*

**executive editor.** The head of the editorial department who is responsible for assigning projects and overseeing the work of the *editors,* who are responsible for the actual shaping of manuscripts. In some companies, the executive editor works as an *acquisitions editor.*

**fiction.** A literary work that is created by imagination rather than being strictly based on fact. This category of literature includes novels of all types and short stories.

**first serial rights.** The rights to publish excerpts of a given work in a periodical such as a magazine or newspaper prior to its first publication. See also *subsidiary rights.*

**force majeure.** An unexpected event that cannot be controlled, such as a restriction imposed by governmental agencies, a labor dispute, or an unavailability of materials necessary for a book's manufacture. According to the standard publishing contract, the failure of the publisher to publish or reissue a work would not be considered a breech of the agreement or give rise to termination if it were caused by events such as these because they are beyond the publisher's control.

**foreign rights.** That subsidiary right under copyright law that allows an author, agent, and/or publisher to sell the translation rights of a work to another publisher located in a foreign country. The right to sell the foreign language edition may apply to a specific country, a group of countries, or any country in which the foreign language is spoken, as specified in a foreign rights agreement. Authors' *royalties* on the sale of foreign rights are usually calculated according to a separate royalty scale.

**foreign sales.** Any international book sales that draw from the original publisher's inventory. Authors' *royalties* on foreign sales are usually calculated according to a separate royalty scale.

**foundation press.** A not-for-profit publisher that is often an extension of an established foundation, and champions the cause of that foundation. Also known as an association press, a foundation press is primarily concerned with producing books that highlight its cause rather than making a profit.

**frontlist.** *Titles* published by a publisher within the last nine months. See also *backlist.*

**galleys.** Originally, long strips of typeset copy created from an edited manuscript. Today, this term may be used to refer to the first set of typeset pages. See also *proofs.*

**ghostwriter.** A person who does the actual writing of the book, but is not credited with authorship on the cover of the book or within its pages.

**how-to books.** Books of instruction, such as books on cooking, gardening, investing, exercise, pet care, photography, and sailing.

**ID.** See *independent distributor.*

**imprint.** The name and logo of a publishing house, or of a division or subsidiary of a publisher, that is used to identify the books it publishes. The imprint normally appears on the book's title page, cover, and spine. A publisher may have more than one imprint.

**indemnity.** A legal exemption from loss, damage, or expense that the author gives the publisher via the contract. The indemnity clause protects the publisher in the event that the author is accused of copyright infringement, libel, or invasion of privacy.

**independent distributor.** Commonly referred to as an ID, a company that inventories and sells the *mass market paperback* books of publishers to high-traffic retail outlets. These include such stores as drugstore chains, supermarkets, discount chain stores, and airport bookshops. Unlike traditional distributors, IDs rip the covers off any unsold books, and provide the publisher with a certified statement that a specific number of book covers have been stripped for credit against the publisher's invoice.

**independent publisher.** Any privately held publishing house that is managed or overseen by its owner(s), as opposed to being a publicly held business entity or a subsidiary of such a public corporation.

**in-house.** Within a specific publishing company. Editors, for instance, often refer to "in-house style"—styles of punctuation, spelling, etc.—followed within that particular publishing house.

**International Standard Book Number.** Commonly referred to as ISBN, a means of book identification used both by publishing companies and by anyone who orders books by those companies. Every publisher buys a book of ISBNs—each of which contains that publisher's unique numerical prefix—and assigns one ISBN to each title. Once assigned, an ISBN refers to only that title—and to only a specific edition of that title.

**ISBN.** See *International Standard Book Number.*

**jobber.** See *distributor.*

**kill.** To reject a manuscript proposal.

**list.** See *backlist; complete list; frontlist; seasonal list.*

**literary agent.** A legal representative of an author who sells the author's work to a third party, such as a publisher, and receives a commission on all monies derived from the work.

**managing editor.** The person in a publishing house who oversees the timely coordination of different departments—such as the editorial department, art department, and typesetting department—to maintain a smooth production process and meet deadlines. The managing editor is sometimes called a production editor.

**market.** The segment of the population considered buyers for a particular type of book;

or a place or system through which books are sold to consumers, such as a bookstore.

**marketplace.** A place or system through which books are sold to consumers, such as a bookstore, library, or other book outlet.

**mass market paperback.** A $4^1/_2$-by-7-inch paperback. Often displayed in book racks, these paperbacks sometimes are reprints of a hardcover edition, and sometimes are published in paperback form without a previous hardback printing. A mass market paperback is both smaller and less expensive than a *trade paperback,* which is sometimes referred to as a "quality paperback." Although sometimes sold in bookstores, mass market paperbacks are primarily designed for sale in high-traffic areas such as newsstands, drugstores, and supermarket chains. See also *trade paperback.*

**medical books.** A subcategory of *professional books* designed to meet the needs of medical doctors, nurses, dentists, veterinarians, pharmacists, and other professionals working in the field of health.

**net price.** The price actually charged by the publisher to any of the customers to whom it sells directly. This can include any book reseller or direct-to-consumer sale. The prices charged by the publisher may be the same as the *retail price,* or may be lower based upon an established discount schedule. The cost of shipping the book is not calculated as part of the net price. See also *retail price; wholesale price.*

**niche market.** A well-defined audience or marketplace that has a specialized area of interest.

**niche publisher.** A publishing house that produces books in one or more specialized areas.

**nonfiction.** A work that contains facts and information rather than being a product of the imagination like *fiction.*

**option clause.** A clause in a contract that gives the publisher an option to acquire the author's next book before it is offered to another publisher.

**out of print.** A term describing a *title* that is no longer available from the publisher. Most publishing contracts define the circumstances under which a book will be taken out of print, as well as what will be done with the remaining copies of the book.

**packager.** A design firm that produces book projects for sale to established publishers throughout the world. These companies are responsible for all editorial content, typesetting, artwork, photography, printing, and binding, as well as translations where necessary. They can offer publishers customized finished editions specifically aimed at their domestic markets.

**page proofs.** See *proofs.*

**print run.** The number of books printed when a book goes to press.

**production editor.** See *managing editor.*

**professional books.** Books that are designed to meet the needs of people who work in a specific profession or technology. This category is divided into several subcategories. *Technical and scientific books* are directed at scientists, engineers, architects, and other professionals in the areas of technology, engineering, and the sciences. *Medical books* are addressed to medical doctors, nurses, dentists, veterinarians, pharmacists, and other professionals working in the field of health. *Business books* are written for business people, accountants, and managers. Other professional books are written for more specific groups, such as lawyers, librarians, teachers, and so on.

**proofs.** Typeset pages created from an edited manuscript. Also called page proofs, they are given to the author and editor to be proofread—that is, to be read for the purpose of finding and correcting typographical errors and other problems.

**prospectus.** A formal proposal designed to summarize a book and excite an editor's interest. Written by an author for submission to a publishing company, the prospectus includes an overview of the book, an analysis of how the book fits into the marketplace, a review of competing *titles*, a biography of the author, and an annotated table of contents.

**publisher.** The person in a publishing house who oversees every aspect of operation of all of the company's departments, including editorial, art, marketing, sales, etc. In some houses, the publisher may also perform the functions of an *editor-in-chief.* Also, a business entity that edits, produces, markets, and otherwise makes available printed and/or electronic material. See also *brick-and-mortar publisher; e-publisher.*

**quality paperback.** See *trade paperback.*

**query letter.** See *cover letter.*

**query package.** See *submission package.*

**reference books.** Books designed to offer readers facts and information in the form of an encyclopedia, handbook, dictionary, or other format that makes the information easy to access.

**religious college textbooks.** Books designed for use in specific religious college courses.

**religious elementary and secondary school texts.** Books designed for use as learning materials in religious elementary and secondary schools.

**religious professional books.** Books designed to meet the needs of people who work in a specific religious profession or job.

**religious reference books.** Books designed to offer readers facts and information on any number of religious topics, in the form of an encyclopedia, handbook, dictionary, or other format that makes the information easy to access.

**religious scholarly books.** Books designed to examine a very narrow religious topic on an academic level.

**religious trade books.** Books designed to sell to the religious or spiritually oriented portion of the general public. Religious trade books—as opposed to trade books on the subject of religion—are produced by religious publishers and are generally geared for people who have a personal involvement in a specific religion.

**remaindered books.** Books sold by the publisher to a discounter for a price that is slightly above or below the manufacturing cost.

Books are often remaindered after their sales fall off.

**retail price.** The full price of a book as marked on the book itself and/or as listed in a consumer catalogue and/or other consumer-oriented promotional literature. This is usually different from the *net price,* and is always different from the *wholesale price.*

**right of first refusal.** The right of a publisher to acquire or reject a previously contracted author's next work before it is offered to another publisher. See also *option clause.*

**royalties.** The money received by an author based upon the sales of his or her book. The publishing contract specifies the royalty percentage for each form of the book being produced; shows whether it is based on the *retail price* or *net price;* and details how the royalty is divided among two or more authors.

**scholarly books.** Books designed to examine a very narrow topic on an academic level. Scholarly books are usually written on an advanced reading level, and are often heavily footnoted and referenced.

**scientific books.** See *technical and scientific books.*

**season.** A specified time of the year for which a publisher presents a new group of *titles* for sale. A publisher may have two or three selling seasons, the most important of which are fall and spring.

**seasonal list.** A publisher's new fall, winter, or spring *titles.* See also *backlist; frontlist; complete list.*

**second serial rights.** The rights to republish parts of a given work in a periodical such as a magazine or newspaper after its first publication. See also *subsidiary rights.*

**self-help books.** Popular psychology, inspirational, and other books designed to improve the inner person.

**slush pile.** Traditionally, the stack of *unsolicited manuscripts* that are usually read by an *editorial assistant* instead of an *editor.* Within large and medium-sized companies, manuscripts that fall into the slush pile are usually rejected.

**special sales.** The sale of books on a deep discount; on a nonreturnable basis; to a *marketplace* that does not interfere with marketplaces such as bookstores, libraries, and book clubs. An example is the sale of a special printing of a book to a company that will offer copies to its customers either free of charge or for a reduced price on a promotional basis.

**sponsoring editor.** A person in a publishing house who is responsible for guiding or overseeing a manuscript through the various phases of production.

**submission package.** A book proposal that is shorter than a *prospectus,* but that, like a prospectus, is designed to summarize a proposed book and pique an editor's interest in the project. The package includes a *cover letter,* annotated table of contents, and book overview. A submission package is also called a query package.

**subsidiary rights.** Those rights derived from the literary work other than the primary right to publish the work. Subsidiary rights may include periodical or newspaper publications; condensations and abridgements; book club publications; foreign-language publications; English-language publications not covered in the "Rights" section of the contract; reprint editions; motion picture, television, radio, and stage interpretations; audio recordings; electronic recordings; public reading rights; and Braille, large-type, and other editions for the handicapped.

**subsidy publisher.** See *vanity press.*

**technical and scientific books.** A subcategory of *professional books* designed to meet the needs of scientists, engineers, architects, and other professionals in the areas of technology, engineering, and the sciences.

**title.** The formal name of a book; or a written work that will be or has already been published.

**trade book.** A book designed for the general reader, and primarily sold in bookstores. Trade books include hardcover books and full-sized (5 1/2-by-8 1/2-inch or larger) paperbacks known as *trade paperbacks.*

**trade paperback.** A 5 1/2-by-8 1/2-inch or larger softcover book sometimes referred to as a quality paperback. Unlike *mass market paperbacks,* which are often sold in drugstores and other nontraditional outlets, trade paperbacks are usually sold in bookstores.

**unagented manuscript.** A manuscript that is not represented by a *literary agent.*

**university press.** A publisher that is affiliated with an institution of higher learning, and primarily publishes scholarly works—professional and technical books as well as periodicals—written by and for professors, scientists, and scholars.

**unsolicited manuscript.** A manuscript that an editor has not specifically asked to see.

**vanity press.** A publisher that requires the author to pay for the cost of production and distribution. Also called a subsidy publisher, author-subsidized publisher, author-investment publisher, and cooperative publisher, a vanity press typically offers editorial and marketing services, as well as unusually large royalty payments.

**warranty.** A legal assurance by the author—stipulated in a publishing agreement—that he is the sole proprietor of the work, and that the work does not contain any material that is libelous or that violates any right of privacy.

**wholesale price.** The price of a book that has been discounted based upon the publisher's established discount schedule, and is sold to only a recognized resaler of the title. See also *net price; retail price.*

**wholesaler.** See *distributor.*

# RESOURCE LIST

Many fine books and periodicals offer insights into the world of publishing; provide helpful guidelines for producing effective submission packages, improving your manuscript, developing your writing skills, negotiating contract terms, self-publishing your work, and effectively marketing your book; and explore other subjects that may be of interest to you. In addition, a number of groups and organizations—including some that are accessible through the Internet—can offer helpful information and support. Keep in mind that this list is intended only to get you started. Your library and local bookstore may provide other helpful readings, and, of course, new online groups and resources are cropping up all the time.

## BOOKS

**Appelbaum, Judith. *How to Get Happily Published: A Complete and Candid Guide*. Fifth Edition. New York: HarperPerennial, 1998.**

This book provides insight into the world of publishing, and offers tips for improving your own material, successfully submitting your manuscript, acting as your own sales force, and more. The self-publishing option is explored in depth, and a truly staggering resource section of over a hundred pages guides you to helpful books, journals, websites, and organizations.

**Bernard, Andre. *Now All We Need Is a Title: Famous Book Titles and How They Got That Way.* New York: W.W. Norton Co., Inc., 1996.**

A fascinating volume rich in publishing anecdotes and lore, this book presents the stories behind more than one hundred of the most famous book titles in the English language, from *Gone With the Wind* to *The Young Lions.* While this may not help you get your book into publication, it will provide you with a window on the publishing world, as well as an enjoyable break from your writing endeavors.

**Boynton, Henry Walcott. *Annals of American Bookselling 1638–1850.* New Castle, DE: Oak Knoll Books, 1991.**

This is a reprint of a title originally released in 1932 to celebrate the 125th anniversary of its then publisher, John Wiley and Sons. Focusing primarily on the development of the book business in Boston, New York, and Philadelphia, *Annals of American Bookselling* provides an early history of book publishing. Be aware that this is not light reading. It is written in a dry, academic style. However, it does offer some interesting information on how it all got started in the United States.

**Bunnin, Brad, and Peter Beren. *The Writer's Legal Companion: The Complete Handbook for the Working Writer.* Third Edition. New York: HarperCollins Publishers, 1998.**

This thorough handbook provides legal advice on contracts, collaborations, working with literary agents, copyright law, and more. Included are a line-by-line review of a publishing contract, and a helpful glossary of publishing terms. Most important, everything is presented in terms that are understandable to the nonlawyer.

**Burack, Sylvia K., editor. *The Writer's Handbook.* Boston: The Writer, Inc., updated annually.**

The first part of this resource offers over a hundred chapters of how-to information from leading writers, including discussions of nonfiction writing. The second part is much like *Writer's Market* in that it presents listings of publishers, literary agents, and publishing and writing conferences. This is a great resource for writers who want to break into publishing.

***The Chicago Manual of Style.* Fourteenth Edition. Chicago: University of Chicago Press, 1993.**

Since 1906, this well-known resource has helped set editorial standards, providing systematic guidelines for editors, proofreaders, indexers, publishers—and writers. Although a bit overwhelming in size, it will tell you where to place the comma, whether you should spell out the number or use a numeral, and if the name of a ship should be italicized or placed in quotation marks. This most recent edition also reflects changes made in style, usage, procedure, and technology in the last few years. Just be aware that your publisher may ultimately edit your book using his own in-house style, which may vary somewhat from that recommended by *Chicago.*

**Cook, Stanley J., and Richard W. Suter. *The Scope of Grammar: A Study of Modern English.* New York: McGraw-Hill Book Company, 1980.**

Still in print several decades after its initial publication, this excellent grammar reference clearly explains such important topics as tense, parts of speech, clauses, nonstandard English, and more. Every chapter is filled with easy-to-understand examples, and ends with a helpful exercise section.

**Dessauer, John P. *Book Publishing: What It Is, What It Does.* Second Edition. New York: R.R. Bowker Company, 1981.**

Dessauer offers an authoritative and detailed look at the history of publishing; the publishing process; book categories; the manufacture, marketing, warehousing, and shipping of books; and the organization, structure, and financial management of publishing houses. This is a wonderful resource for writers who want to understand the inner workings of the publishing industry. Just keep in mind that the publishing world has changed somewhat since the book's publication. And remember to look for *Book Publishing* in your library, not in your bookstore, as this title is, unfortunately, out of print.

**Dickerson, Donya, editor. *Guide to Literary Agents: 500 Agents Who Sell What You Write.* Cincinnati: Writer's Digest Books, updated annually.**

While it doesn't include every literary agency, this annual tome is the most comprehensive of its kind. The more than five hundred agencies listed are divided by type, and cross-referenced by specialty, location, and openness to submissions. Fee-charging agencies are listed separately from non-fee-charging agencies to help you zero in on the type of agent for which you are looking. Also included are introductory articles that focus on queries, rights, and other topics of interest to the aspiring writer.

**Herman, Jeff. *Writer's Guide to Book Editors, Publishers, and Literary Agents: Who They Are! What They Want! And How to Win Them Over!* Rocklin, CA: Prima Publishing, updated annually.**

This invaluable guide lists the names and specific areas of interest of thousands of editors at over five hundred book publishing houses. Also included are more than a hundred interviews with literary agents, who offer sound advice for both aspiring and professional writers. The 2001–2002 edition includes a companion CD-ROM, which provides a database of editors, agents, and publishers, as well as systems for tracking submissions and expenses.

***The International Directory of Little Magazines & Small Presses.* Paradise, CA: Dustbooks, updated annually.**

Although not as user-friendly as the *LMP* and *Writer's Market,* this directory lists thousands of small publishers. In addition to basic contact information, most entries offer payment rates, proposal requirements, and recent publications. Subject and regional indexes are also included.

**Jassin, Lloyd J., and Steven Schechter. *The Copyright Permission and Libel Handbook: A Step-by-Step Guide for Writers, Editors, and Publishers.* New York: John Wiley & Sons, 1997.**

Using clear, jargon-free language, this valuable resource answers virtually all copyright, permission, and libel questions that may arise during the writing of a manuscript. You will learn exactly how you can legally use all types of copyrighted material, including quotations, photographs, and song lyrics. And you will learn how to protect yourself against libel suits, and determine if the material you want to reprint is in the public domain. Included are checklists concerning fair use, copyright protection, and libel, as well as sample forms for requesting reprint permission and writing disclaimers. This up-to-date book also offers the latest information regarding online and multimedia works.

### Jenkins, Jerrold R., and Anne Stanton. *Publish to Win: Smart Strategies to Sell More Books*. Traverse City, MI: Rhodes & Easton, 1997.

*Publish to Win* offers proven marketing advice for both authors and publishers. Early chapters help you evaluate the marketability of your book idea, define your target audience, and test the market. Later chapters guide you in finding a distributor or wholesaler, creating inexpensive but effective publicity, and writing a hot press release. Emphasis is placed on going beyond bookstores and exploiting alternate markets, from book clubs and catalogues to corporations and specialty stores. While helpful for all authors, this is especially important reading for self-publishers.

### Kirsch, Jonathan. *Kirsch's Guide to the Book Contract*. Los Angeles: Acrobat Books, 1999.

Written by an attorney and designed for use by authors, publishers, editors, and literary agents, this book begins with a model book contract. The contract's clauses are organized under topic headings—such as "Introductory Clauses" and "Grant of Rights"—each of which corresponds to a chapter of the guide. This format enables you to turn to the appropriate chapter for a detailed explanation of that portion of the contract. The author provides a wealth of tips for negotiating the deal, as well as cautions about contract elements that may prove problematic. Thorough and truly helpful, *Kirsch's Guide* is a must-have resource for the writer who is serious about participating in contract negotiations.

### Korda, Michael. *Another Life: A Memoir of Other People*. New York: Dell Publishing, 2000.

Drawing from over forty years at Simon & Schuster—most of them as editor in chief—Korda gives you a front-row view of a publishing company's metamorphosis from cottage industry to big business. Through a series of fascinating and often hilarious anecdotes, this memoir will show you what at least one big-city publishing house is *really* like as it entertains you with stories of the many writers who have passed through its doors, from Jacqueline Susann to Richard Nixon, from Truman Capote to Harold Robbins. *Another Life* also provides a glimpse of the egos and politics involved in running a successful business. This is a great book if you want to learn more about how the big houses publish, and an equally good choice if you simply want a "good read."

### Kozak, Ellen M. *Every Writer's Guide to Copyright and Publishing Law*. Second Edition. Owlet Publishing, 1997.

This straightforward text does not overwhelm you with legal terminology, but simplifies confusing terms and issues that arise for new authors. Some subjects that will be of interest are U.S. copyright law, including e-copyrights; fair use; and contract information.

### Kremer, John. *1001 Ways to Market Your Books*, 5th ed. Fairfield, IA: Open Horizons, 1998.

This helpful guide is brimming with ideas, suggestions, and tips for authors—and publishers—who want effective ways to market their books. Illustrated throughout with real-life examples, *1001 Ways* offers inspiration and advice not only for self-publishers, but also for authors who have signed on with publishing houses, but want to take an active role in the marketing process.

**Levin, Martin P. *Be Your Own Literary Agent: The Ultimate Insider's Guide to Getting Published.* Berkeley, CA: Ten Speed Press, 1996.**

Levin provides clear step-by-step instructions for writing a successful book proposal, negotiating a contract, and otherwise acting as your own literary agent. Included is a wealth of model proposals, as well as a helpful glossary and a list of small publishers who, according to the author, are most likely to read and accept your book. Perhaps the most valuable feature, though, is a section-by-section review of a sample literary contract.

***Literary Market Place.* New Providence, NJ: R.R. Bowker, updated annually. www.literarymarketplace.com.**

Considered the bible of the publishing industry, the *LMP* is a comprehensive listing of American and Canadian publishers; literary agents; editorial services; trade associations and foundations; book trade courses; trade books and magazines; book reviewers; book clubs; manufacturers; and more. Although the *LMP's* high price makes it impractical for individual purchase, it can be found in the reference section of any library. Just keep in mind that if you're trying to pinpoint acquisitions editors, *Writer's Market*—although it lists fewer publishers—is more helpful.

**Malone, Eileen. *The Complete Guide to Writers' Groups, Conferences, and Workshops.* New York: John Wiley & Sons, 1996.**

More than a listing of organizations, resources, and educational programs for writers, this book also helps you evaluate your needs and select the group or program that best meets them. Other topics include what you can get out of a writers' group, conference, or workshop; what is expected of a member of a writers' group; how you can give and take criticism; and more.

**Poynter, Dan. *The Self-Publishing Manual: How to Write, Print, & Sell Your Own Book.* Eleventh Edition. Santa Barbara, CA: Para Publishing, 1998.**

Written by an experienced publisher and consultant, this book—considered a leader in the field—is a complete guide to writing, publishing, and selling your own book. Included are a step-by-step system for producing a commercial book, guidelines for getting your book quickly into print, information on setting up your own publishing company, and "secrets" of low-cost book promotion.

**Poynter, Dan, and Danny O. Snow. *U-Publish.com: How Individual Writers Can Now Effectively Compete With the Giants of the Publishing Industry.* 1st Books Library, 2000.**

Written by Dan Poynter, one of world's foremost authorities on self-publishing, and Dan Snow, an expert on new publishing technology, this book shows how you can use the latest technology to publish books at a fraction of the cost of traditional methods. You will also learn how to successfully market your book on the Internet.

**_Publishers' International ISBN Directory_. Berlin, Germany: International ISBN Agency, updated annually.**

Here is the most comprehensive listing of worldwide publishers—including, of course, publishers in English-speaking foreign countries. All in all, some 210 countries and more than 450,000 publishers are included in a format that allows you to find a publishing house by country or name. Like the *Literary Market Place,* though, this book has a prohibitively high price, so look for it in the reference section of a large public library rather than your local bookstore.

**_Pushcart's Complete Rotten Reviews and Rejections: A History of Insult, a Solace to Writers_. Edited by Bill Henderson and André Bernard. Wainscott, NY: Pushcart Press, 1998.**

As its subtitle indicates, this book is a great means of cheering yourself up when you've got the rejection-letter blues. In addition to excerpts from "rotten" book reviews, this collection includes scores of excerpts from rejections sent to the likes of Jane Austen, Gertrude Stein, Chaim Potok, John Le Carré, George Orwell, and more. If you're not blue, *Rotten Reviews and Rejections* makes an even more enjoyable read.

**Ross, Tom, and Marilyn J. Ross. _The Complete Guide to Self-Publishing: Everything You Need to Know to Write, Publish, Promote, and Sell Your Own Book_. Third Edition. Cincinnati: Writer's Digest Books, 1994.**

Written by the cofounders of About Books, Inc.—a writing, publishing, and marketing consulting service—this book gives in-depth advice on the self-publishing of a number of writing genres. Included are discussions of how to take low risks while making profits; e-marketing; and starting your own publishing company. You will also find useful tips for economically designing and printing your own book.

**Strunk, William, and E.B. White. _The Elements of Style_. Fourth Edition. New York: Allyn & Bacon, 1999.**

Considered a classic in the field of grammar and usage, this concise guide covers elementary rules of usage and elementary principles of composition; provides a look at commonly misused words and expressions; and presents tips on refining your writing style. *The Elements of Style* doesn't tell you *everything* you need to know about writing, but it does provide information on many of the basics in a clear and enjoyable way. Many regard it as "must" reading for every writer.

**Venolia, Jan. _Write Right!: A Desktop Digest of Punctuation, Grammar and Style_. Berkeley, CA: Ten Speed Press, 1995.**

Well organized, concise, and actually fun to read, this is a wonderful reference for writers—and anyone else—who needs guidance on grammar, punctuation, and style. This newest edition reflects contemporary usage, providing useful guidelines for communications sent by fax, e-mail, and other on-line methods.

**Wiesner, Karen S. _Electronic Publishing: The Definitive Guide_. Petals of Life Publishing, 1999.**

The author answers all of your questions about e-publishing, and discusses both the positive and negative aspects of this new area of the publishing world. You'll learn how e-publishing works, and you'll find information on selling and promoting your e-book. Most important for the writer who's trying to find a publisher, Wiesner includes a lengthy list of e-publishers.

### Wood, John. *How to Write Attention-Grabbing Query & Cover Letters.* Cincinnati: Writer's Digest Books, 1996.

This guide to writing cover letters, query letters, and book proposals has separate sections geared for authors of articles, nonfiction books, and novels, as well as a chapter on corresponding with editors *after* your project has been accepted. Numerous sample letters are included.

### *Writers' & Artists' Yearbook.* London, England: A & C Black, updated annually. email: sales@acblackdist.co.uk.

This best-selling guide to all areas of the media includes listings of publishers in the United States, the United Kingdom, Ireland, Australia, and New Zealand, including all contact information. As a plus, *Writers' and Artists' Yearbook* is affordably priced, so that you can easily add it to your home reference library.

### *Writer's Market.* Cincinnati: Writer's Digest Books, updated annually.

Similar to the *LMP*, this guide provides listings of book publishers, literary agents, small presses, consumer and trade magazines, and more. While *Writer's Market* has fewer listings than the *LMP*, it is often more helpful for prospective authors as its entries include the names of acquisitions editors, the percentage of titles that come from first-time authors, and other useful facts. Although you'll find it in most libraries, you may want to buy this book, as it is affordably priced.

## PERIODICALS

### *Publishers Weekly*

Publishers Marketing Association
627 Aviation Way
Manhattan Beach, CA 90266
Phone: 310-372-2732
Website: www.pma-online.org

The most important journal within the book trade, *PW* is read by publishers, bookstore buyers, librarians, and other "book people." A sort of window on the publishing world, *PW* provides book reviews, profiles of best-selling authors, an insider's look at book and marketing trends, and much more. Among other things, this is a great place to find out what's hot and what's not.

### *The Writer*

The Writer, Inc.
21027 Crossroads Circle
Waukesha, WI 53187
Phone: 262-796-8776
Website: www.channel.com/thewriter.

Designed for the professional writer, this journal presents interviews with successful writers; lists of helpful books and other writing tools; notices of literary contests, workshops, and conferences; writing tips; and more.

### *Writer's Digest*

F & W Publications, Inc.
1507 Dana Avenue
Cincinnati, OH 4507
Phone: 513-531-2222

Produced by the publisher of *Writer's Market,*

*Writer's Digest* is packed with author interviews and articles on improving your writing, working with editors, writing better proposals, and more. Included are a monthly column on nonfiction writing and a "Writer's Mart" section that guides you to writers' workshops, conferences, and classes; literary contests; professional editorial services and ghostwriters; and literary agents.

## GROUPS AND ORGANIZATIONS

### Association of Author's Representatives, Inc. (AAR)

PO Box 237201, Ansonia Station
New York, NY 10003
Website: www.publishersweekly.com/aar/

A not-for-profit organization of independent literary and dramatic agents, AAR offers a list of member agents through both the mail and its website. In addition, the AAR website suggests topics that should be discussed with a potential agent so that you can better assess if that agent is the right one for you and your project.

### Association of Electronic Publishers (AEP)

Website: www.members.tripod.com/~BestBooksCom/AEP/aep.html.

Formed and run by publishers of electronic books, this organization seeks to insure that certain standards are met among its member e-publishers. The AEP website provides a list of participating publishers, with each entry including complete contact information as well as a list of the genres produced by that company. The site also provides a good deal of other helpful information, such as a list of e-book reviewers and tips for successfully marketing electronic publications.

### Electronically Published Internet Connection (EPIC)

Website: www.eclectics.com/epic

A professional organization of published authors, EPIC was established to provide a strong voice for e-publishing, to help writers learn more about the best publicity opportunities available on the Internet, and to facilitate networking among member authors. Although membership is available only to published writers, the EPIC website offers a variety of resources to nonmembers, including lists of legitimate e-publishers, links to writers' associations, and articles about electronic publishing.

### National Writers Association

1450 S. Havana, Suite 424
Aurora, CO 80012
Phone: 303–751–7844 Fax: 303–751–8593
Website: www.nationalwriters.com

Founded in 1937, the National Writers Association counts both new and famous writers among its members. Membership entitles you to receive a bimonthly newsletter, *Authorship,* and admittance to the National Writers Association's annual conference, held in June. The association also offers support and guidance services in the form of peer review of your work, contract reading and advice, and access to the National Writers Press, which packages and prints books for authors who wish to self-publish. The website includes an online bookstore. Services are provided for members only.

### Publisher's Marketing Association (PMA)

627 Aviation Way
Manhasset Beach, CA 90266
Phone: 310–372–2732
Website: www.pma-online.org

Founded in 1983, this trade association of independent publishers has a membership of over three thousand United States and international publishers—including self-publishers. Through its newsletter, online chat group, and other publications and services, the PMA can guide you to reputable typesetters, printers, editors, and more; inform you of worthwhile publishing fairs, seminars, and workshops; and otherwise provide you with the information you need to succeed as a self-publisher. Services are provided for members only.

### Small Publishers Association of North America (SPAN)

PO Box 1306
Buena Vista, CO 81211
Phone: 719–395–4790
Website: www.spannet.org

Founded in 1996, SPAN's stated mission is "to advance the image and profits of independent publishers through education and marketing opportunities." SPAN offers its members—over one thousand small presses and self-publishers—a range of resources and services, including an information-packed monthly newsletter; a variety of conferences and seminars on publicity and marketing; discounts on health insurance, shipping, office supplies, and industry publications; and a membership resource directory that will allow you to network with other SPAN members. Like the PMA, SPAN provides services for members only.

### U.S. Copyright Office

Library of Congress
101 Independence Avenue, SE
Washington, DC 20559-6000
Phone: 202–707–9100 (to leave a message concerning requests for publications and application forms)
202–707–3000 (to speak to a staff member for information)
Website: www.lcweb.loc.gov/copyright/

If you are worried that a publishing company might steal your work, the U.S. Copyright Office can provide you with legal protection by copyrighting your manuscript. You can either order the necessary forms over the phone or download the forms from the website. Be sure to observe information on the fee involved.

## INTERNET SITES

### Authorlink

Website: www.authorlink.com.

An information service for the publishing industry, Authorlink's primary role is to help writers become published, and to make the job of finding good writers easier for editors and agents. The *Author Showcase* section presents ready-to-submit manuscripts to editors by providing quick synopses, excerpts, and author resumes. Manuscripts are screened by a committee of published writers and must meet strict publishing standards to be listed in this area. The section on *Emerging Writers* lists writers whose work may need more polishing. And for the writer looking for a publisher of a certain category of books, *The Writer's Resources* section shows the areas of interest of a vast number of houses.

### Bookwire

Website: www.bookwire.com.

BookWire is a comprehensive online information source for the book publishing industry. This site's contents include timely book industry news, features, book reviews, guides to literary events, author interviews, thousands of annotated links to book-related sites, and more. Over seven thousand industry-related websites are categorized to make it easy for you to find just what you're looking for.

### Inkspot

Website: www.inkspot.com.

Named by *Writer's Digest* magazine as one of the best sites for writers, Inkspot presents over two thousand pages of information on the craft and business of writing, as well as dozens of discussion forums and other online networking opportunities. This site includes special sections for young writers and teachers. Plus, you can subscribe to *Inklings*—a biweekly newsletter for writers—free of charge.

### LitLine: A Not-for-Profit Website for the Independent Literary Community

Website: www.litline.org/litline.html

LitLine's site provides Internet links to hundreds of small presses, as well as listings of upcoming writers' conferences and events. This is a great website for any writer who's looking for up-to-date information.

### The Nonfiction Writers Workshop

Website: www.members.dialnet/presley/NfMain.htm

A group of The Internet Writing Workshop, this online workshop allows both published and unpublished writers to submit works in progress for critique by other members. The group also recommends helpful books on writing and discusses various aspects of the craft. Not only book-length works, but also essays and magazine articles, are accepted.

### ShawGuides: The Guide to Writers Conferences

Website: www.Shawguides.com/writing/

This remarkably easy-to-use resource can help you find writers' conferences, workshops, seminars, and retreats that meet your personal needs. You simply type in either your area of interest—such as "nonfiction"—or the state in which you live, as well as the month of the year in which you're interested. Using these "filters," the site then provides you with a list of upcoming activities and events. Detailed information is presented on any event that captures your interest. Although the focus is on US conferences, this site also lists events in other countries.

### Writer's Groups

Website: www.writepage.com/groups.htm

This site lists face-to-face—not Internet—writers' groups located not only in the United States, but in other countries, as well. Once you access the site, you merely click on the appropriate region of the country—Western USA, South Central USA, Northeast USA, etc. The site then connects you with the appropriate listings, each of which includes the group's name, description, and a means by which you can contact it. While groups are posted on the site free of charge, not every writers' group in the country is included, of course. Therefore, if you don't find a suitable group through this site, you should definitely try another means of locating one.

# INDEX

## C

## D



## E

## U



## V



## W

## OTHER TITLES IN THE SQUARE ONE WRITERS GUIDE SERIES

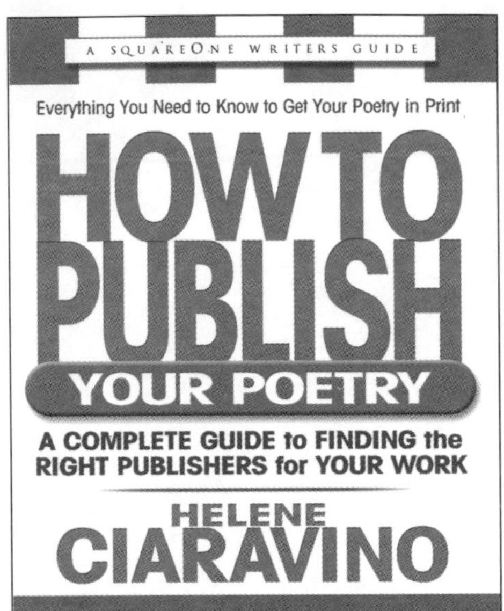


Written for the poet who wishes to enjoy greater success in the world of publishing, *How to Publish Your Poetry* is a complete guide to breaking into the world of print poetry. The book begins by providing a window to the publishing world so that you can see the kinds of publications you should target. You will learn about great market resources for locating appropriate publishers, and you will learn the importance of defining your audience. Following this, the author helps you write a persuasive submission package, and presents a proven step-by-step system for sending your package out—a system designed to maximize results. When the acceptance letters start rolling in, the author helps you select the publications that will help you meet your personal goals. You will even learn of the resources that can help you further develop your special gift.

You've had the passion for poetry for a long time. Now, with *How to Publish Your Poetry*, you have a proven system for making your dreams of publication come true.

*\$14.95 • 192 pgs • 7$^1/_2$ x 9-inch • Paperback • ISBN 0-7570-0001-0*

In today's topsy-turvy world of film production, getting a screenplay sold and produced is no easy task. To play the film game, you need to know the rules. *How to Sell Your Screenplay* not only lets you in on the rules, but also lets you in on the secrets of winning the game.

Written by two veteran screenwriters, *How to Sell Your Screenplay* was designed as a complete guide to getting your screenplay seen, read, and sold. The book begins by giving you an insider's understanding of how the business works. It then guides you in putting your script into the proper format so that you can make the best first impression. Later chapters introduce you to the roles of the "players," including agents, lawyers, producers, and more; guide you in preparing a perfect pitch; provide you with the proven Square One System for query submission; and aid you in getting the best contract possible.

Every screenwriter dreams of getting that lucky break. But the pros know that you need more than luck to succeed—you need to make all the right moves.

*\$16.95 • 288 pgs • 7$^1/_2$ x 9-inch • Paperback • ISBN 0-7570-0002-9*

**For more information about our books, visit our website at www.squareonepublishers.com.**